D0808121

The publisher and the University of California Press Foundation gratefully acknowledge the generous support of the George Gund Foundation Imprint in African American Studies.

# On Black Media Philosophy

# On Black Media Philosophy

Armond R. Towns

UNIVERSITY OF CALIFORNIA PRESS

University of California Press
Oakland, California

Library of Congress Cataloging-in-Publication Data
    Names: Towns, Armond R., author.
    On black media philosophy / Armond R. Towns.
    Other titles: Environmental communication, power,
and culture ; 2.
    Description: Oakland, California : University of
California Press, [2020] I Series: Environmental communication, power, and culture; 2 I Includes bibliographical
references and index.
    Identifiers: LCCN 2021035768 (print) I LCCN
2021035769 (ebook) I ISBN 9780520355798 (hard-
back) I ISBN 9780520355804 (paperback) I ISBN
9780520976016 (ebook)
    |Subjects: LCSH: Blacks in mass media—Philosophy.
I Racism in mass media—Philosophy.
    Classification: LCC P94.5.B55 T69 2020  (print) I
LCC P94.5.B55  (ebook) I DDC 302.23089/96—dc23/
eng/20211110
    LC record available at https://lccn.loc.
gov/2021035768
    LC ebook record available at https://lccn.loc.
gov/2021035769

28   27   26   25   24   23   22
10   9   8   7   6   5   4   3   2   1

To study media is to study more than what we already recognize as media. The beauty of media study should involve the possibility of methodological and theoretical labor that investigates what even constitutes its object of knowledge and the process through which such objects of knowledge are stabilised as the thing that circulates as "media" in academia.

—Jussi Parikka, "To Media Study: Media Studies and Beyond"

# Contents

# Illustrations

# Acknowledgments

Books are not written by individuals, but by a whole host of people, movements, relations, and conversations. This book is no different. It has been debated, discussed, changed, and rewritten based on a world of people who have made both the book and my life better. Some of the people who were important to the development of this book were my thought partners from more than ten years ago. Most important is Sarah Sharma. Her current work continues to inspire me, and I could not have written this without her guidance and belief in me. Also there would be no book without my editors at the University of California Press, Stacy Eisenstark, Naja Pulliam Collins, and Lyn Uhl, as well as my series editors, Phaedra Pezzullo and Salma Monani. They were able to see what I was trying to do with this project when others could not. I am grateful to them.

From my time at the University of North Carolina at Chapel Hill, a host of Triangle-area friends, mentors, and colleagues (some of whom no longer reside there) deserve special thanks: Kashif Powell, Kumi Silva, Jade Davis, Alex Ingersoll, Dana De Soto, Amanda Ingersoll, Ali Brown, J. Beckham, Renee Alexander Craft, Alvaro Reyes, Karla Slocum, Jeremy Packer, Ali Neff, Brett Lyszak, Calum Matheson, Menaka Mohan, Patricia Parker, Carole Blair, Larry Grossberg, Sarah Dempsey, David Monje, David Supp-Montgomerie, Jenna Supp-Montgomerie, Chris Dahlie, Carolyn Hardin, Ted Hardin, Adam Rottinghaus, Alia Wegner,

Daniel Coleman, Andrew Belton, Juliane Hammer, Cemil Aydin, Danielle Purifoy, Eric King Watts, Freya Thimsen, Kurt Zemlicka, Della Pollock, Dennis Mumby, Grant Bollmer, Grover Wehman-Brown, Chris Lundberg, Nova Wehman-Brown, Amy Fallah, Ali Na, Heather Woods, Alex McVey, Jessica Speed Wiley, Lauren Du Graf, Ori Burton, Mark Hayward, Mark Anthony Neal, Michael Muhammad Knight, Mike Palm, Neal Thomas, Neel Ahuja, Pavithra Vasudevan, Priscilla Vaz, Robert McDonald, and Sadaf Knight.

I needed more than just my Chapel Hill partners to complete this project. Since graduation, I have had three important academic homes: first, the University of Denver; second, the University of Richmond; and currently, Carleton University. In Denver, I developed the meat of what would become this book. I have immense gratitude to the homie Raul Perez, who has been talking with me about this project since 2015. Also important was Tayana Hardin, whose leadership of the First Book Group was unmatched. I am grateful to each member of the book group, who read early chapters and provided feedback. I thank my librarian, Jenny Bowers, who helped me obtain access to *The Black Panther* newspaper archives. I also thank a host of Denver homies, some (but not all) of whom remain in the city: Linda Nguyen, Danny Olmos, Paula Martin, Darrin Hicks, Aaron Schneider, Alan Gilbert, Christina Foust, Erin Willer, Carlos Jimenez, Kate Willink, Angela Suell, Ariel Zarate, Beth Suter, Bianca Williams, Cheryl Matias, Frank Tuitt, Erika Polson, Esteban Gomez, Jasmine Pulce, Nicky Reid, Markus Schneider, Michael Brent, Gaby Mohr, Michael Lechuga, Kasey Uchima, Nivea Castaneda, Shadee Abdi, Pavi Prasad, Sergio Juarez, Haneen Al-Ghabra, Thomas Nail, Jere Surber, Dheepa Sundaram, Lisa Martinez, Kristy Ulibarri, Tiara Na'puti, Zoe Tobier, Laurel Eckhouse, and Heather Martin. This project was further developed through many important conversations with graduate student scholars. Maybe most important is Jaime Guzman, the first graduate student who decided to take a shot on me when I was a new professor. Other students remain important, as they go on to graduate schools and beyond, including Daelena Tinnin, Claire Slattery-Quintanilla, Raisa Alvarado Uchima, Tai McMickens, Sara Baugh, Benjamin Boyce, Cody Walizer, Craig Weathers, Kate Hoyt, Misty Saribal, Moana Luri, and Raquel Wright-Mair.

At the University of Richmond a smaller but no less important group of scholars and students helped develop this project. These friends, students, and colleagues include, but are not limited to, Tim Barney, Robin Mundle, Annisa Rochadiat, Lauren Tilton, Taylor Arnold, Mari

Lee Misfud, Justin Madron, Del McWhorter, Dorothy Holland, Jennifer Cable, Nathan Snaza, Julietta Singh, Nicole Maurantonio, Paul Achter, Chaz Antonie, Elinor Frisa, Camilla Nonterah, Caroline Weist, Kayla Corbin, Akeya Fortson-Brown, Shira Greer, Quell Shaw, and T. J. Tann. Last but not least, I'd like to thank my colleagues at Carleton University for their belief in me and this project, including, but not limited to, Liam Cole Young, Chris Russill, Miranda Brady, Ira Wagman, Josh Greenberg, Hannah Dick, Emily Hiltz, Dwayne Winseck, Vincent Andrisani, Sandra Robinson, Benjamin Woo, and Sarah MacLean.

I'd also like to thank friends I met through academia, as well as some outside of academia, who helped with the development of my thinking. One of the most important is my dear friend Corey D. B. Walker, who has been a key Black studies guiding light in my unending growth, and I am forever grateful to him. Others include Carthene Bazemore-Walker and the whole Bazemore-Walker household, Alyssa Stalsberg Canelli, Andrew McLuhan, Simone Browne, Neda Atanasoski, Eram Alam, Jussi Parikka, Lewis Gordon, Malik Spellman, Radha Hegde, Aja Brown, Robin Means Coleman, Karma Chavez, Robin Boylorn, Baruch Gottlieb, Erusla Ore, Fatema Ahmad, Jonathan Sterne, Megan Morrissey, Greg Wise, Dana Cloud, Kent Ono, Jenn Aglio, Joan Faber McAlister, Dylan Rollo, Jody Berland, John Durham Peters, Pete Simonson, Jeff Pooley, Dave Park, Simon Dawes, Korey Banks, Myra Washington, Ronald Jackson II, Lisa Gitelman, R. A. Judy, Alexander Weheliye, Amy Smith Bell, David Peattie, Thomas Nakayama, Kundai Chirindo, Lisa Flores, Chris Poulos, Spoma Jovanovic, Ted Striphas, Rianka Singh, Maryam Arain, Love Jones, Aaron Dial, Joe Lewis, Alfred Lomas, JaTara Allen, Naimah Ahmed, Rory Parker, and E Cram. The following organizations played a big role in the evolution of my thinking around this work: the Watts Tower Art Center, the Library and Archives Canada, the Thomas Fisher Library, and Compton YouthBuild.

Many family and friends were central to the development of this book. I especially want to thank the Husain and the Islam families, specifically Syed Zakir Husain, Sairah Husain, Syed Mazahir Husain, Nasir Husain, Mahjabeen Islam, Afzalunnisa Islam, and Faiza Husain. I also must thank my immediate family for loving me through this work, even as they often had no idea what I was talking about (at times, I didn't know what I was talking about either), particularly my mother and father, Dorethia and Robert Towns. I also thank my siblings, Andre Towns and Kawon Wood; my nieces and nephews, Malika, Octavia, TeeTee, Michael, Robert Jr., DaMorris, and D'Andre; my aunts, Vonnie and Dee; my grandma, Nancy Towns; my cousin Jasmine Taylor; my sister-in-law, Monesha Towns; and so many other family members. You all know who you are.

Last but certainly not least, I thank my partner in all things, Atiya Husain. She has been such a blessing in these times and a consummate editor. Nothing in this book would be possible without her. The expansion, changes, and sharpening of my thought over the years is a product of our relationship. Furthermore, when I needed to step away from thinking about this book, she offered a level of care and thoughtfulness that can never be repaid. She is an amazing scholar and thinker in her own right, which only pushes me to dig deeper. Atiya, life is better with you. Love you.

# Introduction

*The Medium Is the Message, Revisited:*
*Media and Black Epistemologies*

I believe that the establishment of the American universities
should recognize—and they will get nowhere otherwise, but
will do a lot of harm unless they recognize—that black studies is not a concession to black students but a great opening
and penetration into their own intellectual life and understanding. That here is an opportunity to extend the field of
intellectual inquiry which they have neglected up to now, a
chance to penetrate more into the fundamentals of Western
civilization, which cannot be understood unless black studies
is involved.

—C. L. R. James

For the past fifty years an important question has occupied many Black
media studies scholars: What type of media theories should inform our
studies of Blackness? While the question has led to serious engagements
in the racial politics of representation (media content), questions re-
garding Blackness and media form remain far less explored.[1] To ask a
question of media form is to begin not with an episode of a television
series or web series, but to begin with those media technologies and
media infrastructures that make an episode possible in the first place.
And it is unlikely that such a media form approach, Black or otherwise,
can ignore the significant work of the mid-twentieth-century Canadian
theorist Herbert Marshall McLuhan.

From 1946 until shortly before his death in 1980, McLuhan was
a professor of media studies and English at St. Michael's College,

University of Toronto.[2] One of McLuhan's most famous phrases, "the medium is the message," provides a good starting point to think about what constitutes "media" for materialist media infrastructural studies. In this phrase McLuhan pushed back against the idea that the message of any medium was its content (which is where much of Black media studies remains). Instead, he argued that the true message of media involved their transformation of human engagements in the world. According to McLuhan, media are not neutral representations of the world, but they shape the way we come to view the world entirely.

Relatedly, "the medium is the message" also allows for media studies scholars to read continuity into media—another area of difficulty for Black media studies and its overwhelming focus on media representations. For McLuhan, each new medium takes as its content older media, ensuring that there is never really something called new media at all. For example, for him, the content of a book is the phonetic alphabet, not the *Lord of the Flies*; the content of a film is photography, not *Nosferatu*. To focus solely on a book's or a movie's plot as the lone topic of analysis is to miss the centrality of multiple media that can make up the content of a book or movie. In essence, to reduce content to media representations leads to the Black media studies that currently exists—one that often centers analyses of media around the limited question of how racist (or antiracist) a particular representation of Black people is in a book, on television, in a movie, or online. For McLuhan (and for me), representations are not unimportant; they just remain a limited way to think about the fullness of media studies.

Still, it would be a mistake to assume McLuhan's analysis is bulletproof. Although McLuhan's theories allowed for new approaches in media studies, there are legitimate reasons for Black media studies to overlook his work. He had quite a bit to say about race, even as he is rarely remembered for this in much of the contemporary work that takes up his theories.[3] And much of McLuhan's thoughts on race were far from sophisticated, as scholars such as Ginger Nolan and I have written about.[4] However, the outright dismissal of McLuhan in Black media studies may have the effect of producing a body of knowledge in which the episode is overrepresented, while media form is highly neglected. Thus I continue to ask, can a materialist media philosophy, one that is inspired by McLuhan yet that he could never imagine, expand Black media studies further into new questions of materiality and media? And can McLuhan, and the mid-twentieth-century context in which he theorized, provide us with clues for how a materialist media philosophy of Blackness could operate for the future?

What follows is not a book about McLuhan. Yet it is a book very much inspired by his work and cognizant of its problems. This inspiration has led to the development of what I call a Black media philosophy. A Black media philosophy requires recognition of the racial, gendered, sexual, and elemental/natural politics under the surface of McLuhan's philosophy (and McLuhan-influenced studies) and an understanding of the Black challenges to such Western politics. Such a Black media philosophy is made material via pulling together three areas of study. First, there is what Richard Cavell called McLuhan's media philosophy, which, for Cavell, is any study that examines mediation as "the ground of *our* knowing and being."[5] In short, one of McLuhan's important interventions involves his ability to point scholars toward considering media as epistemological: media not only entertain us (representations, e.g., the focus of much of Black media studies); media also frame how we come to know the world and our relation to that world. Yet if we follow McLuhan's lead, as Cavell suggests, the construction of *our* knowing and being reduces being and knowing largely to Western, white, able-bodied, heterosexual wealthy men.[6]

The second and third areas of study that make up Black media philosophy are more important, as both necessarily upend the Western assumptions of McLuhan's media philosophy: Black studies and cultural studies, two distinct yet interrelated mid-twentieth-century challenges to the Western episteme that McLuhan often upheld.[7] Born out of worldwide decolonial, Black radical, Marxist struggle as they are, Black studies and cultural studies would take materiality as one important area of analysis for challenging the Western episteme. It would be the challenge of this moment that C.L.R. James warned must not be ignored—even as scholars such as McLuhan would do just that. The remainder of this introduction centers such alternative epistemologies in my approach to media philosophy. To do so requires highlighting two mid-twentieth-century moments influential for media philosophy: McLuhan's *context* (and his limitations of theorizing race in that context); and questions of *materiality* in McLuhan's theory (which necessarily leads beyond McLuhan to questions of materiality in Black studies and cultural studies). Indeed, even as Black media philosophy remains cognizant of the historical-material context that McLuhan existed in, it also necessarily goes far beyond McLuhan to provide new epistemological questions for media studies.

## MCLUHAN AND THE PROBLEM OF THE MID-TWENTIETH-CENTURY DERIVATIVE

McLuhan's fame in the 1960s and 1970s might be comparable today to such scholars as Cornel West or Noam Chomsky, but largely due to his media analysis, which McLuhan deemed as distinct from any social analysis. Unlike the overtly political West and Chomsky, McLuhan argued in his work and numerous personal letters that his analysis of media was designed to be impartial, so any social analysis that emerged was merely a reflection of the media.[8] Yet similar to West and Chomsky, McLuhan's celebrity exceeded the world of higher education. In 1965 the popular Canadian magazine *Maclean's* dubbed McLuhan the "the high priest of pop culture" because of his prescient analysis of media.[9] McLuhan's fame and his arguments led to open critiques of his work from important scholars of the mid-twentieth century, such as James Carey and Raymond Williams, who both argued that McLuhan was a technological determinist—the argument that technology on its own defines the development of all social structures and values in a society, regardless of human intervention.[10] McLuhan made arguably the most public response to all his critics that any academic possibly could. Though not directly addressed to Carey or Williams, McLuhan made a short cameo as himself in 1977 in the popular Woody Allen film *Annie Hall*, where he delivered a line to an actor (Russell Horton) playing a professor at Columbia University: "You know nothing of my work."[11]

The technological determinism associated with McLuhan's work would be well documented, particularly in another popular phrase attributed to him.[12] In addition to "the medium is the message," another popular mid-twentieth-century phrase that McLuhan would be associated with is the subtitle of arguably his most well-known book, *Understanding Media* (1964): "the extensions of man." For McLuhan, extensions would be a metaphor for all media. Importantly, media do not refer to the "news media," a term often derisively used today to describe television channels such as Fox News and MSNBC. Instead, McLuhan is most famous for arguing that a medium (or the singular of media) referred to any technology that *extended* the human senses. For McLuhan to say that a medium was an extension of the senses meant it would require the attention of specific senses. In his attempt to borrow from anthropological and psychological studies of the early and mid-twentieth century, for example, McLuhan argued (controversially) that the phonetic alphabet was not only a medium, but it extended the eye, meaning the phonetic alphabet required an excessive attention of sight. For McLuhan, each medium similarly facilitated different sensorial involvements—from sight (the eye), to sound (the ear), to multisensorial (the central nervous system). In spite of the controversy, "media as extensions of the senses" was a phrase that pushed against the idea that the sole message of a medium was its content (where much of Black media studies still remains). Instead, McLuhan argued that the true message of any medium involved transformation of human engagements in the world, of which the senses were one example.

Such theorizations would make McLuhan popular in the 1960s. His *Playboy* magazine interview in 1969 is not only one of the more easily digestible pieces you can read of his theory, but it signified his rise as a North American popular intellectual. Although *Playboy* magazine is perhaps best known as a magazine of nude pictures, it also published interviews with influential and controversial figures of the mid-twentieth century. The magazine interviewed Malcolm X in 1963, Ayn Rand in 1964, and Martin Luther King Jr. in 1965.[13] In his 1969 *Playboy* interview, McLuhan argued, among many things, that the changing politico-economic relations of a society were reflective of the media readily available in that society. Specifically, he argued that the 1960s, full of social-political unrest, were "not an easy period in which to live, especially for the television-conditioned young who, unlike their literate elders, cannot take refuge in the zombie trance of Narcissus narcosis that numbs the state of psychic shock induced by the impact of new media."[14]

This meant, for example, that if you wanted to understand the reason why young people were protesting throughout the world in the mid-twentieth century, you would not find an answer in an episode of *Leave It to Beaver*. You would find it in the new media environment that television introduced into society—the medium that the youth grew up with in the mid-twentieth century that their parents did not have in their youth of the early twentieth century. Indeed, one of the main groups inspired by McLuhan during this time were the Youth International Party, or the Yippies. The Yippies were a radical, largely white countercultural revolutionary offshoot of the antiwar movements, who engaged in highly theatrical forms of protests. It would be in the Yippies, and their highly tele-visual forms of protests, that McLuhan would see representations of a new, younger generation, sparked by electronic, involved, multisensorial forms of media, specifically television.[15]

By the early 1960s, 92 percent of U.S. households owned a television set.[16] The new medium's pervasiveness led McLuhan to argue that the content of television was secondary to television's form, which, via the experience of everyone tuning in to watch a show at the same time (no matter its content), was influencing the new, younger generation to view themselves as a part of an electronic, connective whole—or the "global village." Thus in the *Playboy* interview, McLuhan argued that the distinction between the numerous student protests and the repressive state responses to those protests was not a matter of youth ignorance versus adult intelligence, or vice versa, but of the different media that both generations grew up with in the home as children. According to McLuhan, the midcentury unrest was a product of a mere technologically infused generation gap, a distinction between a highly visual, literate, older mechanical generation, and a new, global village generation—the new media environment sparked by electronic media. Electronic children were now young adults, who were politically, socially, and even physically, in some cases, bumping up against their literate-trained, mechanical parents. This was the point of the Yippies, who sought to distinguish themselves from what they saw as a stuffy, mechanical, older generation. In some ways, and despite what some have called his conservativism, McLuhan was able to tap into an energy of multiple youth movements of his time, theoretically at least.[17] While the radical, Black protest poet of the time Gil Scott-Heron famously argued that the "the revolution will not be televised," I would like to think that McLuhan would not disagree, but he might counter with "the revolution will be guided by those who inhabit a televisual media environment." Thus Scott-Heron and McLuhan agree; for both, episodes were not the most important thing to focus on when considering revolutionary change, meaning Scott-Heron was making a media studies argument, too.

Unfortunately, as McLuhan reduced the problems of the 1960s and 1970s to a media problem of the white familial structure of North America (i.e., the generation gap), he could not see that those leading the radical charge of the time were largely influenced by the Scott-Herons of the world (further discussed in chapter 3)—that is, the Black radical and decolonial movements of the time. In short, as suggested in his research archive from the 1960s titled "Negro," even though McLuhan was cognizant of the Black radical movements in the United States and Africa during the mid-twentieth century, his ultimate conclusion of such Black radical movements was that they were representative of concurrent white movements.[18] Black radical movements materialize in McLuhan's publications of the 1960s, then, as indistinct from the white movements—merely derivative. The generation gap sparked by new media—inherently a familial gap—made Black radicalism a stepchild of white leftist movements.

It may not be too shocking that McLuhan's standard for understanding media assumed the white family as the norm. Indeed, he was giving his *Playboy* interview in the wake of the release of the 1965 report *The Negro Family: The Case for National Action,* by Daniel Patrick Moynihan, the former U.S. Assistant Secretary of Labor.[19] Moynihan's report infamously described the Negro family as merely a deviation from traditional families (which meant "white"). McLuhan's attention to media form replicates the dominant mid-twentieth-century, highly racialized approach to Black people in both the academy and politics: a "normal" Black person was either seen as reducible to a mere reflection of what white Euro-Americans used to be in previous eras or reducible to what the most degraded, lower-classed white Euro-Americans are. Pulling more from the midcentury disciplinary assumptions made in anthropology and psychology than explicitly from Moynihan, McLuhan argued the former: that Black people were reflections of what white people once were, meaning that Black people were far more "tribal" than white people. In the disciplines of anthropology and psychology that McLuhan pulled from, often influenced by social Darwinism, humans developed in (technological) stages, and some were further along ("detribal," i.e., no longer tribal) than others (tribal, i.e., "backward," behind the detribal). Here Western Europe and North America presumably looked back at Africa, Asia, the Caribbean, Central America, and South America, as technological reflections of the West's own tribal past, rather than as the colonies from which both natural resources and people were extracted in order to build Western concepts of civilization and development. Although McLuhan was critical of the civilizational assumptions of media, he could not perceive that his weddedness to social Darwinian disciplinary thought during the mid-twentieth century required that Black people (and our presumably tribal media) only acted as measures of where whites once were (further examined in chapter 1).

While McLuhan argued that media could provide an explanation for the protests of the 1960s and 1970s, he implied that the protests were a product of new epistemologies (media split people into different ways of knowing the world); but epistemology remains white for McLuhan, no matter the generation. What he uncritically speaks to is what this book actively asks: How do we refute a media philosophy wedded to a logic of the same? Put simply, media not only teach us how to know, as per McLuhan; they have also been deployed in the West to argue that all of humanity is known through Western media history, which assumes, as Achille Mbembe argues, "It is not okay for them [Negroes] *not* to be like us [whites]."[20] To paraphrase Harold Innis, the Canadian economist who was a central influence on McLuhan, the media that the West deployed produced the West as the monopolizer of knowledge. McLuhan's argument assumed that we are all derivatives of white Euro-Americans, and all media served a Western, temporal, epistemological function: to show white Euro-Americans how far behind them we as Black people were.[21]

My own intervention takes McLuhan's Western media philosophy seriously in order to blow up its limitations, which remain largely under the surface of much of contemporary media philosophy. For me, the "tribal people" and their media, argued to be windows into the past of the West, are indeed *media* themselves, if we follow McLuhan's own in/famous definition of media as "any extension of man." As I have argued, McLuhan's usage of man as a metaphor for the human is largely a sensorial metaphor (an extension of man means media are an extension of the eye, of the ear, etc.); but McLuhan's concept of the sensorial took for granted early twentieth-century (social) Darwinian sensorial orders, which held that Euro-Americans were presumably less sensorial (which meant further from "nature") than Black and brown people.[22] In short, McLuhan's concept of man is, as Sylvia Wynter might argue, often *over-represented* as white, Western, middle-class, able-bodied, heterosexual, and male, building off a Darwinian-influenced sensorial foundation of what it means to be human (see chapter 1).[23]

Here it is not surprising that McLuhan's concept of the tribal mirrors critiques in Black studies of the "Negro," imagined as a figure with a wholly different sensorial ordering than white people.[24] Like the tribal that exists only in McLuhan's mind, what Ronald Judy calls the Negro is not about Black people per se but white imaginations of the Negro: "As a concept, *The Negro* is not an objective possibility; there is no way of knowing whether it is objectively real or not," meaning that the Negro is a "problematic conception that can only be thought; it is an effect of discursivity."[25] While Judy implies it, I explicate it: the Negro is a *mediator* (Judy calls it a "metaphor," which for McLuhan, ever the rhetorician, is the same thing), it is a storage device for white imaginations, used to measure some (white) people's assumed exit from nature and entrance into Western conceptions of humanness and civilization.[26] This is basically McLuhan's definition of tribal media: that which lies in proximity to nature, not civilization and, as such, is a mirror to show how far *we* have come. The Black media philosophy of this book takes seriously the racial implications of Western media philosophy's "we" and "our" to illustrate its limits for understanding Black people.

My work unearths another related, important limitation of McLuhan's media philosophy: What does a media philosophy that does not always already read the West as the measure of all other human's media engagements look like (explored in chapters 2 and 3)? This is neither to say that Western media are unimportant for Black people, nor is it to say that Black people have never deployed such media in important, radical, and joyous ways (indeed, I make no claims of any neat distinction between anything that can be called "white media" versus "Black media").[27] Rather, it is to say that the West's conception of media, as measures of the human, replicates a Western temporal logic that holds no universality for other genres of human. Thus Black media philosophy requires recognition of the racial politics of the Western episteme and a complex understanding of the projects that challenge such an episteme. The inability to understand the challenges is not a problem unique to media philosophy or McLuhan, but it is representative of the problem of the mid-twentieth-century Western academy that McLuhan inhabited.

The limitations of the mid-twentieth-century Western academy would be fully exposed by the exact people that the academy had always deemed as absent of knowledge: Black people. One year after McLuhan's *Playboy* interview, the important Black studies scholar C.L.R. James gave an interview, where he argued that Black studies introduced not simply a critique of Western society but a related critique of the society's order of knowledge—the very institution that McLuhan's work fit so well within. With the rise of C.L.R. James reading groups throughout Montreal, Ottawa, and Toronto in the 1960s, McLuhan would live to see the rise of the Black studies that James would be so central to, that which James warned was necessary if one hoped to comprehend the new epistemological frames that did not rely on white people as the sole carriers of knowledge.[28]

But aside from seeing the founding of Black studies, McLuhan had little to nothing to say about the epistemological critiques that scholars like James would play a role in establishing. McLuhan's inability to understand the epistemological gauntlets that James threw down will continue to haunt contemporary scholars who seek to grapple with media form and materiality unless we name the problem and point toward alternative solutions. This requires a new media philosophy (and history) that is up to the task of examining the interrelations between Blackness, media, epistemology, nature, and materiality. Indeed, Black media philosophy is different from Black media studies because it cannot exist without close attention to materiality and history, or that which includes and exceeds the representation. McLuhan provides some of that materiality and history, but it is necessary to examine how materiality and history are also connected to the development of two major intellectual tests to the Western episteme of McLuhan's time, both of which structure my own intellectual genealogy: Black studies and cultural studies. And, as this book makes clear, the materiality centered in Black studies and cultural studies hold strong yet unacknowledged links with the expansion of the discipline of my training, media and communication studies.

## BLACK STUDIES, COMMUNICATIONS, AND MATERIALITY

Eleven month after the Russian satellite Sputnik entered outer space, the 1958 National Defense Education Act was released with the hopes of encouraging a largely scientific project in higher education, one that would keep the United States technologically apace with the Soviets. The U.S. government hoped the National Defense Education Act would provide another route to replicate the Western epistemological project. In part, the act was designed to provide affordable education to (white) students pursuing higher education, particularly in the realms of science, technology, and languages. Under this act the government sought to "provide that in the selection of students to receive loans from such student loan fund special consideration shall be given to... students whose academic background indicates a superior capacity or preparation in science, mathematics, engineering, or a *modern foreign language*."[29] These particular studies were deemed "necessary to protect the financial interest of the United States."[30]

Notably, despite the context of the space race, scientific engineering was not the sole focus of the 1958 act. In the wake of World War II, and the start of the Cold War, the United States needed a new informational campaign against the Russians as well, aimed at "languages and areas." The urgency of such an informational campaign was directly linked to the fact that the Russians had both beat the United States into space and they were actively calling for all Western nations to abandon colonialism in Africa, Asia, and various parts of the Americas. Of course, as noted in the Central Intelligence Agency's 1948 document "The Break-up of the Colonial Empires and Its Implications of US Security," the financial bottom line of the United States would be hurt by a dying Western colonial regime, as the United States relied heavily on natural resources from Western-controlled colonies, to say nothing of its own colonial relations.[31] The Soviets knew this; in some cases they financially and militarily backed decolonial movements to show the contradictions in the United States's declarations of freedom and liberty.[32] And for these reasons the multifaceted information campaign needed to be swift and effective.

The United States had long been working on such a plan that could easily be translated into the service of an anticommunist agenda. In World War II the Rockefeller Foundation, and later the U.S. government, aided in the development of an interdisciplinary field called *communications*, built from the contracted research of professors of sociology, psychology, and political science.[33] This new field of communications (related to but not to be confused with the later academic discipline of *communication* studies) involved the mostly radio-based attempt to deliver "positive" information about the United States and capitalism to both the larger U.S. public and the populations of war-torn countries that the U.S. militarily entered in order to win the "hearts and minds" of local populations. The main argument for labeling this new area of study "communications" was quite simple: while the Nazis spread partial and biased propaganda, the United States would distribute scientific, presumably impartial communications. However, as Jeff Pooley argues, they were the same thing, with the main difference being that "propaganda" had negative connotations coming out of World War I and the fear of the Bolsheviks, and this meant that "communications" would read more favorably as a terminology for the population in the United States.[34] Thus communications was designed to do different rhetorical work than propaganda, but similar media technological and political work.[35]

In the wake of World War II, the clear communications enemy for the United States was Russia, leading the United States to shift its resources from Nazis to the Soviets. Indeed, maybe the United States's most effective form of communications was to convince the U.S. public that socialism and fascism were synonymous. The communications campaign required specification after Sputnik, meaning that the 1958 act would promote the development of "language and area studies." In other words, while scientists and engineers worked to get "whitey to the moon," as Gil Scott-Heron sang, the act fostered area studies as a specialized provider of communications to newly, and actively, decolonizing locations.[36] Such area studies had as their aim the promotion of expertise in the language and culture of a non-Western geographic area, to slow the spread of socialism to those regions. Put simply, the 1958 act spoke to the need to slow the currently decolonizing people and newly decolonized people (as well as Black and brown people at home) from turning socialist. The area studies scholars were to become experts in their respective geographic/cultural areas and to provide information deemed pertinent to national security.[37] This pertinent information conflated national security with economic stability, denoting what Roderick Ferguson calls the unification of state, capital, and the academy.[38] The act argued that languages provided a "full understanding of the areas, regions, or countries in which such languages are commonly used," allowing for the United States to conduct research on the "more effective methods of teaching such languages and in such other fields."[39] The new focus on areas was a focus on capitalist intervention into the locales where "foreign" languages were spoken.

Communications research begins to fall out of favor for the U.S. government in the late 1950s, moving into universities in the 1960s as a discipline called "mass communication" and later "communication studies," my home discipline (the *s* is dropped in the shift away from the previous more technical studies of journalism and radio, and begins to include more humanistic areas such as speech and rhetorical studies and media studies). As noted by scholars like Rey Chow, in this post-Sputnik, midcentury time period, it is area studies that steps in as the newly funded academic project, with much funding coming from the U.S. government.[40] From the National Defense Education Act we get the full institutionalization of both Africanists and Orientalists as legitimate areas of study both in academia and by the state. It is under this context that Vincent Harding argued that academia was an extension "of the walls of the government, industry, and the military."[41] And, as Robin Kelley argues, by the end the 1960s it is no surprise that universities would begin to fully invest major resources into area studies over Black studies. For example, in contrast "to the militant origins of the Center for Afro-American Studies" at the University of California–Los Angeles during the late 1960s, "African Studies [at UCLA] was founded with unequivocal administrative backing and even more funding," which poured in from a Ford Foundation grant as well as this very

1958 National Defense Education Act, "as part of [the United States's broader] support for area studies programs."[42]

We can consider area studies and communications as two sides of the same coin—both replicated the Western, bourgeois epistemological project as universal and held that the development (a capitalist term) of all the former colonies must follow the West. Indeed, the 1958 act implied that area studies and communications were linked with its Title VII, referred to as "Research and Experimentation in more Effective Utilization of Television, Radio, Motion Pictures, and Related Media for Educational Purposes." Title VII sought to authorize the establishment of an Advisory Committee on New Educational Media that considered the most effective way to use "media of communication for educational purposes."[43] The previous focus of communications scholars (radio, television, motion pictures, etc.) fit right in with the new governmental focus of area studies, so much so that many communications scholars at this time would build off this area studies push, opening communication centers throughout the Global South, as a bridge between the United States and the newly decolonizing nations.[44]

Of course, McLuhan is more area studies than communications (Aniko Bodroghkozy rightly calls him Orientalist).[45] Unlike much of the United States–centric communications scholars, McLuhan did not believe that the hearts and minds of all non-Western people could be changed via any Western bourgeois propaganda project (in fact, I argue that his thought begins directly against this dominant communications paradigm). But McLuhan did believe that the tribalness of non-Western media was central to shaping all non-Western people's approaches to the world. In short, his research focus was unconcerned with learning any African or Asian languages in order to travel and turn former colonies into capitalists; but his research did increasingly rely on twentieth-century social Darwinian scientific scholars who were deemed experts of the "African mind."[46] McLuhan was a part of the mid-twentieth-century Western episteme, which Ferguson argues sought to "absorb" all minority difference for political and economic reasons, and the university was one site for such an episteme.[47] McLuhan is more a cultural relativist (another popular academic project of the twentieth century) than openly racist. For him, all non-Western cultures' media should not be judged against Western frames; but those non-Western media can be deemed as reflective of the West's past, which he could not see was to contradictorily already judge non-Western cultures against Western frames. It is not a stretch to say that McLuhan's philosophy, even as it is a critique of the propagandist/communications logic, replicated another variant of the episteme of post-Darwinian, biocentric, capitalist development that situated the West as the trajectory of all the world's peoples.

No matter if one sees McLuhan as more area studies than communications, or vice versa, what would happen soon after the 1958 act was passed was a game changer for higher education throughout the world. And it was far more complicated than McLuhan's generation gap gives it credit. It was the development of Black studies as a new academic discipline, routed through the philosophies and actions of important figures like W.E.B. Du Bois, Angela Davis, C.L.R. James, Toni Cade Bambara, and Kwame Nkrumah. Referred to by Greg Carr as the "academic extension of what Cedric Robinson has called 'The Black Radical Tradition,'" Black studies is an important cry linked to the material conditions of descendants of African people in Africa, Asia, the United States, the Caribbean, and Europe, whose work was rarely studied in higher education institutions.[48] Though not a reaction to them, it was a call in direct opposition to communications and area studies. These initial calls began in the streets of the colonies and beyond, through a direct challenge to the material conditions of colonization and racism, what Frantz Fanon in *The Wretched of the Earth* called a true analysis of the colonial situation.[49]

In North America, "Black Power" emerged as what Stokely Carmichael (later Kwame Ture) and Charles Hamilton called a direct challenge to "internal colonization," which held that Black people in the United States, like Black people in African colonies, "do not export anything except their human labor," making the U.S. Black ghetto similar to the colonial relationship, only within empire's center.[50] Harding similarly argued that one of the primary contexts to understand for Black studies was "the colonized situation of the masses of the black community in America."[51] Thus Ture, Hamilton, and Harding connected North American Black Power to the Third World, decolonial politics that Fanon spoke about in Algeria. For Harding, part of the vocation of the Black scholar was to figure out why the material conditions of colonization, which included the redistribution of resources and people throughout the world, excessively improved Western, white people's lives but also to consider how Black people have created thought beyond the limitations of such white imagination.

As an academic discipline, Black studies remains in debt to historically Black colleges and universities (HBCUs), particularly the mid-twentieth-century student- and faculty-led calls for the creation of the "Black University." Charles Hamilton would outline such a new university on the pages of the *Negro Digest* in the 1960s.[52] In 1969, the same year of McLuhan's *Playboy* interview, the Black studies scholar Lerone Bennett Jr. delivered his important speech, "The Challenge of Blackness," which would further identify "a Black University perspective" for higher education.[53] For Bennett, the argument for the Black University was threefold: first, that a new education, one called "Black Studies," was necessary to push a politics of Black liberation to better understand the material conditions that Black people throughout the world lived under; second, that because HBCUs were largely located in Black communities, they should serve those Black communities that they reside in; and third, in order to truly fulfill these goals, HBCUs should seek autonomy from the influence of wealthy, white donors.[54] Along with Harding, Bennett became one of the prominent voices for the formation of Black studies as an intellectual project, especially through their work at the Institute of the Black World.[55]

But Black studies was not only a concern of the HBCUs. The call also moved into historically white colleges and universities throughout the United States. The first Department of Black Studies was founded in 1968 at San Francisco State, employing important Black studies scholars like Sonia Sanchez and Nathan Hare.[56] In 1968 an undergraduate student at Yale University named Armstead Robinson organized the conference "Black Studies in the University," which led to the formation of what is now Yale University's Department of African American Studies.[57] In the 1960s, Black studies scholars like June Jordon and Toni Cade Bambara fought for the system of City College in New York City to create "open admissions," a movement that pushed for more Black and Puerto Rican students and a curriculum to reflect the concerns of this population.[58] Outside of the United States, Black studies was influenced by figures like Claudia Jones, the communist Trinidadian, who founded Britain's first major Black newspaper in 1958.[59] In the 1970s, at the University of Dar es Salaam in Tanzania, figures like A. M. Babu, Issa Shivji, and Walter Rodney outlined for the students the centrality of European colonialism to the continued oppression of Africans.[60] Rodney, the radical Guyanese historian who had once tried to start an African and Caribbean studies program while teaching in Jamaica, delivered his now-famous lectures on the Russian Revolution at Dar es Salaam.[61] In these lectures Rodney made connections between the Russian peasantry of the Russian Revolution of 1917 and the peasantry in

Tanzania.[62] In 1972, Rodney also published one of the more important books in Black studies, *How Europe Underdeveloped Africa*, which detailed the centrality of European concepts of development (capitalism) to contemporary African disenfranchisement.[63]

Black studies is born of these very material struggles against oppression, that which McLuhan argued were mere generational gaps, that which communications and area studies argued could be solved merely with the spread of "better information" about the West. Black studies is not concerned with creating a world of Black heroes that would just replace the white heroes studied in the disciplines; it is not concerned with putting a Black face on white theory; it is not a communications/ area studies campaign to teach Black and brown people, both at home and abroad, the benefits of capitalism. It is a full intellectual, epistemological shift in knowledge, one directly articulated to the materialist demands for liberation worldwide.[64] That shift must be thought about via a question asked to media philosophy: What happens if we do not see Western man (white, male, heterosexual, able-bodied, middle-classed, cisgender) and his media as the measure of all humanity? Or better yet, what happens if Black studies opens up a new mode for theorizing the centrality and materiality of media, both old and new, toward the project of Black liberation? Neither area studies nor McLuhan could ask these questions. Like McLuhan noted of media, this intellectual moment was not merely a question of representation but also of form: the entirety of the intellectual tradition would need to be transformed to fit the Black and decolonial demands of the 1960s and 1970s. Of course, this would not fully happen, but it was the initial and continuous demand of Black studies even to this day. McLuhan could not understand that the student protests were the product of the literal realization that Western man held no universal legitimacy, whether in the colonies or in the classrooms. The challenge of Blackness was a project that exploded the racial logics of the Western Negro and opened up something new.

Black media philosophy seeks to think the racial project of man as interrelated yet distinct from the liberatory project of Black people, and it can only do so if Black studies leads the way. But while Black media philosophy builds off the midcentury critique of the Western episteme by Black studies, around the same time period, there was yet another materialist critique of dominant epistemologies necessary to understand Black media philosophy, one that cannot be neatly separated from the Black studies push: cultural studies.

## CULTURAL STUDIES AND THE "NATURE" OF MARXIST MATERIALITY

At Birmingham University, the Centre for Contemporary Cultural Studies (CCCS) first opened its doors in 1964, led by the literary scholar Richard Hoggart. The Centre emerged in a context similar to, yet different from, the conservative context that developed communications as an academic discipline in the United States in the 1960s: postwar nationalist reimagining, only the Centre pushed left against conservatism, while communications leaned into it. More specifically, and unlike scholarship in the United States, the CCCS emerged in the context of a physically destroyed United Kingdom (thanks to Nazi bombing), seeking to rebuild itself after the war and struggling to make sense of the nation's drop on the world's stage and the ascendance of U.S. consumer capitalism. Because it was formed by scholars trained in everything from literary studies to sociology, cultural studies popularized the usage of interdisciplinary approaches to knowledge, meaning that their thought was irreducible to one discipline.[65]

The interdisciplinarity of cultural studies was highly inspired by the early twentieth-century Italian Marxist Antonio Gramsci, whose writings were translated into English in the late 1950s.[66] Gramsci was incarcerated in the 1920s by the Italian fascist regime of Benito Mussolini as a part of the larger right-wing thrust against European Marxism, and his *Prison Notebooks* would push Marxism into new domains, far beyond the economic determinism of the base/superstructure model.[67] With the rise of postwar conservative British politics represented in such political figures as Enoch Powell and Margaret Thatcher, cultural studies took the rising tide of European fascism seriously. Of course such conservativism predated World War II, Powell, and Thatcher in the United Kingdom. Critiques against Marxists like C.L.R. James and George Padmore in Britain during the interwar years were also rampant.[68]

Importantly, cultural studies scholars recognized that Powell and Thatcher represented no neat unbroken connection to prewar conservativism; but their conservativism was so popular due to the way that it spoke to the context of postwar Britain. As such, by the middle of the twentieth century, cultural studies scholars deployed interdisciplinarity to better understand what Gramsci called the "conjuncture," or the immediate political context that one finds themselves in, which cultural studies sought to understand to better negotiate the midcentury terrain of political and economic conservativism. Though not a reaction to Powell or Thatcher, cultural studies scholars argued that it was not merely enough to understand the conjuncture, but intervention in the conjuncture was necessary. Intervention, as Stuart Hall once argued, was necessary to appreciate "how different forces come together, conjuncturally, to create the new terrain, on which a different politics must form up."[69]

In North America, cultural studies approaches would find a home in the more critical pockets of communication and media studies, especially with the work of figures like Hanno Hardt and James Carey.[70] However, what interests me here is the speaking engagements in the United States by Stuart Hall. While they did not start materialist analysis of media and communication studies, Hall's 1983 lectures, delivered at the University of Illinois at Urbana-Champaign, were representative of the mid- to late-twentieth-century rise of materialist-Marxist analyses of media and communication in North America and beyond (indeed, I would argue that Hall's influential visits changed media and communication studies as much as Jacques Derrida's visit changed literature).[71] McLuhan was no Marxist of course, but he did inhabit a North American context where Marxist materialism shaped mid- to late-twentieth century media and communication studies. Often a target of cultural studies, McLuhan remained inseparable from this context of materialist, interdisciplinary investigations of media, only as an English literature scholar who was far more interested in the poetry of James Joyce than the transforming conditions of capitalism and labor. In short, McLuhan was uncomfortably part of the group of interdisciplinary scholars during the twentieth century who, rather than focus solely on media content, were calling for the study of the ways that other relations (like capitalism, corporations, labor, and governments, etc.) were influencing media content.

This concern with media beyond content was the point in Hall's classic 1973 essay "Encoding/Decoding," where he argued that the processes of encoding and decoding messages were not solely about interpretation, but both existed in material power relations that always already ensured relative autonomy: "there is no necessary correspondence between encoding and decoding, the former can attempt to 'pre-fer but cannot prescribe or guarantee the latter, which has its own conditions of existence."[72] According to Hall, not only were encoding/decoding inseparable, but the ruling class's ideology was *not guaranteed* to overdetermine one's reading of a message. While communications remained conservative and anticommunist, a growing contingent of media, communication, rhetoric, and cultural studies scholars turned media more materialist in the mid-twentieth century, in ways that pushed against dominant epistemological structures that assumed that there was some guarantee that media content could turn audiences into clones or cultural dupes of the sender. In many ways, McLuhan concurred with the cultural studies project and its critique of the dominant approaches to media: a radically different materiality of media needed to be considered in cultural studies and media philosophy.

Materiality meant that Marxist-influenced approaches to media and communication (particularly those of us influenced by cultural studies) were never fully distinct from media philosophy. Indeed, as Neil Postman would argue in the 1990s, McLuhan's theory of media pointed toward Marx himself.[73] For example, like Marx argued of the commodity in *Capital: A Critique of Political Economy, Vol. 1* (as can be seen in his famous example of linen—i.e., a commodity made from the fibers of flax plants), capitalism increasingly relied on the destruction of natural resources for the production of its commodities.[74] This concern with nature would be a central theme of Marxist scholars like Theodore Adorno, another figure important for media and communication studies.[75] Likewise, McLuhan would argue that those same commodities that Marx and Marxists talked about were also media. In his classic book *Understanding Media*, McLuhan argued that media, like television and radio, were paid for by other media: *money*, all of which were pulled from natural, raw materials.[76] Interestingly, both Marxists and McLuhan would somewhat concur that commodities/media impacted and were impacted by the natural environment, and commodities/media always spoke beyond themselves to a *surplus* that also impacted the way that people viewed themselves in society. The rise of environmental communication and media studies in the twentieth century would often find its home somewhere in between Marxism, cultural studies, and McLuhan's media philosophy.[77]

And it is in that intimate relation between materiality, media, and nature that I want to stay for Black media philosophy, as it is here that contemporary media philosophy and cultural studies remains, some more Marxist than others. Building off McLuhan's notion that each new medium creates a new environment, such important media philosophers as Friedrich Kittler, Shannon Mattern, Lisa Parks, John Durham Peters, and Jussi Parikka all argue that media are infrastructural, pulled from what we call *nature* and transformative of nature in the process.[78] The production and consumption of media both changes the natural environment, via natural resource extraction, and remakes that environment in ways that often cover up the centrality of nature within our devices. As Parikka argues, we are each walking around with pieces of "Africa in our pockets," as mercury, glass, and golds, often overextracted from African mining, make up our smartphone devices.[79] Building off the long materialist foundations of mid-twentieth-century media and cultural studies, these scholars rightly contend that nature must be theorized not as passive in media philosophy, but maybe as the ultimate medium toward man's invention, as manipulation of nature, toward its destruction, connects to a highly Western anthropocentric, epistemological media project. In short, media lay the ground of our being and knowing, quite literally and highly environmentally. Media are shaped by and continue to shape our physical environments and our conceptions of nature and humanness.

Aside from scholars like Jody Berland, Nicole Starosielski, and Melody Jue, however, the question of the *colonial* foundations of nature is often treated neutrally in these important media philosophies.[80] But the later cultural studies cohort—led by Hall but inclusive of other important Black scholars like Paul Gilroy, Hazel Carby, and Kobena Mercer—would point to the fact that race, civilization, and nature would be inseparable constructs.[81] For Gilroy, there is a Western concept of nature central to the racial project of the West.[82] As Gilroy argues, one's presumed proximity to the natural became illustrative of how civilized one was according to the West, which often worked to equate Black people as more proximate to nature and white people as more proximate to civilization, or distinct from nature and the sensorial. In short, in the lack of analysis of race in philosophies of media, the "natural resources" at the center of dominant studies often abstract out the centrality of race to Western conceptions of nature. However, as Mbembe argues, the "Negro's body is a natural body, a body of needs, a physiological body."[83]

Nature cannot be removed from the Western conception of certain people's presumed proximity to nature—central for Western imaginations of the Negro—and other's presumably heroic emergence from nature. If we accept McLuhan's theorizations (which, again, did *not* ignore the Negro, but took the Negro as given), what his media philosophy does ignore is *how* the Negro becomes a medium. Indeed, it is such Black bodies that are violently ripped from one of the most important Western Euro-American constructs of nature: Africa, that which

McLuhan regularly *tribalized*, or made synonymous with nature and the sensorial. It may not be enough to acknowledge that McLuhan's philosophy of media brushes over its racial implications. Because of the dependence of media philosophy on Western colonial conceptions of nature, we may need to ask whether the Negro (as one secularized, racial, Western-nature construct) remains foundational to any post-McLuhan media philosophy of humanness to begin with. Race, here, is one unstated foundation of Western, McLuhanesque media philosophy.

If media are formed out of nature (particularly as nature is conceived under Western, secularized societies), the ripping of Africans from Africa (nature) can be theorized as one media relation necessary to transform diverse populations into monolithic, captive wholes, particularly in the eyes of white Euro-Americans. Let's say this slightly differently: Western racial violence and ecological violence are inseparable developments, of which the transatlantic slave trade, neocolonial relations, the climate crisis, and the shifting violences of transnational capitalism (each central topics of Black studies and cultural studies) are only a few examples. In this light we can consider the media relation of the Negro as truly a reductive, secular, scientific project—one that conflated several, unique humans into one thing. The Negro is the *middle point*, if we go back to the original definition of media as middles, toward measuring the path from Western tribalism to civilization, which has meant toward white, capitalist, heterosexual, able-bodied maleness.[84]

This is not a radically different position from contemporary media philosophy, such as John Durham Peters and Lance Strate, who both argue that the body is an underexamined medium within media philosophy.[85] However, I contend that the body always does different work when race, gender, sexuality, nature, and capitalism are brought into the conversation. The Negro's media function is to act as Western bourgeois man's self-measure, the placeholder that reuniversalizes man as the self-determined figure, largely distinguishing himself from nature in comparison to those who can never fully get out of nature (presumably Black people). Although such violence is not exceptional to the United States or to Black people, Black media philosophy builds off both the Black studies and cultural studies call for contextual specificity to consider the relationships between Blackness in the United States, nature, and media. There is, then, an inherent relationship between media, ecological violence, racial violence (of which transatlantic slavery is only one variant), and Western conceptions of racial Blackness that Black media philosophy remains cognizant of.

## TOWARD A BLACK MEDIA PHILOSOPHY

How do we rethink the reproduction of the West as the technological end of history, alongside the push of Black studies and cultural studies against such logic? This is what I call Black media philosophy, which takes into consideration both Western man's requirement for the Negro as one medium to reproduce concepts of Western civilization and the ways that we as Black people create our own engagements with media, largely incomprehensible under white supremacy. To Western media philosophy, long concerned with materiality, I bring the radical materiality of Black studies and cultural studies, or the materialities concerned with Black radical, Black feminist, and anticapital politics. Rather than a television, podcast, or web series episode (all important focuses of Black media studies), I reconsider media environments as central to transforming concepts of Blackness. This requires building off Hall's conjunctural approach to research. For Hall, the conjuncture is an examination of the "whole ways of life," which includes, but is not limited to, analyses of the social, cultural, economic, and political elements of the context.[86] Hall concerned himself with how these different aspects of the context "articulated" with one another, meaning there was no deterministic relation between them, but they were "organic unities" that would never "guarantee the outcome of specific struggles."[87] Using archival research, content analyses, and historical-politico-economic analysis, this project is also concerned with articulating differing, constantly transforming media economies to different conceptualizations of Blackness, race, gender, sexuality, capitalism, media, the climate crisis, and Western man—not as fixed guarantees but as multifaceted processes.[88]

This project is divided into two interrelated themes. First, as noted, the connection between McLuhan's thought on media technologies and Darwin(ism), particularly as it pertains to Western conceptions of nature, suggests that race remains central to today's philosophies of media, even when race is not mentioned. For example, in the first chapter I excavate the media philosophical implications of Darwinian theory and Darwin's own work using Black studies and cultural studies. In examining Darwin, I show how his theoretical construct of nature was central to the growth of social Darwinism, and both Darwin and social Darwinism assumed a proximity between nature and the Negro—meaning the Negro was a racialized/gendered construct, by and for white people.

It is the Negro, a Western discursive construct, that functions to mediate man's overrepresentation as human, via categories like whiteness, bourgeoisie, and male. Darwinian thought inaugurated the Negro as a medium by and for man. Of course, my argument is not that there were no captive Black bodies prior to Darwin; instead, the Negro further garners its import as a medium during the nineteenth century, via secularized theories of man's nonmythic control over the environment, necessary for Wendy Chun's theory of "race and/as technology."[89] While Chun implies that Darwin was important for the technologization of the "captive Black body," particularly for the eugenic call to enter into and presumably transform bodies racially, the first chapter points less to Heidegger, as per Chun, and more to Darwin. I use McLuhan to show that (social) Darwinian evolutionary theory holds a flawed media philosophical implication—one that rarely is turned to in media philosophy until now. It is such a social Darwinian, pre-media philosophy that would be necessary for McLuhan's mature, mid-twentieth century theory.

The second theme of the book is organized around the long Black freedom struggle, the challenge to the reductions of our bodies to media functions by and for social Darwinian Western man. Media always hold a creative, "world-transmitting power," a theme accepted in Western media philosophy but ignored in the same philosophies when Black people are placed front and center within them.[90] Put differently, what happens when/if Black people utilize concepts of our bodies as mediators for white self-conceptions against white people? What this has historically looked like is the history of Black radical thought and action (chapters 2 and 3). Chapter 2 outlines alternative concepts of media on the Underground Railroad. The enslaved people's own narratives of their flight from slavery suggested that the Underground Railroad was no unorganized mode of escape, one representative of an inherent relation between Blackness and tribalness but an alternative Black media economy that assisted in Black forms of escapisms from Southern states.

To say that the Underground Railroad was a media economy means that it was a time-space that necessitated a variety of media relations (such as the Negro itself) to facilitate traversals of space by enslaved people in different, though not separate, fashion than the slave catchers giving chase. Although this escape might be degraded as backward or undeveloped, often in capitalist bioevolutionary terms, enslaved people used discriminatory framings of their bodies to sneak past white people. Unlike the slave catchers who relied on media like maps, printed paper, and the phonetic alphabet, the Black enslaved person's media economy was structured around media *not* deemed media by white people, but often deemed natural, such as orality, star constellations, tree branches, and even their own bodies. Alternative media relations were necessary for Black enslaved people to imagine and develop paths toward their own freedom, or at least to escape from racial slavery.

Similar relations would occur over one hundred years later with the rise of the Oakland-based Black Panther Party and their complex understanding of the tele-visual economy (chapter 3). McLuhan once argued that the television would create a "global village," or a world in which hierarchies would diminish as electronic media would eventually make the world into a small, communal village. Interestingly, the concept of a global village was taken up by an unlikely figure in the 1970s: Huey P. Newton, the cofounder of Oakland's Black Panther Party. Using a Black Maoist, anticolonial frame, Newton argued the global village was specifically designed to make the world smaller but only for a small population of people: wealthy, white men. This led Newton to argue that the global village was not only a project of capitalism but also completely inseparable from the destruction of the natural environment, as the ruling class (what he called the "technocrats") required massive expropriation of the world's natural resources and people for the materialization of their global village. With the spread of transnational capitalism came new ways to harm and kill Black people, worldwide, as well as the environment, throwing doubt on the revolutionary potential of the global village of McLuhan's formulation.

Still, Newton did not view the global village as a total waste. He argued that the media central to the global village, like televisions, airplanes, and even nature, held the hidden potential to bring together those fighting racism and capitalism in the United States with those challenging similar forms of oppression throughout the de/colonial world. If there was a global village with any radical potential that could ever be reached via electronic media, Newton argued, it was Black radicals and decolonial fighters who were likely to be the first to enter it, not McLuhan's Yippies. If Black radicals and decolonial fighters did not engage in the global village, then Newton suggested that the environment could turn on man for his arrogance, eventually killing everyone in a world increasingly dedicated to Western domination of the global oil trade and, by extension, environmental destruction.

Chapter 4 walks the line between both themes, showing elements of McLuhan's racialized politics, while pointing toward the ways that Black people potentially disrupt Western man's self-indulgent, racial principles. This chapter examines the increasing popularity of the digital animations of Michael Brown's 2014 killing at the hands of former Ferguson, Missouri, police officer, Darren Wilson. Without video footage of Brown's killing, there has been a related market to digitally animate Brown's killing, largely through Wilson's testimony. Brown is made "information," or property, as the depiction of violence against his Black body is made legible for profit, especially for Wilson, who is rendered nonracist. Yet the proliferation of Brown as information also opened up space for critiques of contemporary conceptions of property itself, in the form of organizations inspired by the hashtag #BlackLivesMatter, which, I argue, challenge both racial violence against Black people but also one of the newest property relationships: the digitalization of ourselves as information online.

Indeed, what the hashtag points toward is the central question of chapter 4, one that suggests that the construct of the Negro has yet to fully disappear online: Does the Negro's historical connection to nature mean that the Negro *matters* way too much in Western society? Rather than Black lives matter, I show that matter (the noun form of the word) is the structure that Judy's Negro rests on, which is why Black lives have been deemed so acceptably killable by the state, both historically and in ways necessarily different today. The contemporary Movement for Black Lives has simply been one of the latest physical (now digital) fights against a long problem of Western concepts of matter—one that, whether on- or offline, keeps the Negro in white minds more than in Black lives.

I conclude the book by turning toward another unthought position within media philosophy: reparations for chattel slavery. With the rise of new groups like the American Descendants of Slaves (ADOS), the discussion of reparations is increasingly turning into a highly U.S.-focused, dangerous, nationalist project. Yet what scholars like Ruth Wilson Gilmore and Angela Davis argue is that reparations cannot be reduced to the U.S. nation alone. Rather, reparations must reverberate throughout the nation and far beyond, transforming the prison as well as U.S.-militarized, colonialist approaches to the world. Building off this position, I want to think about the articulation of the Negro with nature, alongside the violence at the heart of environmental destruction, as all necessarily part of a discussion of reparations. For Davis, reparations exceeds any financial payment, that may or may not come, to include the discussion of what type of planet do we want to live on in the future. Likewise, I connect Davis's question about the type of planet that we want to live on to our need to have a habitable earth, not destroyed by the excesses of capitalism. I conclude by thinking about how reparations exceeds financial payment to those that the U.S. state has classified as Black and speaks to a larger recognition of how racial violence has been articulated with Western bourgeois planetary destruction. We may require new concepts of humanness and reparations, concepts long provided in Black studies and cultural studies, in order to rethink the survival of all people throughout the changing climates of the world.

The historical context in which McLuhan's media philosophy emerged (social and political unrest, the Cold War, social Darwinism, transformations in capitalism, Black studies, cultural studies, area studies, and communications) illustrates that McLuhan often could not see how he both contradicted and fully maintained the dominant epistemological structures of mid-twentieth-century academia. Such limits make scholars like McLuhan useful for contemporary work because they reveal how Western man built Western theory. And most important, Black studies and cultural studies, both of which McLuhan largely ignored, yet could not fully separate from, are necessary to understand media philosophy's weddedness to Western man. In addition, both Black studies and cultural studies can push media philosophy toward new epistemological questions, while also providing us with a lens to think about how Black people have thought about the relationship between liberation and media. In short, understanding McLuhan's context shows the limits of an older epistemology and points toward something new. This project synthesizes these various positions in search of that *newness* that McLuhan pointed us toward, but ultimately missed—a Black media philosophy.

# CHAPTER I

# Technological Darwinism

*I was incessantly struck, whilst living with the Fuegians on board the H.M.S. "Beagle," with the many little traits of character, shewing [sic] how similar their minds were to ours; and so it was with a full-blooded negro with whom I happened once to be intimate.*

—Charles Darwin

Charles Darwin had sexual intercourse with *someone* during his nineteenth-century voyage on the Her Majesty's Ship Beagle (the H.M.S. Beagle). Led by Captain Robert FitzRoy, the H.M.S. Beagle left from England in 1831 on a surveying mission of the Americas. What was supposed to be only a two-year trip turned into five. On the recommendation of J.S. Henslow, the British botanist and priest, the young Darwin was employed as the H.M.S. Beagle's naturalist, using his *Red Notebook* to document geological structures and animal species during his travels.[1] Henson wrote a personal letter in August of 1831 to Darwin, stating that although Darwin was not yet "a *finished* Naturalist," the twenty-two-year-old Darwin "was amply qualified for collecting, observing & noting any thing [sic] worthy to be noted in Natural History."[2] Darwin noted that this voyage to the Americas would be important for developing his later theories in *On the Origin of Species*, arguably his most famous work.[3]

But there were far more violent relations on and around the H.M.S. Beagle that went underexamined in *On the Origin of Species*, the *Red Notebook*, or any of Darwin's personal correspondences.[4] The Fuegians mentioned in the chapter epigraph were on board the H.M.S. Beagle because FitzRoy sought to return three captives that he had kidnapped from Tierra del Fuego on the first mission between 1826 and 1830. Indeed, the Fuegians also provide one of the more important entry points into many discussions of Darwin's complex and contradictory positions on race.[5] However, there is another, even less examined entry point into Darwin's position on race in the same quote. You could read the epigraph as a representation of Darwin's belief that there were few racial differences between white and Black people, particularly as Darwin was clearly willing to be *intimate* with a Black person. But, as Black studies has long taught us, we should not confuse intimacy with abolition.

The end of the epigraph is worth repeating. As Darwin was noting the similarities between himself and the Fuegians, as all human, he likewise wants to note they all share the same human commonalities "with a full-blooded negro with whom I happened once to be intimate." It is almost a throwaway line, and it is not clear if the intimate act happened while in Tierra del Fuego or elsewhere. But the line also reveals much about Darwin's context: he lived in a world that situated him as a figure with racialized/sexual power over the non-Western, colonized, and enslaved people in the Americas. To assume that his intimate report was representative of a critique of racial differences requires not asking an equally central question: What to the full-blooded Negro, forced into this intimate act, did Darwin's criticisms of racial differences mean? Nothing, as the Negro was an object of sexual desire by and for Darwin. Under the captivity of the Americas that Darwin admittedly hated, a full-blooded Negro's choice about a sexual encounter with a white person was always determined by the violence of slavery that made that encounter with the Negro in the Americas possible in the first place. It was such forms of sexuality that were part of multiple colonial ventures of Western Europeans, situating non-Western people who were violently colonized and enslaved as hypersexual in relation to the civilized, rational colonizer (i.e., white men), who could partake in the fabricated hypersexuality of colonized and enslaved women.[6] Intimacy for Darwin was rape for the full-blooded Negro.

It is with the full-blooded Negro that we can reexamine Darwin's own abolitionist position, one of the most consistent positions he took on slavery, such as in his book *Voyage of H.M.S. Beagle*.[7] This is not too surprising, as Darwin came from an abolitionist family. His grandfather, Josiah Wedgwood, was a "master potter, designer and manufacturer," but Wedgewood was also a part of the middle-classed abolitionist group, the Committee for the Abolition of the Slave Trade, or simply the London Committee.[8] Thus when Darwin ended *Voyage of H.M.S. Beagle* by expressing his joy that he was finally leaving Brazil, vowing that "I shall never again visit a slave-country," it was not out of character.[9] This abolitionist position also informed Darwin's later concept of variation, where he argued that species (of all kinds, humans included) were not as distinct from one another as popularly thought. Instead, all species differed from one another by degrees, not kind: "From the strong principle of inheritance, any selected *variety* [of a species] will tend to propagate its new and modified form."[10] It would be the propagation of selected varieties, which could only occur over long periods, that would lead to changes in a species's skin, hair, eyes, teeth, nails, and more. Put into explicitly racial terms, Darwin's theory of evolution shuns popular, nineteenth-century polygenetic arguments, which held that different races are the product of very different species. Alternatively, Darwin argued that the nineteenth-century conflation of the Negro with monkeys was "almost ludicrous" and that the human "races agree in so many unimportant details of structure and in so many mental peculiarities, that these can be accounted for only through inheritance from a common progenitor."[11] In other words, Darwin was in favor of monogenism, meaning that Black people and white people were different varieties of the *same species*.

Despite Darwin's monogenetic argument, later social Darwinists used his work to make racist arguments against Black and brown people; in the United States these critiques would extend to white immigrants as well.[12] This has led many to argue that social Darwinists misread Darwin, applying his work in racialized and gendered discussions of human groups that survive better than others. The assumption that lies between these two areas is a distinction between "real" science (Darwin) and "pseudoscience" (social Darwinism), ultimately obscuring "the political nature of much of the biological and human sciences."[13] But such distinctions between social Darwinism and Darwin himself breakdown when we pay attention not to Darwin's abolitionist position, not to Darwin's disgust at the act of capturing the Fuegians, but when we give our full attention to the overlooked full-blooded Negro who haunts Darwin's notes.

The only way to give the chapter epigraph the full violent weight that it deserves is to acknowledge that Darwin's intimacy was attached to what Saidiya Hartman once referred to as the "simulation of consent in the context of extreme domination."[14] Darwin's intimacy was inseparable from a racial/gendered relation of power that he held over that Negro with whom he was intimate. As Candice Jenkins argues, intimacy means different things depending on the races of those involved in the intimate act. For her, the dominant, Western discursive production of the Negro is often a history not of Black people per se but of white desires and imaginations of Black people. For example, the systematic rape of Black women, both during and after slavery, was justified via reference to the "promiscuity" of all Black women, itself a white fabrication based on Western conflations of Black people with nature and emotion.[15] As per the dominant, nineteenth-century racist arguments, people of African descent were wild, highly emotional, and sexually licentious, thus "dooming the larger black population to depravity and disease," particularly under nineteenth-century "republican family ideals."[16] To rape a Negro, at Darwin's time in the Americas, often made little sense, as the Negro was not deemed human (at least in legalistic terms) but property.

When we fully break down Darwin's intimate act, we cannot even see this as intimacy in any consensual way.[17] We can say that Darwin had a sexual encounter with what we can guess was a Black woman (although this is just an assumption, as he does not state whether he was intimate with a woman or a man); but we cannot say this encounter existed outside a context in which the full-blooded Negro, as a construct of the white imagination, served a *media function* for Darwin's sexual urges, no matter his criticisms of racial slavery. As per Brian Hochman, the media function in the West was anything that continued (Darwin's) colonial, civilized power.[18] For Hochman, the phonetic alphabet, the printing press, and the gramophone could each stand as measures (or media) of how far the presumed former tribal Western man had come out of nature to reach *his* civilized, colonial, rational (de/retribal) state in the present. The full-blooded Negro was likewise one measure of where civilized people like Darwin used to be: highly sexual, wild, and natural. Darwin was not returning to a previous state through his intimate act with a Negro, but he was reaffirming his civilized ability to take advantage of (or select) those who remained emotional, sexual, sensual, and close to nature. For Hortense Spillers, the captive Black body has historically existed to function not by or for itself, but by and for others, meaning, for me, that the Negro can be thought about as a medium that does work for what we now call white people. Indeed, the Negro is one central route (mediator) for some to become white in the first place.

Although nothing more than a short line in Darwin's notes, what would it mean to reposition this intimate act with a Negro as representative of a larger project of Western media functions? It would mean that Darwin's antislavery positioning would not undo the racialized and gendered context through which Negroes were deemed useful, not for themselves, but by and for another (Darwin). Following scholars like Banu Subramaniam, but also Darwin's own words on intimacy, I want to take a different position from those who critique social Darwinism as a misread of Darwin. Instead of considering Darwin's intimate act as representative of his belief that humans only differed slightly, I argue that his theories suggested that the full-blooded Negro could be *artificially selected*, fundamental for Darwin's continued self-conception as civilized and evolved Western man—a metaphor for whiteness, capitalism, and maleness.[19]

Darwin argued that artificial selection was how man, like other animals, selected objects from nature and turned them into items that could be used for his own survival. Despite Darwin's presumably neutral theory, it cannot be ignored that it was assembled in the same conjuncture where the Negro was one of those items, what Sylvia Wynter once called one "primary empirical referent category" for Darwinian, Western man's self-concept.[20] The Negro was that which Darwin could be intimate with before going on about his life. While Darwin may have despised racial slavery in the Americas, he also nevertheless considered the Negro as fully capable of serving a function by and for himself. This function was always already in excess of sexual acts but nevertheless intimate, as intimacy, for Lisa Lowe, was "the property of the possessive individual."[21]

Darwin's intimacy with the full-blooded Negro did not require naming or even gendering the Negro, but a full ungendering, as per Hortense Spillers, in order to justify Darwin's self-concept. What was required was Darwin's capacity to select for himself the media function that that same Negro must serve. Darwin lived in a world in which the Negro was a medium toward extending his presumed monopolization of civilized humanness, and his overall bioevolutionary theory reflected such a view. In ways that mirror Richard Cavell's argument of media philosophy as the study of *our* knowing and being, the Negro was a medium, or in McLuhan's terms, an extension, of Darwin's self-being and knowing. Indeed, I argue Darwin's artificial selection is a media philosophy itself, well before a thing called media philosophy ever existed. And this nascent media philosophy lay the foundation for McLuhan's later, mature twentieth-century media philosophy. No matter who the nameless, full-blooded Negro was, they were a medium by and for Darwin during that intimate act. It is for these reasons that I believe that the medium or Negro long ignored in Darwin's story and studies of Darwin deserves a reckoning.

## HOW (SOCIAL) DARWINIAN THOUGHT INFLUENCED MEDIA PHILOSOPHY

Although Darwin publicly voiced abolitionist leanings, his own intimate act suggested that he would not be fully against some elements of the later social Darwinian theoretical project. But social Darwinism and Darwin cannot be conflated because the conjuncture is far from static. Although social Darwinism existed during Darwin's lifetime, a burst of social Darwinian theory proliferated in the twentieth century in a context that Darwin would have likely found unfamiliar: both the increasingly tense debates about the legitimacy of Western colonial rule in Africa, Asia, and the Americas, and Black and brown people's growing calls for self-governance during the early and mid-twentieth century. For example, Black and brown people all over the world would be alarmed by the fascist regime of Benito Mussolini invading Abyssinia on October 3, 1935. The violent Italian invasion was a part of the country's wider expansionist strategy in the wake of World War I and the League of Nations inaction, despite the organization being formed to prevent exactly what Italy was doing. The invasion would come to serve as "a flashpoint for anti-imperialist and anticolonial agitation and organization" for Black and brown people throughout the world.[22]

With the embarrassing, hands-off approach to Mussolini from the West—around the same time the West also took a noninterventionist approach to the rise of other fascist regimes led by Francisco Franco and Adolf Hitler—places like Britain would see a rise of anticolonial thought, led by figures like C.L.R. James and George Padmore. In James's 1938 book, *The Black Jacobians*, he wrote about the eighteenth-century Saint-Domingue Revolution with twentieth-century Africa on his mind.[23] The book marked a shift in character for Black and anticolonial feelings throughout Africa and the diaspora, as calls for increasingly more radical responses to Western colonization and racism arose, calls that would violently materialize in the colonies throughout the twentieth century. Of course, the United States would find such Black radical positions increasingly alarming—more alarming than fascism—as it was invested in Western colonialism for its own financial bottom line.[24] Fascism often did not threaten the West as much as decolonization, Black radicalism, and anticapitalist thought and action.

While the United States's and Nazi Germany's related eugenics projects are often held up as epitomizing twentieth-century social Darwinism, another figure landed closer to the theoretical home of McLuhan.

In a context where Black and brown people throughout the world called for the end of Western colonial rule, colonial psychiatrist J. C. Carothers was representative of the Western social Darwinian context of the twentieth century, arguing, for example, that Kenya's Black population was dependent on Western colonial rule, in part, due to Western technological superiority. In 1955, two years after what the West called the Kenyan Mau Uprising, where Black Kenyans rose against British colonial rule, Carothers wrote his report, *The Psychology of Mau Mau,* to be reviewed by the government in the capital city of Kenya, Nairobi.[25] In the report, Carothers argued that the Europeans were well acquainted with change, as the "solid world of Newtonian physics is melting before our eyes and its place is being taken by a more fluid world of probabilities."[26] However, the jolt of change via Western colonial rule in "Africa is much more drastic," leading to rebellions throughout Kenya that Carothers said most people "realize by now...will fail."[27] Carothers's solution was simple and would match the efforts of other Western colonizers and their attempts to slow decolonial efforts: in order for the Nairobi government to stop the rebellion, it should provide people in Kenya with some "rights" (under a Western logic of rights), which would "help certain rehabilitation problems," and also further materialize British colonial rule in neocolonial ways.[28]

Carothers's 1955 report on Kenya was informed by his earlier work. In 1953, for example, he wrote *The African Mind in Health and Disease: A Study of Ethnopsychiatry,* published by the fairly newly formed World Health Organization (1948). In it, Carothers argued that the "Negro's conditions" were largely alien to Western Europeans, and such conditions were so strong that they could carry over, well beyond transatlantic slavery and Africa, to effect the mentalities of Black people in the United States, even those of us who had never stepped foot on the African continent.[29] Carothers's presumed African mentality, inside all black people, would organize McLuhan's thinking as well, though Cartohers's work would have far more violent implications than McLuhan's. For Carothers, racial violence was not the problem of Black people; the African mind was, whether healthy or diseased.

In his *African Mind in Health and Disease,* we see Carothers's version of the temporalized, evolutionary, racial logic of social Darwinism: there is a group that is behind the West (tribal) and that same group can be used as a measure of where the West once was. Such logic would be critiqued by Johannes Fabian in his classic 1983 text *Time and the Other,* as the "denial of coevalness," or the Western inability to think about time outside of its own Western epistemological frameworks.[30] In other words, as Bernard Stiegler argued, time, technology, and epistemology are linked in the West.[31] Presumably for Carothers, there is *one time*, and all others not only must catch up to Western time, but those others also provide empirical examples for the study of Western human evolutionary, technological development. In Carothers's formulation of development he used a term that Fabian critiques—one that was popular in the social Darwinian anthropology of the twentieth century: "tribal man," the position of the "underdeveloped" (i.e., those people close to nature), uncivilized, without Western technology. What Carothers would add to this conversation is "detribalism."

Here, Western Europeans had come out of the tribal, they alone had distinguished themselves from a previous, mythic, magical, oral world and moved into a highly technological, literate, objective, secular, and scientific world—the detribal. They had, in other words, removed themselves from their own tribalism, becoming *de*tribal men. For Carothers, it was technology and capitalism that separated detribalism from tribalism, ensuring that detribalism was the presumable peak that Black people always wanted to reach, but could not without white people's help. Indeed, as Walter Rodney argued in his classic *How Europe Underdeveloped Africa*, whether linked to technology or racialized assumptions of the mind, "development" was always structured by Europe as a metaphor for capitalism.[32] In *The African Mind in Health and Disease*, Carothers would argue that tribalism always permeates "the lives of many [African and diasporic] people who at first sight seem totally detribalized," but they (Black people) cannot fully detribalize, as only Europeans can truly escape the backwardness of tribalization—which is to say, develop toward the social production stage of capitalism.[33]

Of course, Carothers would be noted as an important influence on McLuhan, in both McLuhan's documented six personal correspondences between Carothers and in McLuhan's famous 1962 book, *The Gutenberg Galaxy*.[34] Much of the mid-twentieth century anthropological and psychological theories that McLuhan based his media philosophy on would be disproven as faulty social Darwinian theory. As noted, Carothers would not disappoint on this account, as his theories exceeded the hypothetical and materially justified British colonialism in temporal, social Darwinian terms: Black people were tribal, or highly close to nature, largely oral cultures with little technological development; and white Westerners were detribal, highly technological and far more developed and civilized, or outside nature. In short, the tribal (Black) is a measure of where the detribal (white) once was. Furthermore, the tribal is not just a measure, for Carothers, but the tribal always holds a relation between nature, emotion, and the senses.[35] For example, Neda Atanasoski and Kalindi Vora argue that Darwin biologized the human senses in ways that were popularized in the twentieth-century academy but have carried over into contemporary digital products.[36] For Atanasoski and Vora, Darwin's theories assumed a strict dichotomy between the more emotional, highly sensual humans *(tribal,* close to nature) and less emotional, sensually isolated humans (*detribal*, the figures distinct from nature). Those more emotional beings were presumably in touch with their senses and thus less civilized; those less emotional beings were more civilized based on the fragmentation of senses.[37]

Similar frames would arguably organize McLuhan's midcentury media philosophy. McLuhan once argued that media were any extension of our human bodies, specifically our senses; this meant that the media content always exceeded a television show to include the full materiality of the medium itself. Orality illustrated tribal, or acoustic, natural environments, meaning media environments that extended the ear, or sound and touch, as sound vibrates (multisensorial, those beings in touch with their senses). Alternatively, the phonetic alphabet and Gutenberg's printing press represented more mechanical, detribal media environments, which is to say a detribal environment housed media that often extended one sense (often the eye, for McLuhan), articulating sight and detachment with knowledge in the West, all distinct from the emotional, the natural, and the multisensorial. Thus McLuhan and Darwin agreed in some ways: the less civilized/tribal were more emotional and sensorial; the more civilized/detribal were less emotional and sensorial. And such agreement makes sense in a context where social Darwinian theorists, such as Carothers, were highly influential on McLuhan's media philosophy.

For McLuhan, each new media environment, from tribal to detribal, resulted in new scales "introduced into our affairs by each extension of ourselves, or by any new technology."[38] Yet McLuhan's read of media as extensions of the senses was no neutral, scientific engagement, but pulled from the social Darwinian context that he lived in, which conflated a presumed control over the senses and emotions (or lack thereof) with outdated distinctions between culture and nature. Like Carothers, McLuhan's tribal man was designed to say more about what the West imagined itself as than what Kenyans or Black people in the United States were. The tribal, here, shares a lineage with the Negro:

both existed more in white people's imaginations than in the lives of Black people. Like the phonetic alphabet or Gutenberg's printing press, the tribal/Negro serves a function in early media philosophy, one that has little to do with Black people and more to do with Western needs of self-creation and preservation as detribal. In this light, McLuhan has a direct connection to Darwin: these two scholars assumed that the tribal/Negro was not inferior to white people per se but measurable by and for white people, which for me means the tribal/Negro was a medium, central to building Western raced-gendered self-imaginations.

### AGAINST SEXUAL SELECTION; OR ARTIFICIAL SELECTION AS A BASIS FOR MEDIA PHILOSOPHY

The data that we have on the full-blooded Negro of Darwin's retelling remains incomplete. But what we do know is that Darwin lived in a context of racial slavery and colonization—one that Carothers and other academics of the mid-twentieth century were trying, yet failing, to hold onto. Under such a context, only people like Darwin had the legit capacity to select, or consent, to the intimate act. It is without surprise, then, that an unnamed, ungendered, "full-blooded negro" haunted Darwin's later theories and their implementation beyond himself.

Still, while we may have difficulty finding the full-blooded Negro of Darwin's past, that does not mean that we should stop looking. Indeed, we can reconsider Darwin's intimacy for its raced, gendered, and mediated implications. Specifically, we can reconsider Darwin not only as a theorist of evolution but as an unexamined media philosopher, one that lay the foundation for a later McLuhanesque philosophy. Indeed, because we started with McLuhan's social Darwinian influence, we can think about the full-blooded Negro as a medium, one whose function was to be a measure of how far Darwin, and the like, had come out of nature (detribal). However, if we are not careful, one way that Darwin's intimate act might be viewed is under the domain of what the famed naturalist called "sexual selection." For Darwin, sexual selection was representative of the manner through which members of one "biological sex" made themselves attractive to partners of the other "biological sex" in order to mate and continue on their different, unique forms of variations.[39] As John Tyler Bonner and Robert May argue in their introduction to Darwin's The Descent of Man, and Selection in Relation to Sex, under sexual selection "certain traits in the male (or, less commonly, the female)" make "him (or her) more successful in mating."[40]

The important philosopher Elizabeth Grosz has tried to rethink discussions of race via Darwin's sexual selection. For Grosz, one mode of attracting sexual partners is the capacity for language, in the broadest sense (speech, songs, grunts, etc.).[41] Sexual selection led to the continuation/reproduction of some variations in species over others. In short, sexual selection is Darwin's agential, largely heterosexist process of selecting a partner to mate with. It is via sexual selection that Darwin argued that racial differences may be re/made, as race could be deemed something of a preference when selecting partners. He is worth quoting at length:

> We have thus far been baffled in all our attempts to account for the differences between the races of man; but there remains one important agency, namely Sexual Selection, which appears to have acted as powerfully on man, as on many other animals. I do not intend to assert that sexual selection will account for all the differences between the races....Nor do I pretend that the effects of sexual selection can be indicated with scientific precision; but it can be shewn [sic] that it would be an inexplicable fact if man had not been modified by this *agency*, which has acted so powerfully on innumerable animals, both high and low in the scale. It can further be shewn [sic] that the differences between the races of man, as in colour, hairyness, form of features, &c., are of the nature which it might have been expected would have been, acted on by sexual selection.[42]

Grosz likewise follows Darwin's lead: "sexual selection, that is, relations of sexual difference, may have played a formative role in the establishment of racial differences."[43] If we follow both Darwin and Grosz to their end, the Negro may be mistakenly read as a choice via sexual selection: racial groups are the product of an ability of certain humans with specific variations to linguistically communicate better with those who may have similar forms of variation (like skin tone).[44] But as Cedric Robinson argues, this ignores the long-held interrelationship between Africa and Europe, via Moorish and Roman colonization of Europe, well before the fabrication of the West.[45]

Europe did not wake up one day with "races" who only preferred those from similar racial backgrounds. Instead, Europe is a product of the history of what Cedric Robinson called *racialisms*, in which sexual preferences ebbed and flowed, given that what we now call Black people were part of both the Roman and Moorish Empires and living in European centers much longer than Europe cares to acknowledge.[46] Today's Black and white people, under biocentric logics of sexual selection and "full bloodedness," are relatively recent inventions in this long view of race. Thus Darwin's intimacy with a full-blooded Negro cannot be read as a product of any mutual, agential communication (sexual selection), but as a product of racialized-gendered violence that functioned by and for Darwin, toward the establishment of the West and its newly invented biocapitalist, secularized whiteness. Because that enslaver was why the full-blooded Negro was in the Americas in the first place, Darwin held his mutual, agential communicative relation not with the full-blooded Negro but with the enslaver, not with the property of his intimate imagination but the owner. It is the Negro, a fabrication aimed at rewriting Western history as the only history, that transmits to Darwin and the enslaver a shared and increasingly biocapitalist form of whiteness and maleness, which social Darwinism presumes existed prior to 1492.[47] Thus we will not find the entirety of the full-blooded Negro within the theoretical account of Darwin's sexual selection.

Rather than sexual selection, Darwin's raced and gendered media philosophy can be divined from another important component of evolution: his theorization of "artificial selection," that which links Carothers and McLuhan. Whereas sexual selection was the process where organisms better adapted to their environments could survive and produce more offspring, artificial selection involved the ways that man, like other animals, selected natural objects from the natural environment and turned them into items that could be used for his own survival.[48] Scholars influenced by Darwin would theorize artificial selection in similar ways, adding far more racial framings. Infamous social Darwinist Herbert Spencer argued that the "supplementary limbs," or advanced tools of Western man, marked the conditions necessary for the development of "higher forms" of human beings.[49] Spencer noted that humanness could be objectively measured via technology. And, again, Carothers would talk about the import of Western tools for human development, as distinct from the naturalness of the tribal African.

These Western tools, for Carothers, were central to African dependency on Europe. Here (social) Darwinism was a myth about the mythlessness of artificial selection. These were epic tales about Western man's mastery over the colonial construct of nature, which would be central to artificial selection. Indeed, artificial selection was the allusion of how nature was open to selection by man (most specifically Western man) in ways that other humans and animals could presumably never reach.[50] Such control led to Western man artificially turning nature into something new: once tamed (technologized), nature could *extend* Western man above all beings because only he could manipulate nature in secular ways that other beings could not. Indeed, this highly anthropocentric, colonial position is the unthought foundation of nature in contemporary media philosophy, particularly that which lies closest to McLuhan.[51]

Thus we have already spoken to one of the questions that lie at the heart of the Darwinian-McLuhanesque media philosophy: If the captive Black body is a medium, then what is its content? McLuhan argued that all media have content, even as we largely misunderstand what that content is. For him, that content is not solely a media representation, but other media, like the phonetic alphabet in books or photography in film. I argue Darwin gives us more insight into the content of the Western construct of the Negro for media philosophy: the content of the Negro lies not solely in a radio show or a new Netflix special, but in Darwin's colonial construct of nature. Nature-as-content is not too distinct from contemporary media philosophy. According to John Durham Peters, all media have an *elemental* legacy, meaning that the history of media must be rewritten to include air, water, fire, and earth as media; natural elements always mediate experiences of human life.[52] For Peters, McLuhan's argument that all media are environments can be flipped: environments (air, water, earth, weather, elements, or nature) are also media.

But what is obscured in many media philosophical positions is my central focus: that media content is inseparable from the Western colonial construction of nature, which means the highly Western logic that nature, as a construct, lies in excess and gendered waiting of Western man's control and manipulation of it toward his own necessity.[53] As fabricated by everyone from Darwin to McLuhan, Western man positioned some people as closer to the colonial construct of nature (and by extension, media) than to himself. Put simply, the content of the Negro *is* Western nature. This content is a highly anthropocentric construct that presumed nature to be measurable and secularized, to be overexamined and overmanipulated for Western scientific and capitalist overuse.[54] The Western construct of nature ensures that the Negro, the construct of Darwin's intimate act and his imagination of that act, has more similarities with Western media than both the Western people who kidnapped Africans and those who fought for the end of enslavement.

If we buy the argument that media are always elemental, that media are pulled from natural materials, then what is the transatlantic slave trade, or the rape of an enslaved woman, or slave breeding, other than man's artificial selection of natural elements to reproduce his own imagined evolutionary superiority? We have now made the Negro a central concept of media philosophies in the West—one, like other media, that holds nature close. This can begin to account for why early racial classifications of the Negro situated "it" as a completely separate species from the human, closer to apes, monkeys, and chimpanzees, which Darwin fully disagreed with; yet this relationship between the Negro and natural elements also accounts for why the Negro, apes, monkeys, and chimpanzees were deemed as closer to nature than to man, which Darwin was far more ambiguous about. The longue durée of Western man's classification of Negroes shares an isomorphism with McLuhan's media: both are deemed *items*, initially pulled from nature, that extend Western man's monopoly over humanness, they were and the tools with which to measure all other forms of humanness. These Western colonial concepts of nature, elements, and raw materials function as the metaphorical content of the Negro. As such, the Negro's historico-political conflation with elements, with matter, with nature, makes it not merely a human among all other humans but an undertheorized medium by and for man.[55] Black people would have none of this, of course, but this does not mean that we have not been largely theorized in Western, white imaginations as closer to Western man's nature than to man himself.

Today the Negro is rarely explicitly contemplated in media philosophy. Still, the elemental component of the Negro—located in Darwin and Carothers and, as such, McLuhan—can be called forth by Western man when need be, similar to Heideggerian modern technology.[56] This is not a choice made by Black people; it is a selection, productive of the Negro as medium to begin with. What better description of nature being called-forth from the Negro do we find than in Frantz Fanon's description of his own body? In the fifth chapter of *Black Skin, White Masks*, Fanon described what would go on to be one of his most written about interactions as a Black man living in France, surrounded by mostly white people. One day, while traveling by train, Fanon was interrupted by a small white child who noticed him and cried to its mother, "Look, a Negro! *Maman*, a Negro!"[57] In that moment Fanon implied that his Negro-ness was called forth, not of his own doing, but by and for another. Although coming from a small child, Fanon's Negro-ness, called forth, mirrored the psychological approach to Black people at the time—as nonhuman or naturalistic objects rather than as humans.

It is for similar reasons that in *The Wretched of the Earth*, Fanon openly criticizes Carothers (McLuhan's influence) for his bioevolutionary invention of tribalized African minds.[58] On the train Fanon was no longer Fanon per se; he was *the* Negro (he says he was "spread eagle"), in closer proximity to nature than to Western man, and laying violently at standing-reserve for any white person's distributive utilization when necessary.[59] Likewise, Fanon (or rather Fanon's spread eagle body) was productive of the white people around him, he served as a measure for them. In his own words, Fanon was a "toy," or what I am calling a medium, necessary to extend whiteness, maleness, heterosexual-ness, and middle-classness as the representative of all forms of humanness.[60]

Fanon ruptured any hopes of race- and gender-neutrality in Darwin's or McLuhan's philosophies. Fanon's Black body was an extension, pointing toward the normality of the media function of the Negro as selectable, by and for the other, but also (like all media) as a body productive of the selector's self-conception.[61] When a Black person is stopped and frisked by the police because they "fit the description," they know Fanon. When a Black person walks into a store and is followed by the white store clerk, they know Fanon. And when a Black person has campus police called on them for sleeping in their own dorm's lobby by a white dormmate, Fanon returns yet again.[62] In these different situations, as Spillers teaches, the Negro haunts Black people well into the present.[63] To artificially select was never solely the privileged ability of Western man for Darwin but artificial selection was something done at differing levels of sophistication, depending on the being; as such, it is representative of the racialized/gendered violence that turned certain humans into items and others into what Darwin and McLuhan called man.

Multiple scholars have noted that Darwin was critical of racial categorization in his research.[64] Yet to prove or disprove Darwin's racism is not my point here. Instead, I find it more important to illustrate that Darwin's theorizations never sought to displace the centrality of North American and Western European monopolies on humanness, development, and evolution. And just as important, such Western monopolies were so pervasive in the Western episteme during the nineteenth and twentieth century that they even found their way into my area of study, media philosophy and communication studies (among multiple other areas of study), even as their racial relations are brushed over. Some celebrate Darwinian, modern, evolutionary knowledge to tell us that race and gender do not exist biologically. However, they ignore this more important point of Darwin's canonical work: the attempt to prove whether or not race or gender exist biologically presumes biology is *story-less*, to paraphrase Sylvia Wynter.[65] Furthermore, it brushes over the fact that the Negro remains one elemental medium to extend man (white, capitalist maleness) as *the* genre of humanness for the West. The artificial selection of certain Africans from Africa, itself a construct inseparable from Western nature and colonization, is required to reshape some people into Negroes, those made to function whenever man required a reminder of his authority as white, male, and capitalist. With a Darwinian, colonial understanding of nature reframing our studies of media philosophy, Blackness is no longer tangential to media philosophy; indeed, Blackness may actually be a central, yet wholly ignored, theoretical concept of the field.

Going forward, I pull from and leave behind McLuhan. I am less concerned with McLuhan's extensions as largely sensorial transformations—which is not to say the senses are unimportant here. Instead, I want to consider McLuhan's extensions as more closely associated with his discussion of the transformation of the human. To say that the Negro is an extension of man is not to say that the Negro has changed the senses of man. It is to say that the Negro is a medium that transmits conceptions of Western civilization in highly selective ways. McLuhan's definition of media as any extension of man can be utilized in excess of the sensorial: each new medium transformed what it meant to be human for Western Europeans and North Americans in highly racialized ways, in which the senses (or lack thereof) represented levels of civilization. There may be few media that have had such a drastic transformation on Western humanness than the Negro—that unnamed, ungendered medium that normalized whiteness as an epistemological racialized relation, overrepresented as the human in Western scientific and philosophical grammars. These relations continue to remain ignored in Darwin's and McLuhan's writings, while also intimately haunting their every move. As such, it is to Darwin that I must turn to next to understand the raced genealogy of a contemporary largely white, male media philosophy.

In Darwin's intimate act (alongside the long history of racial-sexual violence in the Americas), we can see the beginnings of a contemporary (white) media philosophy, or the opposite of my study: the full-blooded Negro, always in close proximity to nature, is an extension of man, is an empirical construct of Western man's raced, gendered, sexed, classed self-creation. Here I also want to offer an imaginative, fictional counter to Darwin, one that, to some extent, I argue may be representative of the enslaved person of Darwin's documented intimate encounter, while always exceeding said intimacy: the fictional, eponymous character of the enslaved woman of the nineteenth-century novel *Clotel*. Still, like the Negro that Darwin was once intimate with, to call Clotel a counter to Darwin is not exactly accurate: the Negro only exists by and for the Darwins of the world within the Western context of the media function; but the Negro can never be solely reduced to such a function and nothing more. Neither Clotel nor the full-blooded Negro are counters per se. Instead, even as a medium, one central to Western self-conceptions, the Clotels of the world exist despite the Darwins of the world. The Negro of Darwin's intimate imagination similarly holds a radically alternative concept of humanness that Darwin's theory (like Carothers's and McLuhan's) could never fully comprehend. It is here that we can see Blackness as an alternative conception of humanness, one never reducible to Western epistemological structures. And these alternative concepts of humanness lead to radically different approaches to media (see chapters 2 and 3).

## *CLOTEL* AND THE ARTIFICIALITY OF THE MEDIUM'S CONSENT

It is with artificial selection that I metaphorically locate the full-blooded Negro that Darwin left behind on his journey through the Americas. In other words, while the Negro is not named or gendered by Darwin, maybe we can couple Darwin's theories on artificial selection with a different, though related, factional character that was named and gendered in the Americas around the same time. Not long after Darwin began his voyage to the Americas in 1831, the third president of the United States, Thomas Jefferson, died at his home in Monticello, Virginia, in 1826. Jefferson was known for many things: president, philosopher, "Founding Father," enslaver, and rapist. What has been referred to as the Jefferson-Hemings controversy has been debated since the nineteenth century, after it was revealed that Jefferson fathered several children with Sally Hemings, an enslaved Black woman on his estate.[66]

One of the first iterations of this story can be found in the fictional retelling of Clotel, published in 1853 by former enslaved person, William Wells Brown. Brown created Clotel in his novel by the same name (*Clotel; or, The President's Daughter*) as the fictional enslaved daughter of Thomas Jefferson. We can only speculate as to whether Darwin left behind any children in the Americas. However, we can be sure that both the full-blooded Negro and Clotel served a media function: rather than of their own sexual will (sexual selection), both were violently artificially selected to further the detribal, rational, civilized character of Darwin and Jefferson. Hemings, who has been wrongly catalogued as Jefferson's "mistress," points to the limitations of sexual selection addressed above: If Hemings is a mistress, she and Jefferson *chose* an intimate relation of their own, mutual volition that resulted in multiple children. Yet for us, Hemings existed in a context of white supremacy, which left her less a choice than made her a violent selection of Jefferson's, not unlike Darwin's intimate act. Likewise, it is in the story of Clotel, which is inseparable from Hemings, that we may find a small semblance of the full-blooded Negro, morbidly disappeared by Darwin, like all media, toward the transmission of both Darwin's (his evolutionary theory) and the enslaver's whiteness and maleness.[67]

Six years before the publication of Darwin's *On the Origin of Species*, Brown's *Clotel; or, The President's Daughter* was published. Although popular in its own right, *Clotel* would not receive the same fanfare as Darwin's research. As a Black abolitionist who also escaped his enslavement, Brown wrote *Clotel* as a critique of slavery. Brown starts Clotel's factional story on the auction block, where she is sold by her father, Jefferson. Standing naked, she awaited sale to the highest bidder. Many of the bidders did not understand why Clotel was on the auction block at all, as "that girl so young and fair" could not have been enslaved.[68] No matter; the auctioneer sold everything she had: "bones, muscles, sinews, blood, nerves, and *sexuality*" sold "for five hundred dollars," while "her moral character sold for two hundred dollars; her improved intellect sold for one hundred dollars; and her chastity and virtue sold for four hundred dollars."[69] Though fiction, Black studies scholar Katherine McKittrick argues Clotel is important because of the historical articulation of raced/gendered violence that mapped onto Black life in the Americas. Clotel stands as representative of the rape and torture that existed as material realities for enslaved Black women throughout the Americas.

If we take McLuhan and Darwin as starting points for theorizing Blackness in media philosophy, then (social) Darwinian tools, McLuhan's media, and Clotel's Negro-ness all start to sound alike: each are concerned with extending Western man out of a mythic nature and into his secularized civilization. Indeed, for Darwin, later social Darwinians, and McLuhan, this man was assumed as representative of all humans despite his truly Western allegiances. In short, like all media, the Negro holds a "mediality," meaning it is a medium that does not promote dialogue but begins to reflect who the human is in Clotel's scenario.[70]

Clotel's sexuality and race, listed as items sold, quite literally extended the political-economic status of the enslavers, particularly the wealthy Richmond, Virginia, socialite, Horatio Green, who purchased Clotel. In short, Clotel's sale transmitted a white human lifeworld not to Clotel (whose father was white, of course), but to Horatio Green and the other people seeking to buy and sell her. Clotel's technological life and death suggest that the Darwins of the world must be rethought when considering media, race, and gender. As Darwin argued, to artificially select is something multiple species can do but largely something that only certain human populations can do at a sophisticated level—the assumed actions monopolized by Western man. Rather than the discerning selection of two agential sexual partners (similarly suggested by Darwin's retold intimacy), Jefferson's rape of Hemings, violently initiated by and for Western man, produced another violent artifice toward Western man's civilized self-image: Clotel, not as a person for Jefferson per se but as property. In *On the Origin of Species*, Darwin made an argument that forever, and maybe unintentionally, linked his Western constructs of nature and artificial selection with Clotel:

> We cannot suppose that all the breeds were suddenly produced as perfect and as useful as we now see them; indeed, in several cases, we know that this has not been their history. The key is man's power of accumulative selection: nature gives successive variations; man adds them up in certain directions *useful to him*. In this sense he may be said to *make for himself useful breeds*.[71]

Of course, Darwin's discussion of breeding in this early section of *On the Origin of Species* is largely about what he referred to as the *lower animals*: the dog, the horse, the game-cock, the camel, and more.[72] However, we cannot ignore the context in which this discussion of man's intervention in the breeding of animals occurs, one that draws anthropocentric boundaries between humans and nonhuman, natural entities.[73] W.E.B. Du Bois would argue in *Black Reconstruction in America* that such breeding was presumably designed to "improve the human stock of strong and able workers."[74] It is here that Darwin provided what could be retroactively interpreted as a scientific justification for a long, related history of racial/sexual violence: man's privileged, artificial selective capability to breed plants, animals, and enslaved people by and for himself. Indeed, it would be such an assumption of racial breeding that would situate the full-blooded Negro in the Americas in the first place—part of the project of colonization and transatlantic slavery. Despite Darwin's abolitionist leanings, his intimate, nineteenth-century interaction (notable enough to write about) rests on the normalization of such racial/sexual violence.

Darwin suggested that certain human beings (man) can intervene in nature in more advanced ways than others, and that advanced intervention was not distinct from technological concerns. The question of advancement and development was maybe most evident in Darwin's argument that the Negro differed not in kind from Western man but "so greatly in *degree*, from the corresponding powers of man."[75] At the time of *On the Origin of Species*, this hierarchal relation between the artificial selective capacity of man versus the Negro ensured not only that man had presumably more advanced media, but man could equally select the pieces and parts of the Negro that most benefited himself: Clotel's bones, muscles, sinews, blood, nerves, moral character, chastity, and her sexuality were all on sale. Like man's ability to breed animals, Clotel and other slaves were deemed closer to animals and plants and open to man's intervention based on her proximity to animals and other natural entities, all artificially selectable/manipulatable.

The Negro of Darwin's brief time in the Americas was expropriated from Africa in ways similar to the minerals that currently power our iPhones, still extracted from African mines today.[76] Both were elements, given new life, via the labor that went into their new Western media form. For later social Darwinists like Carothers, it did not matter if Clotel was born in the Americas or Africa, it did not matter if she had a white parent or not: her biological relation to Africa ensured that she would always be deemed as open to artificial selection. Here Clotel's association with nature not only made her open to racial and sexual violence, but it ensured that she was there largely to create "new media," or enslaved children of use in the maintenance of the plantation economy. Gender was given to Clotel not as a sign of freedom or subjectivity but for the racial-economic imperative of rape by white male enslavers and/or for slave breeding with other enslaved Black people—the forced copulation made possible by the enslavers and for their continued wealth under an increasingly biocapitalist project. Profit, nature, media, gender, and race all intertwined. Clotel could never fully excavate her elemental legacy for her enslavers.

What happens when a white man is the figure who can legitimately select a Black woman's sexual partner (breeding), or rape a Black enslaved woman (the full-blooded Negro or Hemings), for that white man's financial, social, political, racial/gendered benefit, regardless of the Black woman's sexual desire or attraction to him or his language?

Another way to ask this is, What does it mean when an enslaved woman comes into existence as a Western epistemological object not through her own agential, self-owned, sexual selection but by Western man's artificial selective violence? Sexual selection presumes that taste and preference account for all racialized difference; yet taste and preference do not account for the sale of Clotel's blood, or the selection of Africans that would eventually become Negroes because of the plot, the auction block, or the transatlantic slave trade. To say that sexual selection accounts for racial difference is to say that racial Blackness has existed across time and space—lying dormant in certain people, gradually emerging based on the preferential selection that some people have made to choose to continue their long-held, unchanging racial Blackness. I reject this position, which is not to say that sexual selection is unimportant. Yet it is to say that in its post-bioevolutionary, post-divine, post-Renaissance iteration, racial Blackness becomes the product of man's artificial selection, the transformation of secularized, colonial nature into a medium for his own self-determined use.

Further distancing Clotel from sexual selection, she was deemed "improved" based on her racial mixture of Black and white parentage. Interestingly, the racial improvement that was associated with Clotel sounds similar to the words of one of the more popular philosophers at the time Darwin was writing: G.W.F. Hegel. Maybe more explicitly than Darwin, in Hegel's vastly important lectures, *The Philosophy of History* (originally published in 1837), Hegel promoted a common description of the Negro of the late-eighteenth and early nineteenth centuries, one that located the Negro in closer proximity to nature than to Western man, or himself: "The Negro, as already observed, exhibits the *natural man* in his completely wild and untamed state."[77] But just as interestingly, the Negro for Hegel was assisted by Western colonization and slavery. Racial violence moved the Negro out of a state of natural man—it was a form of minor improvement. After turning his nose up at the frequency of cannibalism among Black Africans, Hegel argued:

> Another characteristic fact in reference to the Negroes is Slavery. Negroes are enslaved by Europeans and sold to America. Bad as this may be, their lot in their own land is even worse, since there a slavery quite as absolute exists; for it is the essential principle of slavery, that man has not yet attained a consciousness of his freedom, and consequently sinks down to a mere Thing—an object of no value.[78]

Racial violence was one mode of bringing the Negro out of nature into society, a potentially beneficial move that improved the morality and virtue of the Clotels of the world. This bringing of the African into Western society, out of nature, was the central *mediamaking* process for the Negro. Thus white enactments of racial violence took certain Africans and forced Negro-ness on them, presumably bringing them into (Western) history. Negro, a term that both Sylvia Wynter and Cedric Robinson show was used only for some people prior to the rise of the West, becomes associated immobily with Black Africans after the West.[79] In terms that media labor scholars like Christian Fuchs and Vincent Mosco might find familiar, racial violence here is a media labor process—one transformative of diverse groups of African people into a Western construct of the Negro.[80] If Western man's labor of processing pulp out of wood, for example, goes into making newspapers (violence against nature), then racial violence is also labor, central to reducing diverse groups of Euro-Americans (and certain Asians) to whites and diverse groups of Africans to Negroes, presumably more civilized in the Americas than in Africa, via their forcibly removed, violent selection. Of course, this labor of racial violence would not be limited to transatlantic slavery, but for Clotel such racial slavery would be central. In short, for Hegel and many others, racial violence was deemed as a *gift*. While bringing the Negro out of nature was a myth, one structured on accepting Western colonial constructs of nature, nature remained one of the dominant epistemological frameworks for the West to think about the Negro long after Hegel had died. There is little about Black people in this framing, and much more about what Western society imagines itself to be, a central theme of the mediality of all media for the philosopher Sybille Krämer.[81]

Darwin held similarities to Hegel. While Black and non-Black people of color differed greatly in degree, but not kind, from white people, racial violence could be an improvement to the mental faculties of Black and non-Black people of color for Darwin. Though not talking about the Negro, Darwin's experience with the Fuegians, with the captured, suggested that Hegel's model of improvement applied to all who lacked Western mental capacity: "The Fuegians rank amongst the lowest barbarians; but I was continually struck with surprise how closely the three natives on board H.M.S. 'Beagle,' who had lived some years in England and could talk a little English, resembled us in disposition and in most of our mental faculties."[82] Captivity changed the Fuegians for Darwin in similar ways as it changed the Negro for Hegel, and, likewise, Darwin's sexual intimacy with the Negro might have had the same effect. Darwin called this change civilization, the full step up out of the state of nature that Western Europeans had long made. We would see similar positions grounded in the mid-twentieth-century social scientific thought of Carothers. We could just as well call this civilizing effect the production of Clotel's and the full-blooded Negro's racial Blackness and the Fuegians' racial Indian-ness, that which mediated or extended Western conflations of white maleness with human civilization.

The important take away is this: If the Negro is a medium, in the media philosophical sense, then it extends what we call whiteness and maleness. The argument is not that the Negro has existed forever, extending humans immemorial, which seems to be Western man's historical, epistemological argument, as best theorized in Hegel's history and later biologized in Darwin's science. Instead, the argument is that with the invention of what we call the West, the Negro has served an important media function—namely one that equates the epitome of all humanness with Western geohistorical registers. As a medium, the Negro extended man's self-conception of civilization, rationality, and human evolution.[83] Darwin largely conflated all human evolution with Western man's artificial selective capacity.[84] Nature survived by and for Western man's artificial selection and that selection was a concern with the self-representation of Western development, with Western advancement as a metaphor for all secularized human evolution. Furthermore, such nature, as a colonial construct, has never been fully disarticulated from the Negro—even when the Negro goes unmentioned.

Necessary for the creation of media, man's selection from nature was a process of presumed self-creation, and not discovery. In this light my work remains aligned with much of the tradition of media philosophy, from McLuhan to Kittler: Western man's media have led to the reproduction of himself (which both McLuhan and Kittler would agree with); and that self is largely white and male, that being who self-interestedly measured his human evolution based on the presumed capacity to leave behind nature for domestication, which the Negro was assumed to be incapable of (which McLuhan never considered and Kittler, it could be argued, only hinted at). Social Darwinian, colonial constructs of nature were not only the media content of the Negro, but the presumed lack of self-determination and agency of the African/nature has also functioned to produce what has been called man by Darwin, Carothers, and McLuhan, particularly man's post-Darwinian, biological, capitalist, technological iteration.

## THE NEW RACIAL CLIMATE

Darwinian tools and McLuhan's media philosophy both suggest an underexamined medium of what Darwin and McLuhan both called man: the Negro. The Negro serves a media function; its connection to nature extends man into what he now takes for granted as his white male superiority, progress, and development out of the natural. Like McLuhan's media, man's selection, or artificial selection, occurs via selection of "those characteristics that appeal to *us*," and through "careful breeding with similar individuals, *we* can produce crops and animals that suit, perhaps while transforming, *our* needs and wants."[85] Where I hesitate can be surmised with a question: Who encompasses the pronouns "us" and "we" necessary to sustain "our" needs and wants within Darwinian theories and, by extension, media philosophy? To understand the Negro as a medium requires adding a cognizance of race, gender, and sexuality to Kittler's important question of who is the "so-called Man" in media philosophy.[86]

Clotel points to similar questions surrounding the identity of this so-called man. Her story ends in tragedy, though, maybe surprisingly for the Darwins and Jeffersons of the world, on Clotel's terms. Ultimately, she escapes slavery but is recaptured when she returns to Richmond to free her daughter, Mary, who remained as enslaved/a daughter of Horatio Green. In Richmond, Clotel is recaptured and imprisoned. She managed to escape imprisonment and fled northward away from Richmond, but with the slave catchers too close on her heels, Clotel decided to jump into the Potomac River and drown herself, rather than return to enslavement. She died not far from the White House, the onetime residency of her father.

What does it mean to be human in Clotel's world? We might ask the same question of what Darwin called the full-blooded Negro of his youthful adventure to the Americas. Clotel's and the full-blooded Negro's humanness are not the same as Jefferson's, Green's, or Darwin's in the Western epistemological project, but not fully separate from their forms of humanness either. In fact, the biggest affronts to Jefferson's and Green's humanness occurred as Clotel escaped and drowned herself. It was here that she poked holes in the solidity of the Western monopolization of humanness—showing that the inanimateness of her Blackness could animate in ways beyond and outside their anthropocentric control. Still, Clotel's enslavement and her intimate relations (which can only be thought about as "consensual" with the use of scare quotes) meant that the dominant concept of humanness in her world was simple: It meant whiteness and maleness. To be human—at the time of Clotel's or the full-blooded Negro's rape—was to historically enact violence against the Negro and nature, a violence necessary to turn some into media. Historically there has been little distinction made between the Negro and nature: each has at times been used to enrich and enliven the human life of Western man. It is nature and the Negro that were media, which could be organized to illustrate the civilized, developmental stranglehold that man held over the world. In this light, Indigenous people like the Fuegians and the full-blooded Negro, as well as the Clotels of the world, were not much different from the notebooks Darwin used to classify them: Once existing in a state of nature, each could be domesticated/technologized toward the continual representation of white maleness as the epitome of humanness.

In popular culture there remains a hesitation, not with connecting the human to technology and the natural environment, but with thinking how each relates to racial violence. And that ignorance of racial violence takes work because there are no shortage of examples of the interconnection between the human, technology, nature, and racial violence. For example, in 2019 a few popular articles were released that linked climate crisis to colonialism, imperialism, and technology.[87] Each showed that technological Darwinism exceeded Darwin, to structure the technological and colonial invasion of Western Europeans throughout the Americas well before Darwin. Reporting on a study conducted by University College London, the articles featured interviews with researchers who were arguing that Western European colonizers killed so many Indigenous Americans that it changed the global climate. In the wake of Columbus's violent journey to the Caribbean, Western Europeans began frequenting various parts of the Americas and killing Indigenous people via genocide and/or spreading foreign diseases. This violence not only lay the foundation for Western occupation of the Americas but it also left large tracts of agricultural land untended. The lands became overgrown with vegetation, and this regrowth soaked up so much carbon dioxide from the atmosphere that it cooled the entire planet in the sixteenth and seventeen centuries.[88] The climate cooled so much that it resulted in what was called a "Little Ice Age," regularly freezing over the River Thames in London, creating snowstorms in Portugal, and disruptions of agriculture that caused famines in other parts of Europe.[89]

While these scientists illustrate the way that the global climate cooled due to colonial violence, they are far more silent on the heating of the environment that occurred in the wake of the establishment of Western colonization. One of the study's coauthors, Chris Brierley, argues that what is *most important* to take away from the study is proof that the climate can cool, which to me is akin to saying that genocide "shows us what reforestation can do" to save everyone.[90] Such a position works only if there is no complex approach to man's media foundations. After the "global cool"—which is unsurprisingly marked in the University College London study by a little ice age in Western Europe—the mass extraction of natural resources from the colonies, or hyper-artificial selection, led to the climate heating up around the "industrial revolution." Of course, as Jussi Parikka reminds us, the heat up and massive extraction of natural resources from the Americas, Asia, and Africa underlie much of our current media technologies.[91] Furthermore, humans were also extracted as a result of these different yet intersecting projects. This Western technological militarism led to today's climate crisis heating the globe.[92]

Harold Innis would argue that such militarism is also characteristic of "spatially biased media" cultures, ones that privilege media that are light and easily transportable in order to traverse vast distances and hold military power over distant lands.[93] The preponderance of Western media were central to expansion and the establishment of a plantation-colonial labor economy based on the Western idea that the colonized were lagging behind human development. In this light, anti-Indigeneity, anti-Blackness, and environmental destruction are inseparable. Both Black and Indigenous people have been imagined as clearable "foliage."[94] This connection to foliage and nature is also important to the conceptualization of the Negro as a *medium*, both artificially selected and necessary to clear and domesticate the lands of the Americas via plantationization (i.e., to continue more artificial selection).

Not only is Darwin's nature the content of the Negro, but those Black bodies are the media toward reflecting the presumably objective Western world order of knowledge and its institutionality. In this light the Negro's radicalism opens spaces for an interruption of Western man's being: Clotel's suicide ruptured Western scientific and philosophical thought and action. Specifically, Clotel's suicide was a radical act, not as a celebration of death, but as a hope for a new life. It challenged and threw into question the solidity of Western human dominance, control, and taming of nature. Likewise, the University College London researchers might be dealing less with "climate change" and more with the radical result of widespread acceptance of the Western colonial construct of nature, of which Clotel is only one part. Like the full-blooded Negro, Clotel is an example that suggests we would be mistaken to assume that Western man, and his multiple violences, monopolized all forms of humanness.

Though brushed over by Darwin and Jefferson, what the Clotels and the full-blooded Negroes speak to is not a world of only slavery, but new worlds beyond the materiality of this life (Clotel was willing to die for)—increasingly unthinkable for the Darwins and Jeffersons of the secularizing West. Herein lies the problem that *On Black Media Philosophy* points to: What happens if Clotel's suicide is not proof of any mental incapacity (Carothers's "African mind"), but a radical act? What happens when media resist? What *media* do the *media* use? Ultimately, Black people use our own bodies and other media forms (orality, electricity, star constellations, newspapers, the web, etc.) to unhinge man's place in the white world that he fabricated. Around the time that Darwin was traveling and writing, there may be fewer better examples of alternative Black media economies in North America than on the Underground Railroad.

# CHAPTER 2

# Black Escapism on the Underground (Black) Anthropocene

We—readers of books such as this—are so literate that it is very difficult for us to conceive of an oral universe of communication or thought except as a variant of a literate universe.

—Walter Ong

The Detroit River is the nautical borderline between the metropolitan areas of Detroit, Michigan, and Windsor, Ontario. The two cities are so close that Windsor friends often jokingly tell me that any popular photographs that depict Detroit were actually taken in Windsor. The two cities are connected by bridges that go over and through the river. During the nineteenth century it was through this same icy river that many enslaved people attempted to cross to reach the "free" city of Windsor (ironically, geographically south of Detroit), away from chattel slavery in the United States.[1] The harsh conditions of Black escapism are easily forgotten today, as both sides of the river are lined with expensive bars, restaurants, and hotels—all geographically near downtown Detroit and Windsor. For runaway enslaved people in the nineteenth century, however, the river functioned differently: it was a safe haven, a northward (though southern) marker, or even a place to die, free from racial enslavement. In all cases, the river signified alternative experiences of Black liberation, very different from the realities of enslavement. The dangerous traversal of the Detroit River during the nineteenth century by enslaved people was part of a larger secret network that we refer to as the Underground Railroad, which reached its height between 1850 and 1860.[2] But the Detroit River was also a medium, a middle point between remaining captive or getting free, between being by and for another or being something else.

As I noted in chapter 1, a highly Westernized media philosophy is recognizable within the horrors of slavery. Accepting the premise of media philosophy—that media are the product of the laborious transformation of nature into media—means accepting that the artificial selection (or kidnapping) of African diasporic people as natural resources was one labor process that transformed Africans into media/Negroes in the Americas. Such equations of the Negro with nature/inferiority would exceed the nineteenth century, infusing the dominant white historian accounts of Black escapism during the twentieth century and well beyond. The white historian critiques often mirrored the racialized terrain popularized under social Darwinian terms, which is to say, a world where racial inferiority was normalized. For example, some scholars of the early twentieth century attributed any successful Black escape on the Underground Railroad to the superior intellect and efforts of white abolitionists, crediting the (media) technological savvy of the white abolitionists as the best method for Black spatial traversal.[3] Of course, Black escapisms equally relied on the collaborative energies and ingenuity of Black runaways, free Black people, Indigenous people, and Mexicans (to name only a few). Still, these white historians deemed Black, brown, and Indigenous spatial traversal as secondary to white people's spatial traversal (i.e., the true mediamakers).

Katherine McKittrick debunks early white historian views of incorrect Black mobility, instead referring to the Underground Railroad as a "Black geography," or a dynamic network of secret routes, safe houses, and hidden messages (what I call media) that Black runaway enslaved people used to escape enslavement and imagine spaces beyond their commodification.[4] Much has been written on the harrowing narratives of runaways. For example, the narratives and speeches of Frederick Douglass—who became an abolitionist, an adviser to President Abraham Lincoln, and founding editor for the antislavery newspaper *The North Star*—have often been considered as foundational for Black studies, providing one theory of abolition.[5] But despite the important research on the Underground Railroad, less work has asked the main question that McKittrick points to and this chapter is organized around: What media were crucial to the Underground Railroad? To paraphrase Simone Browne, what media did runaway enslaved people use to deterritorialize their Blackness as property?[6]

The answers to these questions are numerous, but it is hard to imagine that phonetic writing and orality would be absent from the answers. Walter Ong famously argued that orality and the phonetic alphabet were media. He contended that orality was not subordinate to phonetic writing; instead, writing alters orality, never fully displacing it.[7] Of course, Ong would develop such a position after he was tutored at Saint Louis University by a young Marshall McLuhan, who supervised Ong's thesis in the 1940s.[8] Ong would be part of the cohort of U.S. scholars highly influenced by McLuhan in the mid- to late-twentieth century, such as Neil Postman and Paul Levinson. Many of these scholars would play a central role in bringing McLuhan into more contemporary media studies discussions in the United States, such as the important work by Levinson on the relevance of McLuhan's work for theorizing the Internet.[9] However, much of their analyses would be limited to the same terms of man that haunted McLuhan's theories.

For my purposes the tactics that the runaway enslaved people used to reach Windsor, among other places, reveal an underexamined media economy or media environment, one that was fully materialized in the nineteenth century via the project of distinguishing phonetic writing from oral communication. The assumption that orality was less developed than phonetic writing in North America is fairly new, and it entangles with a conversation on race largely unexamined by Ong and media philosophy. For example, Brian Hochman argues that an "evolutionary theory of language" developed in late-nineteenth century, situating Western phonetic writing as "more evolved" than orality.[10] In short, evolutionary theories of language would position both Black and Indigenous people as not different in kind, but as different "so greatly in *degree*" from white people.[11] Under this new, post-Darwin, evolutionary theory of language, scholars increasingly assumed that Western European and North American people were the sole (or at least the most sophisticated) groups that could technologize language in written, phonetic form, and thus the theory held that white people were the most evolved race.[12]

Here epistemology was a media concern: those who could phonetically read and write monopolized all knowledge. If Black and Indigenous people had the ability to write phonetically, then the evolutionary theory of language was presented not as faulty, but such forms of writing were often presented as due to white people's benevolence to teach Black and Indigenous people. There are similarities here to what Carmen Kynard calls a myth of "academic-discourse-as-material-access."[13] That is, the only forms of legitimate literacy are those reducible to the white bourgeoisie. If Black people engaged in Western forms of writing and speaking, it was deemed a *media gift*, provided via the violent

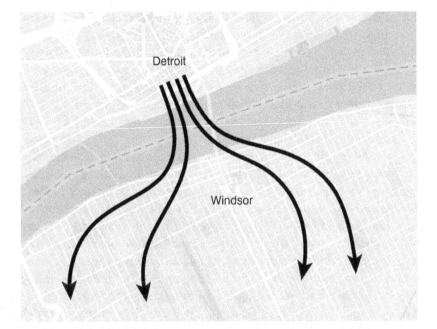

FIGURE 1. Map of Detroit/Windsor and surrounding area, showing the city of Detroit north of Windsor, separated by the Detroit River, marking movement across the river into Canada. Map created by Justin Madron of the Digital Scholarship Lab at the University of Richmond. Special thanks to Justin for the rights to reuse this image.

selection of enslavement by the developed (white) to the underdeveloped (Black).[14]

As Ronald Judy argues, the slave narrative must be thought about as no pure route to emancipation but as a new opportunity for actions against slavery.[15] The dangers of assuming that the slave narratives signified a self-conscious freedom were seen in white abolitionist and white enslaver statements that Black phonetic writing was proof of white civilizational good, development, and benevolence. Certain media were assumed as markers of effective movement and thus intellect, while others were seen as inefficient and thus not really media at all. The point being: For many white people the Detroit River was no medium, unless it could be reduced to the mapped image in figure 1; it was just a river, either a barrier in the way of smooth and efficient movement or of use for smooth and efficient movement, via shipping. Here Black people did not have the media function, meaning they did not use media that white people saw as developed, but they used media deemed as backward, or even tribal, for McLuhan. But this is exactly what I want to emphasize: to ignore the river (among other things) as a medium is to ignore the entirety of an alternative Black media economy. Western conceptions of tribal and detribal, or Harold Innis's time- versus space-biases, mirrored Western conceptions of orality and phonetic writing, of primitive/natural (water) and civilized (steamboat), respectively.[16] And an understanding of both media forms was important for Black people to navigate the Underground Railroad.

If the Negro functions as a medium, as an extension of whiteness and maleness, what happens when the medium decides not to work? Black people have not solely been reducible to commodity relations, but we have also pointed toward new futures and new forms of human-ness, unexamined by those highly invested in the racialized extension of Blackness.[17] On and off the Underground Railroad, new Black lives were sought beyond commodification, which challenged Western, nineteenth-century media economies and their conception of human development. The Black people fleeing enslavement understood the power relations inherent in writing, in printing, and in mapping, and they created alternative, overlapping forms of mediation to get around the people in pursuit of them.[18] To escape enslavement, Black people relied on a variety of media, oftentimes not deemed media by those in pursuit of them. Songs, messages stitched in quilts, flagpoles, star constellations, their own bodies, and even rivers were media for those fleeing their enslavement toward places such as Windsor. In hindsight, such media may have reinforced early twentieth-century social Darwinian, anthropocentric, racial conceptions for white historians of the twentieth century, which held that white people moved beyond nature, while Black people were closer to nature due to a lack of human development. But why would an enslaved person fleeing for her life in the nineteenth century ever care to prove her human development to those seeking to reenslave her or to those seeking to academically disprove her capacity for escape? For many enslaved people there were bigger problems to face. Their media may have been deemed undeveloped or even backward by those giving chase; yet evidence suggests that Black people also used assumptions of their underdevelopment to work toward self-emancipation.

The Underground Railroad functioned as a media economy, specifically in the sense that it could not be reduced to one medium alone, but a complex interweaving of mediations that produced both Black liberation and sometimes man's self-image.[19] In other words, Black people on the Underground Railroad might necessarily use media that their pursuers deemed inferior, reflecting back the presumed superiority of the pursuers and their concept of the Negro; but such white technological arrogance may have also been exactly what was needed for Black people to sneak by. On the one hand, the media that allotted linear, efficient movement continued to be the media that were associated with Western man, or forms of phonetic writing, print, and mapping that would be deemed by social Darwinists, such as Lewis Morgan, the late nineteenth-century anthropologist, as proof of Western man's racialized evolutionary superiority.[20] On the other hand, the exact same Western media could prevent Western man from comprehending Black geographies and alternative media outside his own purview. While implied in Black studies, I explicitly argue that Black geographies *assume media*, as media and communication have always been connected to questions of transportation and geographic space.[21] The runaway enslaved people sought to extend themselves not into Western registers of man, but into the materiality of their own self-abolition. The runaways did not care to reflect the West back unto itself, they did not seek a Western recognition of their humanity. They sought to outrun the West completely.

## FOR "UNORGANIZED" MEDIA

For a racialized example of the technologization of language, we need look no further than the early twentieth century, during a time period of increased debates around racism in the United States and colonialism abroad. Much of this period, of rising criticism against Western racism, would be met by a reactionary push that promoted the importance of Western and white benevolence to historical development. For example, in 1933 historian E. Delorus Preston Jr. maintained that the accomplishments of the Underground Railroad were largely due to the efforts of white abolitionists and their technological ability. For Preston, there were roughly two eras of the Underground Railroad: the first was largely unofficial or *unorganized*, occurring prior to the nineteenth century and involving the nonliterate actions of free Black people, Indigenous people, and Mexicans (Preston refers to this as the "underground," purposefully lowercase); the second was official or *organized*, during the early nineteenth century by white abolitionists who could read and write (he capitalizes this form as the "Underground"). His shift from "underground" to "Underground" is not insignificant as it marked a temporal, evolutionary trajectory of media development, from one era to the next. While the former was important, the latter period was presumably the most technologically developed form of escapism in the history of the United States:

> [William Lloyd Garrison's American Anti-Slavery Society] organized the most ingenious system ever devised by the brain of man for the relief of the weary and disconsolate slave. They offered him respite from the system, gave him guidances [sic] and transportation on his journey, provided him with shelter, protection, food and clothing, gave him surcease from the wintry blasts, asylum from the slave catcher and the bloodhounds, and escorted him to Canada and to freedom. Such was the Underground Railroad.[22]

For Preston the unmatched white organization of the Underground Railroad could be conflated with terms like rationality and order. Specifically, he argued that the white establishment of the Underground Railroad ensured that Black people fleeing for their lives scarcely stayed outdoors overnight, rarely went hungry, and traversed space efficiently, largely thanks to the efforts of benevolent white abolitionists.

Of course, the time period that Preston was writing about white benevolence cannot be overlooked. The year before he published "The Genesis of the Underground Railroad," the U.S. government began recording the voices of former enslaved people in the important Voices Remembering Slavery project in 1932.[23] After her studies with anthropologists like Franz Boas and Margaret Mead, Zora Neale Hurston, the Black anthropologist and novelist of the early twentieth century, played an important role in the collection of some of these Black voices. Some of the recordings included songs; others included graphic descriptions of the harsh conditions that Black people endured while enslaved. Likewise, the Federal Writers' Project began its related recording project in 1936, *Born in Slavery*, gathering more than twenty-three hundred first-person accounts of enslavement and taking five hundred black-and-white photographs of former enslaved Black people.[24] In a country dedicated to arguing that there were little to no problems for Black people during racial slavery, works like these shed new light on the harsh realities of enslavement and its continued relevance for the United States in the 1930s.

Of course, these two projects cannot be viewed as the first time slave narratives were given attention: what the United States did in the twentieth century had already been done in the nineteenth by Black abolitionists, such as William Wells Brown and Benjamin Drew. These Black mediamakers recorded the tales of runaway enslaved people upon their successful escape to places such as Pennsylvania and New York. Many of the tales account for the violent reality that Black people endured during slavery but also provided a limited look into how some Black people escaped enslavement. By changing a detail here, a name or location there, the narratives of escape threw off anyone trying to put a stop to Black self-liberation.

Such important Black perspectives on racial slavery and its aftermath would not end during the nineteenth century. For example, at the time that Preston was making a name for himself as an expert on the Underground Railroad, W.E.B. Du Bois published his classic book *Black Reconstruction in America* in 1935. In the wake of the Great Depression and the failure of the "talented tenth" to lead the Black race (Du Bois later replaced this group with the "Guiding Hundredth" to match his Marxism), Du Bois wrote *Black Reconstruction* with the future of Black liberation in mind. Du Bois's book was not solely about the way that Black people in the nineteenth century pushed the country's democratic promises forward during the era of U.S. Reconstruction, but also about how white people's racist backlash to such reconstruction organized twentieth-century Black poverty and sharecropping.[25]

White benevolence, then, was shown to be largely fictional. With the rise of Black challenges to presumably objective history in the nineteenth and twentieth centuries, the white challenges to such Black thought and knowledge required loud and consistent voicing.[26] It is in a long context of white apologia that we must understand Preston's interest in white benevolence on the Underground Railroad: at a time of increasing challenges to white benevolence during the 1930s, the white abolitionists needed to be rewritten as aspirational, kind figures who held organized media—a truly literate, detribal guiding light for all Black people, contradicting Du Bois–like arguments of white liberals as complicit in Black oppression.

What was Preston's marker of "organized" escapisms? It was paper documentation. In other words, Preston's gift of the technologization of language structured his entire theory of the Underground Railroad in ways that merged racism and white liberalism with media. For Preston, media were inherently an epistemological concern, one that mirrors what Lisa Gitelman critiques in *Paper Knowledge*: Western knowledge was always situated as transmitted textually via paper documentation.[27] As Judy similarly argues, the modern university also assumed all authoritative transmission of knowledge is that of the scholar to the text, and such thinking would likewise conflate all previous forms of knowledge with the capacity to write.[28]

Academics of the early twentieth century, like Preston, affirmed the position that Gitelman and Judy critique: written documentation of the Underground Railroad *was* the Underground Railroad for Preston. Documentation included, but was far from limited to, printed paper, phonetic literacy, and mapping, or what Harold Innis called "space-biased media." Space-biased media were light and easily transported, lending themselves to highly aggressive forms of militarism and colonial ordering of space via state-sanctioned legislation.[29] For early historians of the Underground Railroad, we can say that spatially biased media were the central, often unnamed, modes through which they understood all forms of successful spatial traversal by Black people, though not *of* Black people; such successes were always reducible to the developed, benevolent, and technological efforts of white people.

Preston was consistent in his assumption: Western phonetic writing was the main technology of legitimization and transmitter of objectivity on all statements for and against slavery. Of course, in order for Preston's argument to work, he had to ignore the importance of African Arabic-speaking and -writing people who were enslaved in the Americas, those who Judy argues had long examined questions of rationality.[30] Non-Arabic, Western phonetic writing and reading was established as a true technologization of language. On the one hand, according to Preston, to catch an enslaved person required a paper trail littered with Western phoneticism: sheriffs posted descriptions of runaways on courthouse doors and in newspapers; laws were passed warning of fines, jailtime, or even slavery for those who assisted the runaways; and the passage of fugitive slave acts designed to return property to the enslaver.[31] On the other hand, to fight slavery also required a paper trail littered with Western phoneticism: the 1774 declaration to end the importation of more slaves in North American colonies; the abolition of slavery in northern states during the eighteenth and nineteenth centuries, all marked by state laws; and the forging of slave passes that marked enslaved people as legally traveling north at the request of a white enslaver.[32]

For Preston the Underground Railroad and its restrictions were organized by those who were the most capable of tracking and freeing slaves—other white people, or that group most capable of the effective technologization of language. In this light, the organization toward both reenslavement and Black emancipation were structured by Western media (phoneticism and mapping and printing systems). Preston argued that because "many [runaway slaves] had seldom left the plantation on which they were born," they "were so completely *ignorant of geography* and relative distances" that they could not find the most efficient path northward and were most likely to be caught without any white assistance.[33] Preston's concern with ignorant geography matched with what McKittrick calls the "ungeographic," a colonial fiction that assumes that Black geography is a nonhuman construct.[34] Alternatively, McKittrick argues that Black geographies are not just ungeographic but radically different spaces, which white people could never wholly understand. I want to add to this: Black geographies also hold a media concern.[35]

To traverse space in other fashions required alternative conceptions of media. As many enslaved people did not write down on paper their methods of escape, this did not mean that they were less proficient in the usage of media than their white abolitionist counterparts. It just meant that they had more to hide, and the reliance on inscriptive media was not the favored method for hiding escape routes. Racial violence ensured that Black enslaved people required media that could also hide in plain sight, preferably illegible to those white people giving chase. Those fleeing enslavement did not have Preston's concern: rather than a hierarchy of organized over unorganized media, their concern was with differing media economies routed in whatever it took to get away from enslavement. Another way to say this is that the enslaved people sought to kick, scratch, claw, punch, run, swim, and trick their way away from the plantation.

If, as per McLuhan, media are any extension of man, then the Negro, as medium, presents a crisis for McLuhan's Western man.[36] Not only does the association of the Negro with temporal backwardness and nature function for Western man, but both the Negro and the media used by enslaved people to navigate the Underground Railroad challenged the anthropocentric, classificatory power of Western man altogether. For the runaway enslaved people, media were constellations, sticks, rocks, and more. Though deemed inferior by some, and maybe because they were deemed inferior, the sticks, rocks, and constellations were media that *extended* Black people into alternative, Black futurities outside the purview of the people giving chase to them. To fully comprehend a Black media economy like the Underground Railroad, we must note that it both extended Western constructs of a narcissitic man and revealed his limited applicability to Black people, those who sought their own forms of emancipation by utilizing media not deemed media at all. The maps, the slave passes, and the content of slave narratives were not unimportant but were also not the only media; others included make-shift mediations, such as orality, sticks, trinkets, and even bodies.

## BLACK GEOGRAPHIES, MEDIA, AND THE ANTHROPOCENE

Western media philosophy's contemporary approach does not allow for a critical discussion of the Underground Railroad. We would do well to take a page from the Black enslaved people to rethink both media content and media form in relation to race. In short, what we see within the discussion of the Underground Railroad is a central theme of today's media philosophy, though largely unacknowledged by its scholars. What some might call nature (sticks, the North Star, etc.) were media for the Black people fleeing for their lives on the Underground Railroad. While such concepts of nature have found themselves a home in media philosophy, Blackness has not.[37] For example, Anthropocene research has focused on "extraordinary burdens of toxic chemistry, mining, depletion of lakes and rivers under and above ground, ecosystem simplification."[38] Likewise, media philosophers have concerned ourselves with the relationship between the Western, capitalistic need for new media and the depletion of the earth's natural resources toward the creation of those same new media. Indeed, the extraction of natural, raw materials from non-Western locales has been important for the powering of laptops, cellphones, and flat screens of disproportionately Western use.[39] Thus for decades, media philosophers have flirted with the interconnections between technology, capitalism, and planetary destruction.

Although delving into the Anthropocene literature is important, another related term may remedy the problem of Blackness in media philosophy research: the "Black Anthropocene." Kathryn Yusoff argues that the Anthropocene under investigation in academia is truly a Black Anthropocene, meaning that the Anthropocene assumes a racial, gendered, sexual assemblage as its organizing principle, even as much of the research on the Anthropocene does not acknowledge this.[40] Like the Anthropocene, the Black Anthropocene relied on largely Western resource depletion of non-Western resources, but such forms of depletion cannot be distinguished from a world in which the Negro was also an important part of the same natural resource depletion, a body deemed to be closer in proximity to nature than to civilization. The Anthropocene always held raced and gendered conceptions of nature, even as race and gender are ignored in much of the contemporary media philosophy that focuses on the Anthropocene. It would be similar positions that would distinguish between "the underground" and "the Underground" for Preston: not only were Black people deemed closer to nature, but such proximity to nature also presumably justified a tendency toward unorganized media. There is a link, then, between Western conceptions of nature, capitalist resource overdepletion, racial Blackness, and media.

Whereas the Anthropocene is often presented as a nonracial project, Yusoff rejects this position and also rejects the alternative *cenes* of the Anthropocene, such as the Capitalocene, the Chtulthocene, and even the Plantationocene.[41] The Black Anthropocene, which assumes the plantations and the colonies, is irreducible to the other *cenes* because it also holds alternative, radical potentialities. In other words, the Black Anthropocene can point toward new conceptions of humanness and freedom. Likewise, enslaved people on the plantation (as well as those who fled from it) engaged in new modes of thinking about human interaction with the nonhuman world to foster multispecies well-being.[42] This new multispecies well-being is a narrative, a "plot," as per McKittrick, that never stayed on the plantations but moved with Black people, on and off the plantation, as they traversed alternative space-times toward abolition—that which white people often cared little to interrogate in any serious way.[43]

McKittrick argues that the plantation was indeed "a location of black death," but to assume that it was nothing more brushes over the new, alternative futures that Black people imagined and created. On the plantation, the locale of the Negro, there were dreams of a struggle for life, far beyond white imaginations of the Negro.[44] Because there were certain elements of the plantation, and its racial violences, that continued on (such as slave catchers, Fugitive Slave acts, etc.), for McKittrick, the plantation also demanded transforming "decolonial thinking," predicated on new forms of human life from the start.[45] In other words, the enslaved people, and those who escaped, were radical thinkers. The plantation functioned as a blueprint for the spatial-temporal imaginations of those enslaved Black people who fled from it; it was a simultaneous reification of and rejection of commodification—a rejection of the Negro of white imagination and an expression of alternative concepts of time, space, and life.

The Black Anthropocene was both a factory, one highly productive of our current overextractive processes that structure Western media (including the Negro as a medium), but it also pointed toward new futures than what white enslavers, slave catchers, and liberals were fully aware of or prepared for. In other words, Black people used their bodies and/as alternative media toward freedoms that fully exceeded Western humanism's frame.[46] As I see it, we have a chance to remake media philosophy in at least two ways, though likely far more. We could relocate our discourses of contemporary media technologies away from the Anthropocene, toward the Black Anthropocene, which is to say toward the plantation and the colony. In the process we could fully resituate the destruction of the natural environment not solely in the destruction of both flora and fauna but also in racial violence.[47] If we focused on the Black Anthropocene in media philosophy, we could also better understand the centrality of the white, Western imagination to the raced and gendered construction of nature, that which would make up our contemporary media devices as well as the contemporary racialized order of knowledge.

Second, and far more important for me, we can also think about how those media, inseparable from the plantation and colony (and the flight from both), continue to plot out new worlds than what Western man could ever fully comprehend—they create radical, alternative conceptions of Black life. If media have potentialities underthought by Western man, they are not only his trusty tools, but they are also technologies that he can never fully monopolize or comprehend, especially in the hands of Black people. There may be few better examples of a rejection of, yet full comprehension of, man's anthropocentric media environment in North America than the alternative mediations of the Underground Railroad, where media and Black liberation collide outside the limitations of white, Western epistemic imaginations.

## BLACK GEOGRAPHIC MEDIATIONS

What we have from the Underground Railroad today is largely written documentation, particularly from enslaved people's autobiographies and abolitionist interviews with former enslaved people after they had escaped. Here some may argue that we largely reside in a similar context that we are critiquing Preston for not critically seeing: phonetic writing is one of the most important modes through which we come to learn about the Underground Railroad. Furthermore, the online proliferation of information about the Underground Railroad is massive. Virtual tours are now available of routes taken on the Underground Railroad, and many tourists continue to sign up online to take plantation tours,

itself a big industry, which often teaches about how many enslaved people fled the plantation.[48] Yet there are clues about alternative traversals
of space in the enslaved people's narratives themselves. A close reading
of the narratives of enslaved people illustrates that their media were not
considered media by those chasing them. Black people's forms of media
were necessarily deemed primitive, natural, or tribal by scholars like
Preston (and I argue even McLuhan), compared to the media forms associated with white, Western Europeans and North Americans. As a by-
product, primitiveness, naturalness, and tribalness provided a needed
cover for Black escapisms.

While slave catchers, academics, and scientific racists considered the
lack of writing and mapping as proof of racial inferiority, it could also
reveal enslaved people's understanding of the importance of such media
forms for white people. The enslaved people often did not use writing
and mapping to escape slavery; this was essential, as scholars like Paul
Gilroy argue that writing and mapping may have undermined Black
escape attempts if paper routes were ever discovered by those pursuing them.[49] Alternatively, Black escapism required media based on the
particulars of the situation, not a paper trail. Enslaved Black people
and their sought-after freedoms often required illegibility/illiteracy. Although many enslaved people wanted to learn to read and write, and
many did so, the current negative associations with illiteracy were not
viewed in the same light for those on the run. Inseparable from the enslaved people's understanding of spatially biased media, both illegibility
and illiteracy could assist the runaways to navigate space in alternative
fashion, often ignored by white enslavers and catchers. Simultaneously,
the white assumptions of Black illiteracy furthered white monopoliza-
tions of the media function, or the presumed ability to sophisticatedly
technologize objects, pushing forward arguments of Black undevelop-
ment.[50] However, what these assumptions ultimately showed was that
Black people had long expressed alternative conceptions of humanness
and knowledge, blurring distinctions between human and nonhuman as
a necessity for survival.[51]

Under the terms of Black media philosophy, we find a plethora of
long ignored media on the Underground Railroad. The most famous
example of alternative media forms involved the frequent personifica-
tion of the North Star or Polaris, the brightest star in the constella-
tion of Ursa Minor. The abolitionist and author William Wells Brown
factionalized a mode of travel for Clotel, a fictional enslaved daughter
of Thomas Jefferson, in his book *Clotel; or, The President's Daughter*

(chapter 1). But beforehand, Brown had to actually escape his own enslavement. In recounting his experience, he argued that finding the North Star was like finding a lost friend: "I knew not which way to go. I did not know North from South, East from West. I looked in vain for the North Star; a heavy cloud hid it....I walked up and down the road until near midnight, when the clouds disappeared, *and I welcomed the sight of my friend,—truly the slave's friend,*—the North Star."[52] Josiah Henson similarly argued that the North Star was not only his personal savior but likewise a divine signal, provided to him by God: "I knew the North Star—blessed be God for setting it in the heavens! Like the Star of Bethlehem, it announced where my salvation lay. Could I follow it through forest, and stream, and field, it would guide my feet in the way of hope. I thought of it as my God-given guide to the land of promise far away beneath its light."[53]

Frederick Douglass, in a retelling of one of his attempts to escape, famously stated: It "was our purpose to turn our canoe adrift, and follow the guidance of the north star till we got beyond the limits of Maryland."[54] Upon successfully fleeing to New York, Douglass went so far as to name the newspaper that he founded in 1847 *The North Star*, an homage to this medium. In another retelling of a runaway slave named Margaret's escape path, abolitionist Eber M. Pettit recounted that when Margaret saw the slave catchers approaching, she "then pressing her child to her bosom...fled with all the speed of which was capable toward the North Star."[55] The North Star was a guide; or even better, the North Star was the medium through which the Underground Railroad conductors and those fleeing slavery effectively stunted mapping and writing as the privileged modes of spatial traversal.

The North Star was not the only medium used to navigate space. In the abolitionist Benjamin Drew's interview with runaway enslaved person Edward Hicks, Hicks stated that he created makeshift markers to note where and when he should start moving: "I travelled on about twelve miles, when it was so dark I dared not walk any further. I made for a bush, and laid a stick with the big end the way I was to go. That night, about dark, I got up and started again."[56] A stick could be just a stick, or nature, for someone in pursuit of an enslaved person; however, for a Black person it was natural material repurposed to extend them toward a life beyond slavery. The naturalness of the stick served a purpose: it both was easily ignored by a slave catcher (and such ignorance was of necessity for those seeking escape) and artificially selected by someone on the run to mediate their way toward liberation. The Black

Anthropocene both assumed such a Western, white arrogance of nature but also Black people's ability to make a way out of presumably no way. It is here that we can say that Western man held no monopolization over media, even as we often associate the term media with specific Western technologies today.

In another instance, makeshift markers noted when it was safe to move or when it was not. Runaway James Adams, for example, told Drew about the warning signs that abolitionists would give him on his travels. One time in particular, while Adams and fellow runaways were hiding in a thicket of trees near an abolitionist safe house, the abolitionists used flagpoles to communicate the danger in the area: "then we [the other runaways and Adams] saw a little girl come out and climb up on the fence, as if she were playing about, and she knocked down the flagpole,—which meant that we were to look out for ourselves."[57] Knocking over flagpoles was one mode through which space was navigated, but in a different space, state, or at a different safe house, the flagpole might go unused. These strategies were completely dynamic, which was not to say they were ineffective but constantly changing. They had to be in order to maintain confusion for the catchers and to facilitate new modes of mediating space for those fleeing.

Other examples illustrate that the trinkets people carried could be mediators between enslavement and abolition. In his attempt to free the family of James Lightfoot, abolitionist and former enslaved person Josiah Henson revealed a token of Lightfoot's in order to convince the Lightfoot family that he was no enemy: "I was an entire stranger to them, but I took with me a small token of their brother who was gone, which they at once recognised; and this was to let them know that he had gone to Canada, the land of freedom, and had now sent a friend to assist them in making their escape."[58] While skeptical of any words that Henson could use to convince the Lightfoots, an object owned by their family member represented freedom for them. In short, the trinket was a medium that extended the physical and metaphorical kinship of the Lightfoots to Henson himself, letting them know that their kin was safe and they, too, could potentially make it out of slavery.

As noted at the start of this chapter, a consistent "friend" of the runaway was another natural resource: water. No matter which geographic direction the runaway enslaved person faced, water was one medium, meaning it was a middle point between the experience of being reenslaved and freedom.[59] At times, crossing water, whether north or south, was necessary to escape catchers in that particular moment.

While catchers may have joked that an enslaved Black person was too dumb to know which geographical direction they were headed when they entered the water, the catchers did not take into consideration the extra hours of freedom this allotted a person until after they finished laughing. Put simply, water was a medium that suggested that there were not only spatial power relations for those escaping but temporal relations as well.[60] Water could increase temporal freedoms, as its difficulty to traverse did not allow for easy white interrogations or surveillance of Black people. For Douglass, water was both a space of freedom, one not easily accessible by slave catchers, and a time of freedom, as it could prolong recapture if spotted by catchers. Recounting one of his many attempts to escape with two other enslaved Black people, Douglass argued: "Our reason for taking the water route was, that we were less liable to be suspected as runaways; we hoped to be regarded as fishermen; whereas, if we should take the land route, we should be subjected to interruptions of almost every kind."[61]

For Douglass the people fleeing could use water to keep up appearances. For anyone looking for runaway enslaved people, water presumably maintained what Sarah Sharma in her book *In the Meantime* calls the "temporal order of things," whereby the laboring body maintains the profit of others by always being in the time of others.[62] Enslaved people on a boat, for example, were assumed to be making profits for white enslavers, while enslaved people on foot were probably wasting an enslaver's time and thus open for interrogation. Slave papers, a privileged medium of scholars, were used by enslavers to keep tabs on enslaved people, especially easy to check when on foot or on horse. When in the absence of their enslavers, enslaved Black people were required to carry slave papers on their person at all times, and oftentimes even those papers could not stop them from harassment. The slave papers listed the specific reasons why they were traveling away from the plantation. The slave papers allotted all white people the power to stop, question, harass, and surveil all Black people.[63]

Water prevented such interrogations, if only for a short time period; it could not be scaled like land, making it a time-space in which to remake oneself. While water was a natural resource and mode of travel for white people, water acted both similarly and differently for enslaved Black people: it was a medium, a physical and metaphorical do-over that they could use to draw out potential recapture and/or escape recapture all together. Even if crossed in the wrong direction, water's malleable characteristics stunted recapture, if only for an hour or two. While viewed as a temporary annoyance for the slave catchers, water was a medium for those who were fleeing to toy with their pursuers and to potentially free themselves. If water allowed for a white slave catcher to consider the enslaved's escape futile, and a waste of time, a prolonging of the inevitable, water also allowed the enslaved a longer temporal experience of freedom.

Of course, water could be a medium of eternal kinds of freedom. From the extreme reports of runaway enslaved people crossing water on blocks of ice with their children in hand, to enslaved Black people drowning their children to prevent recapture, water also mediated the complete boundaries of freedom and slavery.[64] The potential to die must be considered another media relation between enslavement and freedom. For many enslaved Black people, drowning to death (whether they drowned themselves or their children) was the ultimate, Black Judeo-Christian- and Muslim-inspired freedom for themselves and their children—an entrance into heaven and out of the hells of racial enslavement.[65] Not only did Black spiritual relations ensure that the Western phonetic writing project held no necessary legitimacy over Black enslaved people (as some could write and speak Arabic), it also ensured that many Black people saw this material world as secondary to the next. While Western man secularized, seeing this life as all there was, many enslaved Black people believed their lives were irreducible to slavery, as would be revealed in the next life. We cannot underestimate this view as representative of a backwardness associated with spirituality, as to do so would be to accept McLuhan's terms of tribal sensorialness. Instead, in the face of a rising Western, white, secular push against the history of religious thought, which Friedrich Nietzsche lamented as the death of God, enslaved Black people saw God as a philosophical articulation of why their lives were no more or less than their white counterparts and thus proof of the illegitimacy of slavery. Under these conditions water was not suicide, drowning one's children was not murder. No, water was the medium through which to send oneself and loved ones toward divine, unending liberation.[66]

The physical presence of some people also mediated freedom dreams of full emancipation on the Underground Railroad. In other words, the presence and disguise of certain people on the plantation could increase the confidence that enslaved people felt in their own ability to get free. This means that the physical body could be another medium, but not only by and for white people's artificially selected self-concepts (the Negro or the captive Black body), but also one medium for Black liberation. For example, Harriet Tubman was not just the most famous conductor of the Underground Railroad. She was also the living embodiment of Moses for countless enslaved Black people, both male and female.[67] If Moses parted the Red Sea to help the Jews escape Pharaoh's pursuing army and their reenslavement in Egypt, Tubman was viewed as parting the traps laid by enslavers, leading to the freedom of hunderds of enslaved people.[68] Tubman's physical body extended religious narratives of Exodus from Egypt to the time-space of nineteenth-century enslaved Black people. Whereas some white people (unlike those who had totally secularized) may have viewed the Bible as documented, written proof of enslaved Black people's inferiority in the eyes of God (the "curse of Ham"), Black people saw it as the dynamic, oral/written medium in which the bodies and spaces of the past were affecting their lives well into the present. Likewise, Tubman was the physical medium between the tyranny of the South/Egypt and the North/Promised Land; more than any lyrics Tubman sung, her presence extended the bodies of others into new physical and metaphorical spaces that connected Black people to a long narrative of God-ordained freedom.

Furthermore, Tubman revealed that on the Underground Railroad gendered norms were challengeable and sexual roles were far from stable, a necessity for the secret network's success. Dominant male leadership was supplanted in favor of freedom from the hells of enslavement. On the Underground Railroad white male patriarchal worldviews of the enslavers and catchers were both useless and useful. At times Black male slaves may be leaders; at other times they may be followers. For one man fleeing enslavement, Austin Steward, a Black enslaved woman named Milly, and her "burning desire" to escape, made him push up his escape plans. Even though "the time [Steward] had set for [his] departure was near at hand," he figured he might as well "accompany [Milly] in her flight."[69] Likewise, abolitionist Benjamin Drew reported that another enslaved woman, Mrs. James Seward, saw her husband's ferocious determination as a new route toward self-emancipation. Mrs. James Seward's husband personified the freedom that she awaited: "I have been wanting to come away for eight years. I waited for Jim Seward to get ready. Jim had promised to take me away and marry me."[70] While a slave owner may have viewed them as merely commodities, the Sewards relied on each other as physical and metaphorical crutches to push northward and away from slavery.

One of the more important gender- and race-bending examples of using the body comes from the account of wife Ellen Craft and her

husband William Craft, a central story examined by Black studies scholars. In his report William Still, a conductor of the Underground Railroad, elaborated on the extensive, challenging escape plan of the Crafts.
It involved dressing the fair-skinned Ellen up as a sick, white male enslaver, while William was to be the enslaved Black man who was assist-
ing her/him. In line with the Black creativity of transness summarized
by C. Riley Snorton, Ellen cannot be deemed as a recoverable trans
representation in the past that is worthy of celebration in the present,
but more as an openness that is necessary for Black fugitivity.[71] Ellen
underwent the significant changes to rearticulate a new and highly misunderstood form of freedom. In particular, she had to pull off her transformation from Black woman to white, disabled man and thus facilitate
her and William's escape:

> Ellen being fair enough to pass for white, of necessity would have to be
> transformed into a young planter for the time being. All that was needed,
> however, to make this important change was that she should be dressed el-
> egantly in a fashionable suit of male attire, and have her hair cut in the style
> usually wore by young planters. Her profusion of dark hair offered a fine
> opportunity for the change. So far this plan looked very tempting. But it oc-
> curred to them that Ellen was beardless. After some mature reflection, they
> came to the conclusion that this difficulty could be very readily obviated by
> having the face muffed up as though the young planter was suffering badly
> with the face or toothache; thus they got rid of this trouble.[72]

Ellen and William Craft's story is one of many in which people's physical bodies were mediators of space. As Simone Browne argues, Ellen's
"passing in terms of race, passing in terms of gender, passing in terms
of class, and passing in terms of disability all played a role in her and
William's passing into freedom."[73] Ellen's body was a medium through
which she and her husband reached the North, out of the South, on
the one hand; but, on the other hand, her body was also the medium
through which white masculinity was contested, toyed with, revealed
as a sociopolitical production that was performable, even by Black enslaved women. To escape the plantation, enslaved people had to reimagine what media could be, often in ways that did not align with the
gendered constructs of their pursuers. Rather than solely sight-oriented,
the Crafts showed that sound, sight, clothing, textile, and performance
mediated experiences of race, gender, space, and freedom. As such,
they materialized McLuhan's media philosophy in ways he could never
imagine.

The runaway enslaved people often used the tools of the master to disrupt "his house," speaking to the nuance of one of Audre Lorde's most famous lines, which we can rephrase as: the master's house may not be undone by his tools, but they just might put a crack in it.[74] As necessarily undocumented/unmapped, the Underground Railroad manipulated the master's tools right under his nose as a means of achieving liberation by using messages and signs "hidden in constellations, quilts, landmarks, songs, [and] enigmatic newspaper advertisements."[75] From the perspective of some white historians, enslavers, medical doctors, and slave catchers, the lack of posters, maps, and writing reproduced conceptions of Blackness as ignorant, abnormal, primitive, close to nature, and underdeveloped. Yet for Black people fleeing enslavement, spatial and temporal power relations ensured that they held different conceptions of media, while also wholly understanding the functions of media most important to those people chasing them, whether they could read and write phonetically or not.

### WHAT'S THE CLIMATE ON THE PLANTATION?

What to the slave was white, Hegelian recognition on the plantation or the Underground Railroad? It was to die. What to the slave was an attempt to show white people that they were all human? It was to die. To "steal oneself away" was not a call for fairer labor conditions, in hopes of an equal democratic distribution of labor, but a radical call to destroy the raced and gendered world on which anthropocentric constructs of man rested in the first place.[76] The runaway enslaved person did not register along the lines of social Darwinian (or McLuhan's) man but appeared as his limitation. For the West, the Negro held more consistency with nature than the social Darwinian man. For the West, both the Negro and nature were *things* that lacked any self-determination and that could be denigrated to prove man's monopoly over evolution. Because of the classifications of the developed (writing) and the undeveloped (oral), which Preston built his career as an expert on the Underground Railroad on, we can say that Western man would situate a lack of phoneticism with being ungeographic, as per McKittrick. But far more important, the ungeographic would ensure that man doubted enslaved people's self-determined capability to escape from enslavement, without his media. And it is this doubt that would open up not only new worlds but also new media, knowledges, and possibilities.

The Underground Railroad's success relied on its improvisational nature. Here media became whatever was necessary at the time. Since the writings of McLuhan and Ong, arguments have been made that oral communications are media, much like books or movies.[77] For me, such media have not only spatiotemporal implications, as per both McLuhan and Ong, but racialized and Black radical implications as well. For example, while it was not uncommon for people who freed themselves from enslavement to record their narratives in written form (whether by their own hand or others), it was also common for the same people to refuse to reveal their birth names and specific routes of their escape in the narratives. Indeed, as Judy argues, although Douglass's narrative is held up as the quintessential slave narrative for the attainment of freedom (both physically and self-consciously), Douglass warned Black people about the dangers of the slave narrative, suggesting that he saw no direct link between literacy and freedom.[78] This was because Douglass recognized how important written mediation was for the white enslavers and catchers. Writing, mapping, and recording were far from apolitical—they were the media used by slave catchers and enslavers, the media monopolized by those whom the enslaved sought to flee from. As one survival tactic within a white supremacist world, media had to be something different for the runaway enslaved people than the catchers.

On/off the plantation, what more consistent example of Western man's incapability to fully bend the Negro/medium to his own wishes do we have other than the Underground Railroad? As noted in chapter 1, we can see within *Clotel* (William Wells Brown's fictional story of Thomas Jefferson's daughter from his rape of Sally Hemings) and her drowning a sort of freedom, not lifelessness, even as her story may end as she deathly floats down the Potomac River. Not only was the Negro made into a medium of Western man's self-extension (also in chapter 1), but that medium never worked out as smoothly as he hoped for. In other words, Clotel was unpredictable. We know what white historians like Preston thought about the Underground Railroad. They were predictable. Decades before Preston, we also know what the white slave catchers and enslavers thought about the same Underground Railroad. They were predictable. In both cases the Black enslaved people were captives, commodities needed to extend white male concepts of self-determination and autonomy (man).

However, if we reframe the enslaved person who fled the plantation within the futures of the Black Anthropocene, we can begin to see that enslaved people always imagined other worlds. Indeed, to presume Clotel as nothing but Black death is to accept a secularity of thought inherent in the Western project under critique here in the first place.

Let's say this slightly differently as a question: What if in Clotel's physical death, she reached an eternal life, one routed not in any perpetual Black death, no matter what she does or where she goes, but in Black liberation from a white supremacist world?[79] What if the radical politics often associated with Western secularity (i.e., the idea that there is nothing after death, so one must do everything in this life) actually illustrate not radical transcendence but a limited approach to radical politics? It is here that we would do well to remember one of Du Bois's lines from his classic 1935 book, *Black Reconstruction*:

> Foolish talk, all of this, you say, of course; and that is because no American now believes in his religion. Its facts are mere symbolism; its revelation vague generalities; its ethics a matter of carefully balanced gain. But to most of the four million black folk emancipated by civil war, *God was real. They knew Him.* They had met Him personally in many a wild orgy of religious frenzy, or in the black stillness of the night. His plan for them was clear; they were to suffer and be degraded, and then afterwards by Divine edit, raised to manhood and power.[80]

What Du Bois points to is no cycle of pure, unending Black death but a mediation between one world and another. I cite Du Bois here less as a call for religion as the overarching way to think about media and Blackness on the Underground Railroad, but more as a way of pointing out the importance of other worlds, beyond the physicality of racial slavery, Black death, Black bodies, and Negroes. If the Black enslaved people could imagine those other worlds, they also could imagine media where there were none.

For the enslaved people, the plantation was both a time-space where Blackness and flora and fauna were often conflated, distinct from man, as well as a time-space for alternative forms of meaning-making.[81] People fleeing enslavement (and even those who never ran at all) engaged in thinking beyond man's anthropocentric, secular concept of the world. Likewise, we could also say that enslaved people engaged in some of the earliest critiques of the contemporary climate crisis: they recognized that they were chattel, and, as such, they fashioned alternative stories about everything that assisted in self-liberation, away from the extractive death that gave the plantation life. To escape was to not only critique the fabrication of the Negro as an extension of Western man's whiteness and maleness; it was also to articulate alternative forms of mediation, often overlooked by that same Western man who narcissistically could not think about a world outside his own narrative creation of technological progress.

If we reduce the media of the Underground Railroad to the media of the catchers, enslavers, and white abolitionists, then the central importance and urgency will be located in that of the slave posters and maps. However, if we expand conceptions of media, then rivers, sticks, rocks, and people held significant meaning for enslaved people fleeing the United States as well: in order to get to places like Canada, many of them had to traverse space in undetectable and untrackable ways, often through the usage of media that would go unrecognized by those in pursuit of them. This ensured that runaway enslaved people would be further considered less-than-human, as they lacked the media function; yet with the threat of being reenslaved, this did not matter for those on the run. What mattered for enslaved people were alternative genres of humanity expressed in these alternative forms of mediation. Such thinking would not die with racial slavery.

Black people would continue to toy with, play with, and rearticulate Western media conceptions in ways that would go unrecognized by white people. By the twentieth century, electronic media would move from solely a commercial and militarized enterprise (electronic telegraph of the nineteenth century as utilized by the railroad industry, for example) into the everyday lives of people throughout North America.[82] In other words, electronic media—such as light bulbs, radio, and eventually the television—would come to organize new conceptions of media. Indeed, as electronic media would rise, we would see the invention of the media concept itself in the late nineteenth and early twentieth century, one that we can now apply back to the Underground Railroad.[83] Thus unlike the runaway enslaved people, the transformation in media in the twentieth century ensured that Black radical philosophies had a very different conjuncture to operate in, one that would be organized around a new media economy that increasingly made the Western traversal of space feel easier than ever before. Television, for example, could privately transfer its viewer to new worlds that once only existed in photographs or film; airplane travel could physically move travelers to new locations in hours that used to take months to reach by ship. And interestingly, McLuhan and Huey P. Newton, cofounder of the Oakland-based Black Panther Party, would both call this new, increasingly tele-visual media economy the "global village."

# CHAPTER 3

# Toward a Theory of Intercommunal Media

African American, New Left, and Native American movements all made their voices heard, both behind the scenes and
on the screen. Sometimes this generated reactionary responses
from conservative broadcasters, network executives, or even
local governments. Television was often a site of struggle
between contending social factions, but it also served as a
barometer of changing social mores.

—Lynn Spigel and Michael Curtin

In a packed hall filled with college students, professors, staff, and lo-
cals at Boston College in 1971, Huey P. Newton outlined his thesis on
contemporary capitalism. The cofounder of the Oakland-based Black
Panther Party argued that United States's capitalism was in the midst of
a transformation from industrialism to consumerism, where new "free
markets" were sought outside of the United States in the Second and
Third Worlds. For Newton, this shift in capitalism signified the death of
the United States as a nation and the birth of it as an empire, different
from previous empires. Unlike old models of imperialism, the United
States sought not to be an empire that coexisted with other empires
but *the empire*, to which all the world was subject, often via capitalist
linkages.

At the height of the Party's popular image as Black militants, one of
Newton's goals in Boston was to illustrate that the Party also had a highly
theoretical platform.[1] Prior to this time, the Party had been wrongly but
popularly framed by television, radio, and newspapers as angry, largely
Black male militants, with little intellectual structure.[2] This popular image coincided with massive, violent state repression in the late 1960s.

Just a few of the well-known examples of this state repression include targeted political assassinations of members such as Fred Hampton and Mark Clark in Chicago in 1969; the arrest of twenty-one Panthers in New York City, accused of planning to coordinate bombings and sniper attacks against police stations in 1969; and the incarceration of the Party's other cofounder, Bobby Seale, who was a member of the "Chicago Eight"—a group of antiwar, anti-imperialist protesters, who were arrested after the riots in the wake of the 1968 Chicago Democratic National Convention.[3] Himself newly released from prison due to a hung jury on voluntary manslaughter charges, Newton sought to illustrate how the Party developed its political and theoretical foundation so as to ease the state repression. Furthermore, he sought to position himself as the intellectual of the Party, a figure conversant in Third World and Black radical thought, Marxism, continental philosophy, environmentalism, and, I argue, media philosophy.

Much of the contemporary work on the Black Panther Party interrogates its critique of empire and its development of solidarity between U.S. Black people and Third World radicals.[4] Yet we should also ask what *mediated* the context in which U.S. Black people came to view their own antiracist struggle as consistent with the Third World's decolonial project, and vice versa? Indeed, such a relation of transnational solidarity was the norm in the mid-twentieth century. For example, as the Vietnam War was the first televised war, the Party positioned its solidarity not with the U.S. government or military but with the North Vietnamese fighters, who they argued had pushed out French colonialism and were now unfairly forced to fight against the new, U.S. free-market form of colonialism.[5] Of course, the Black Panther Party was not the only group in the United States to feel this way. Students for a Democratic Society and others all critiqued the U.S. involvement in the Vietnam War for similar reasons.[6] Likewise, the Party made important cross-racial connections, organizing with radical Asian American and Latina/o/x communities that held similar anticolonial goals, many of which connected the oppression they faced in the United States to Western imperialism throughout the world. The United States was not the only place where the Party formed anticolonial solidarities: Party members, such as Newton, traveled to the People's Republic of China, based on their admiration of Mao Zedong; and the Party, of course, built off the larger Pan African-Asian anticolonial project occurring throughout the revolutionary mid-twentieth century, maybe most popularly culminating in the Bandung Conference in 1955.[7] In short, the Party was not an isolated, U.S.-focused, exceptional organization but influenced by a larger transnational movement of radical politics.

That night in Boston, Newton provided what he saw as an answer to the question of what mediated the context of such transnational solidarities, an answer that remains largely underthought in his legacy: advanced and electronic media transmitted the struggles of the Black population in the United States to Third World populations, and vice versa.[8] These transmissions were not merely metaphorical. Newton argued the solidarity between U.S. Black radicals and the Third World was an unintended result of the United States's technological arrogance. The connections that the Party made with decolonial movements cannot be separated from the global, electronic media environment that increased the capacity for Black radicals in the United States to see and hear, at increased speeds, what the United States did to Black and brown people worldwide. In short, electronic media technologies helped to transmit a new world of camaraderie, where people argued that the United States's racism was different from, but also similar to, various Western colonial relationships.[9]

Of course, none of this is to say that electronic media were the first media to make transnational solidarities possible. In the eighteenth and nineteenth century, Black people throughout the Americas were inspired by stories of the Black revolution in Saint-Domingue, which was spread via newspapers and word of mouth.[10] Electronic media were not even the only forms of media to create transnational solidarities in the twentieth century: other media—like underground newspapers, books, and magazines—all circulated toward the creation of new forms of comradery. Yet since the late nineteenth century, even nonelectronic media were circulating at increased speeds within an increasingly global, electronic economy—one that forever blurred the lines between print and electronic, as local and underground media reported quickly on important events from distant locales based on the electronic transmission of information.[11]

What I want to examine is not an exceptionality of electronic media but Newton's technological argument: electronic media played one role in opening up spaces for the Party, as it was conceived by Newton, to view the Vietnamese, the Chinese, the Cubans, the Algerians, and more as comrades in a similar struggle against U.S. imperialism, racism, and capitalism. Thus in the solidarities drawn between different radical voices, Newton developed an underexamined media philosophy, one that can be gleaned from his summary of the Party's development. In the

Boston College speech in 1971 he dialectically summarized for the audience the four stages that the Party had undergone before Newton came to realize the importance of media for U.S. imperialism. In 1966 the Party started out as *Black nationalists* based on a shared but outdated notion: "most people in the past had solved some of their problems by forming into nations."[12] Problems emerged as the Party came to realize that to become a nation they needed to become a dominant faction in the United States, and racism made that unlikely.[13] The Black population in the United States would likely never outnumber the white, making true nationalism impossible.[14]

These contradictions of nationalism led to a second Party shift, to *revolutionary nationalism*, meaning that the Party had to join "all of the other people in the world struggling for decolonization and nationhood."[15] In line with what Kwame Ture and Charles Hamilton (and others) called *internal colonialism*, the Party's synonym for their new nationalism was a "dispersed colony," because Black people in the United States were disproportionately segregated and ghettoized by the mid-twentieth century.[16] As the Party argued, not unlike Western European colonial military forces that produced segregated apartheid conditions throughout Africa and Asia, Black people in the United States were largely prohibited from leaving their own communities by an increasingly militarized police force. However, Newton realized that the contradictions of Black nationalism had not been eradicated by the Party's revolutionary nationalism: all forms of nationalism were complicit in the colonization of people worldwide.

The Party's third stage came as they realized that they were not nationalists. They were "individuals deeply concerned with the other people of the world and their desires for revolution"; and to fully show solidarity with Black and brown people worldwide, the Party decided to call themselves *Black internationalists*.[17] Of course, there was one final contradiction that existed even in the Party's shift to internationalism. On that night in Boston, Newton revealed to the audience: "Our mistake was to assume that the conditions under which people had become nations in the past *still existed*."[18] Newton claimed that previously nations were structured by "natural partitions," such as "water or a great unoccupied land space," alongside violent conquest. At this time, new technologies like gun powder, mapping, and ships were expanding Western European nations, furthering the "phenomenon we know as colonialism."[19] But Newton argued even these conditions of colonialism were dying (or at least almost dead).

At Boston College, Newton announced that the final stage of the Party involved two, interrelated parts, both based on the transforming technological interests of empire; one of those parts was representative of the new stage of capitalism and the other was the required response by radicals to that new stage. The first stage already existed: *reactionary intercommunalism*, or the white supremacist, masculinist structure that sought to profit from a new techno-transnational capitalism. The second was what the Party needed to become: *revolutionary intercommunalists*, or those radicals who could mobilize the reactionary's technologies to create the new conditions critical of reactionary politics. For Newton, U.S. Black people and Third World peoples could now engage with each other to new degrees based on intercommunalist technologies (e.g., electronic media, advanced transportation technologies, digital media, etc.), against reactionary politics.

Newton argued that the technologically savvy, wealthy, largely white figures were driving the rising reactionary electronic, computational transformations, and the Party would have to understand this if they wanted to keep up with the transformations in capitalism. It is no surprise that the reactionary intercommunalists sounded like what Charlton McIlwain calls "Committeemen," or those mid-twentieth-century, largely white male figures who, "at the behest of their government, set America's founding principles of white supremacy loose to run amuck in new computational systems they designed and built."[20] No matter the important disagreements within the Party about the use of intercommunalism as an ideology, Newton felt that evidence for shifting the Party to intercommunalism had been there from the start.[21] Beyond any nationalized allegiance, electronic and digital media technologies were increasingly creating a world newly mediated in ways designed to expand white bottom lines via the transnational expansion of the market to Black and brown people.

Intercommunalism was not the only term Newton used to describe this new media economy that night in Boston. Newton also stated that, via their technologically expansive domination, the reactionary intercommunalists had "created the '*global village*,'" or a space mediated by technologies for capitalism's interests, not the U.S. nation's.[22] Of course, not long before Newton's Boston speech, Marshall McLuhan argued that electronic media, such as radios, telephones, computers, and televisions, had turned the world into a global village in the twentieth century. In McLuhan's important 1962 book, *The Gutenberg Galaxy*, the global village ensured that nations would come to matter far less, as all the world's people could be intimately, sensorially involved in each other's lives.

Electronic media introduced a new worldview, drastically different from the detribal, civilized, mechanical one that came earlier. While McLuhan held that older mechanical media (like Gutenberg's press) were extensions of one sense, such as the eye, electronic media (like the television) produced "an extension of our nervous systems," supposedly reintroducing multisensorial engagement into the Western world.[23] For McLuhan, electronic media *retribalized* Western man, presumably removing him from the detribal and returning him back to the tribal (but never fully), only now via the electronic creation of increased information circulation and participation with people from different parts of the world. In overly optimistic fashion, McLuhan hoped that in the global village racism would die out, altering "the position of the Negro" so that "they can no longer be *contained*, in the political sense of limited association. They are now *involved* in *our lives*, as we in theirs, thanks to the electronic media."[24] However, in Newton's recasting of the global village, he might ask McLuhan, when exactly was the Negro not involved in *our lives*? In fact, Newton foresaw the Black media philosophy question asked throughout this book: Who are the our, we, and us assumed in media philosophy?

Despite McLuhan's hope that the global village would diminish racism, Newton illustrated that when media are thought apart from the raced implications of the human, it is an error symptomatic of Western racial violence. In other words, reactionary intercommunalism was McLuhan's global village, while revolutionary intercommunalism was Newton's. Neither McLuhan's nor Newton's global village fully eradicated discrimination. In fact, the hierarchies worthy of challenging for Newton were often limited to racism and classism, with little emphasis on patriarchy, gender, and sexuality.[25] However, Newton does point toward a critique of media philosophy unthought in the work of McLuhan and useful for my own. McLuhan's frame of the global village assumed one human representative of "our lives"—Western man.[26] But Newton also saw a continuation of social Darwinian, Western man's artificial selection in new form: not only were Black and brown people still deemed closer to nature than to civilization but we could increasingly be targeted as consumers on the globalized capitalist market. According to Newton, this was symptomatic of a new man, one that he called a *technocrat*, who, like the new electronic media he created, was not bound to a nation, but capable of the dispersed transnationalization of markets everywhere—from the (former) colonies to the ghettoes.

Newton's project was to expose to oppressed people of the world that Western man would now enter their lives not solely by physical presence but by marketing commodities from afar to those once viewed as commodities themselves. Indeed, in the middle of the Cold War, fearing the influence of Russian communism on Black political organizing, at home and abroad, the United States had long opened the market as a basis of democratic practice. Democracy was not going to be based on the distribution of equal protections of all people under the law in the United States but on the presumed equal capacity to buy and sell. Such thinking would reach the very top of the political spectrum: President Richard Nixon ran his 1969 campaign on "law and order" and "Black capitalism," two interrelated policy points that would get him elected. The first point (law and order) was designed to conflate Black radicalism with criminality, while the other policy (Black capitalism) sought to financially boost the Black middle class, positioning them as representative of racial equality for all, with no concern for poor Black communities.[27]

Newton showed in his 1971 speech that, despite massive technological changes, expansion of markets, and the potential for Black people to get in on such markets, not much would change politically for most of the world's Black people. He argued that Western man's raced/gendered background was far from universal but looked like McLuhan. Newton adds that the new technocratic man of the global village would electronically bring together not the world per se, but Western, white, and wealthy men from the United States and other Western locations. Or maybe more accurately, the bringing together of Black and brown people in the global village was an afterthought to the bringing together of Western, white profit-seeking, technocratics. Furthermore, Newton argued that the global village would be *without national affiliation*, bringing together the wealthy white populations only so that they could expand their own bottom lines by electronically entering into the lives of as many people as possible, no matter their race and no matter where they lived (reactionary intercommunalism). In short, the new man was responsible for creating a new, transnational, capitalist form of consciousness.

But importantly, the reactionaries did not monopolize politics. Remember, McLuhan imagined that the global village might diminish racism. Alternatively, Newton argued that the global village may be implemented for racist and capitalistic purposes (reactionary), while also unintentionally reinforcing comradery between people in the U.S. ghettos and the Third World peoples (revolutionary). In other words, the Black and brown people throughout the world, who were afterthoughts of the reactionary's profit margins, could mobilize against reactionary politics via the newly available technologies. Racism would not end via magically waving an electronic wand; instead, racism may end via electronic formation, or rather transmission, of connections between seemingly separate (geographically and politically) people. Newton argued that the global village created the new potential for revolution against a small, white, rich group of men who deemed the global village necessary to consolidate non-nationalistic, capitalistic power. As an unintended consequence of Western technological arrogance, Black people in the United States were no minority, but a village, a global majority, or a "multitude," as Michael Hardt and Antonio Negri would much later argue, mediated by technologies of reactionary intercommunalism.[28]

This chapter offers a particular rereading of Newton's intercommunalism with the objective of recasting Western media economies as constitutive of his theory of imperialism. For my purposes, this is a Newton not meant to be the sole, historically accurate representation of the entire Party—a group historically shown to be led by the work and leadership of Black women, even as it is often popularly depicted as a Black male organization (to say nothing of the massive political rivalries within the Party's leadership structure).[29] Instead, this is an interpretive chapter that argues that Newton's philosophy—at times seen in his own words, or in the writings of other members, such as Elaine Brown, or even in the Party's newspaper—is not only a sign of what he wanted the Party to be, but representative of Black media philosophy's challenge to the Western, white, and dominant media philosophy, as per Darwin and McLuhan. For those unsure of where to find Black media philosophy, Newton can be turned to as one mid- to late-twentieth-century Black media philosopher—which of course is not to say he is the only one.

I put forward that Newton was not only influenced by the anti-imperialist work of Fidel Castro, Mao Zedong, or Frantz Fanon, but also an unexamined area of study in histories of the Party and Newton: Herbert Marshall McLuhan.[30] For Newton, the global village was both an imperialist and (potentially) an anti-imperialist economy, one that held Blackness at its core. And, as McLuhan could not see this, we would need people like Newton to point media philosophy toward Black political thought and power.

## NATURE AS CONTENT: ON THE DIS/ASSOCIATION OF
## THE COLONY WITH THE GHETTO

Newton situated his political activism directly within the West Oakland community in which he grew up. Near the docks of the San Francisco Bay, West Oakland was once the largely Black and working-class industrial center of Oakland, California. This community is important less for any biographic information about Newton and more for what it represents: a continuation of anti-Black racism in postslavery, migratory Black communities.[31] In short, well after racial slavery, the violent artificial selection of some people as the Negro drove the logics of migration, racialized segregation, and ghettoization for the descendants of enslaved people.

Thus we must remember that the context that the Black Panther Party emerges in matters. Founded in 1966, the Party develops in the wake of the signing of civil rights legislation, which suggested that such legislation did not fundamentally transform the lives of a significant number of Black people in the United States. Indeed, Party members would argue that much of the civil rights legislation did not reach the Black and brown ghettos of the northern and western United States. By Newton's youth, jobs and social programs had diminished in Oakland, contributing to rising Black unemployment rates and precarity of the community. This mid-twentieth-century moment would come to be marked by related economic shifts, like deindustrialization, cuts to welfare, and white flight.[32] Thus a major contradiction emerged in the mid-twentieth century: while the United States passed crucial civil rights legislation that benefited some Black people, it also demonized all social welfare programs that could help much of the Black population as home-grown, Cold War–era socialism. While the mid-twentieth century saw booms in the Black middle-class, a large portion of the United States's Black population remained underemployed while living in increasingly deindustrialized, highly segregated ghettoes.[33]

At the same time as Black poverty surged, civil rights legislation inspired many white conservatives in the 1970s to argue that Black people no longer had the right to complain about societal failures. In 1973, the Heritage Foundation, the highly conservative think tank, emerged with the goal of crushing legislation that was perceived as a "handout" to the poor—which often meant they worked to kill legislation that helped Black people.[34] In the wake of massive funding for the Heritage Foundation, Black radicals like Newton needed to craft a narrative to demonstrate what appeared fairly easy to show, but many were now doubting: that racism was not solved via civil rights legislation, and that the inner-cities were increasingly spaces for the U.S. government to forget about the harms inflicted on Black people.

For Newton and numerous Oakland residents, the ghettoes were occupied territories, surveilled by a violent police force designed to keep Black people in check. Indeed, not long before the Party moved to intercommunalism, its second political position was that the ghetto was comparable to European colonization (internal colonization). While Newton and the Party moved away from this position, I argue it deserves some attention to understand Newton's Black media philosophy. Newton never provided a sophisticated definition of media, but one can be excavated if we take seriously his reading of the ghetto, alongside his thinking of the colony's relationship to nature.[35] Newton made the connection between colonialism and the ghetto, based in part on Kwame Ture's and Charles Hamilton's important 1967 book *Black Power*, an influential work for Newton that would never leave his thinking. In their book, Ture and Hamilton argued that due to white extraction of Black labor from the ghettoes (via both mass incarceration and cheap, exploited labor), the Black community was just like a colony, with resources not for its own use but for the utility of white capitalists. Ture and Hamilton conflated the raw materials, extracted from Africa, with those cheap and incarcerated workers extracted from the inner cities, all of which were necessary to maintain the Negro construct:

> Under classic colonialism, the colony is a source of cheaply produced raw materials (usually agricultural or mineral) which the "Mother Country" then processes into finished goods and sells at high profits—sometimes back to the colony itself. The black communities of the United States do not export anything *except human labor*. But is the differentiation more than a technicality? Essentially, the African colony is selling its labor; the product itself does not belong to the "subjects" because the land is not theirs. At the same time, let us look at the black people of the South: cultivating cotton at $3.00 for a ten-hour day and from that buying cotton dresses (and food and other goods) from white manufacturers. Economists might wish to argue this point endlessly; the objective relationship stands. Black people in the United States have a colonial relationship to the larger society, a relationship characterized by institutional racism.[36]

Apartheid-style policing, white extraction of labor and capital from the Black community, and a lack of social programs to denounce socialism at the height of the Cold War all ensured that the Black ghetto in the

United States mirrored the colony for Ture and Hamilton. Importantly, social Darwinian conceptions of nature resided inside both the colonies and ghettoes: each locale comprised extractable raw materials, selected and turned toward (Western) man's utility.[37] The colonies and inner cities served as factories to continue to reproduce the Negro by and for white people.

If McLuhan's man is overrepresented as white and male—and I argue reliant on the Negro-as-medium—then hyperpolicing, segregation, redlining, and other reproductions of the Negro continued to extend whiteness and maleness in mid-twentieth-century forms.[38] The ghetto is a form of racial violence after racial slavery (far from the only one, of course), designed to prevent the Negro from fully removing the media function by and for the West. Whether the colony was a good metaphor for ghettoization or not, the problem for Newton was that Black people were treated in both systems as tools—what I call media—of a larger white supremacist society.

For contemporary media philosophy, media often are built off the anthropocentric intention of depleting nature in excess, as nature is the content of media. Likewise, in his 1974 essay, "Dialectics of Nature," Newton held that the West was structured off the social Darwinian depletion of raw materials in excess. As I have been arguing, this works similarly for the Negro after captivity: Western colonial conceptions of nature act as the Negro's content, which, in turn, reflect what the West imagines itself to be. In the white imagination, "nature" increasingly turned away from mainly Africa and increasingly became associated with the U.S. ghettoes. The ghetto was deemed both factory for the reproduction of the Negro *and* natural habitat, from which the Negro could be called forth for new twentieth-century purposes. As Martin Heidegger argued, nature was "challenged-forth" for "modern" anthropocentric ends.[39] Similar to Heidegger's technology and McLuhan's media, Newton argued in "The Technology Question" that "man is becoming less dependent upon the natural forces of nature" for his use as need be, and more dependent on the *excessive* technological stressing of nature, demonstrating "how the crucial issue of our time is the control of technology."[40] Rather than the moderate use of nature to sustain oneself, the West used nature far beyond its own needs.

The definition of technology that Newton critiqued adopted the Western assumptions implicit in Darwin's artificial selection (which again is to say, Darwin's media philosophy): man held a capacity to artificially select nature and transform it into artificial items/media, for his own maintenance and far beyond. In addition to language, it would be this excessive use of nature that would make Darwin's man unique. Like McLuhan or Darwin, Newton argued that nature lay the foundation (or was the content) for media and their relationship to Western humanness; unlike McLuhan or Darwin, Newton also argued that media, humanness, and Western conceptions of natural materials were representative of a *specific* human interest, impossible to consider outside racism, capitalism, and ghettoization. If media philosophy speaks to the relation between technology and the human's being and knowing for McLuhan, Newton suggests a contradictory question that McLuhan had no answer for: Within Western media philosophy, is the Negro more legible as the Western human or as that human's media? Newton would answer such a question by pointing to the importance of the colonial construct of nature to Western man: the ghettoes in the United States were full of *natural resources*, extracted for the re/production of more and more Negroes for white profit. It is in the ghetto that the war on drugs, mass incarceration, and more become not only articulations of an assumed, natural, racial depravity, but profitable for white people, toward replicating fabrications of the Negro as a medium.

Just as important, for Newton, intercommunalism spoke to a new shift necessary to understand this chapter going forward: not only were the colonies full of raw, natural materials (both resources and the Negro) that could be extracted, but now, those same people, who were once deemed natural, raw materials, could be *marketed to* by the reactionary intercommunalists. Increasingly in a post–civil rights world, one supposedly without racism, Black consumerism was presented as evidence of racism's end, even as racist policies and economic exploitation had yet to disappear. Internal colonialism did important work for Newton's intercommunalism: while the elemental association of the Negro had not died in the ghettoes or colonies, the Negro could be made a consumer, which was supposed to be proof of the end of white supremacy.

In the United States, no longer was the Negro viewed as solely a medium, via the social Darwinian, violent artificial selection of Africans. No longer were captive Black bodies produced and violently worked only on the plantation, based on self-determined decisions of the colonial-political-economic, white elite few. Instead, the Negro was situated in the ghettoes/colonies, and this increasingly meant that Black people were viewed as impaired based solely on their own politico-economic decisions. To become increasingly targeted consumers, of course, meant that Black people would need to make better decisions to improve our own lot, rather than to blame racist politics. Similar racist arguments about poor economic decision making and consumption stretched back well into the nineteenth century, with, for example, governmental failures of the Freedmen's bank during the United States's reconstruction era.[41] What differed for Newton in the 1970s was that the intercommunal technologies not only helped to globalize Black consumption, but in the process they effected an end of white capitalist national allegiance and thus the end of any need for the nation to take care of those not keeping up with the intercommunal transformations. No longer did dominant white arguments about slavery as a gift to Black people make sense (as discussed in chapters 1 and 2). By the mid-twentieth century, arguments about Black people's conditions needed to be reread within social Darwinian claims of natural depravity, of which many whites argued that they had no role in producing.[42] The politics mirrored the technocracy of the global village: Black poverty was no national problem, but an individualistic problem of inherently bad decision making. The nation was increasingly not responsible for *your* problems within an intercommunal world.

Newton outlined a theory of technology that was necessary to continue the racial capitalist relationship under new terms of twentieth-century technological development. He would also challenge the reduction of the Negro to a medium of white society. Unfortunately, Newton could not see fully how gender and sexuality were always entangled with racism and capitalism.[43] But Newton does provide a read of what happens to Western man under reactionary intercommunalism, and he does so in ways that hold important implications for understanding how central media have always been to Western resource extraction and thus the current climate crisis we are in. For the rest of this chapter, I interpret Newton, far less as a historical figure that is representative of the Party, and more as a theorist to think about media philosophy differently. In short, rather than a fair reading of the Party, or even Newton for that matter, I am interested in Newton as a midcentury theorist of Black media philosophy: he critiques the reduction of the Black body to Western man's media while also illustrating alternative media uses designed to fully challenge the West altogether. And Newton does so by building off an important theoretical legacy for both twentieth-century Black radicalism and media studies: Marxism.

## DIALECTICS OF A BLACK VANGUARD AND THE MOVE
## AWAY FROM INTERNAL COLONIALISM

Contrary to those who have argued that Karl Marx and Friedrich Engels felt Russia could not have a revolution, in their Russian preface to *The Communist Manifesto*, Marx and Engels argued Russia could be the "vanguard" of the revolution.[44] Such phrasing would not only inspire Vladimir Lenin and the Bolshevik Party that he led in the early twentieth century, but the word *vanguard* would be central to the way that many Black people throughout the world saw themselves, especially after Lenin's death and the rise of Stalinism. The vanguard suggested that the underdogs would not only rise but point to the revolutionary destruction of the capitalist system. Newton was not immune; he situated the Party as the vanguard in the United States. This was not merely symbolic Marxism. From Marx to Lenin to Mao, Newton tapped into a dense, anticapitalist, anti-imperialist theoretical legacy that he, in part, viewed as necessary for a Black revolution. Marxist dialectical materialism was a theory that Newton felt would provide a new worldmaking potentiality, one that revealed the Party's own contradictions that it needed to address and point the way forward to the end of capitalism. Newton was always "interested in the ever-changing status of things," which Mao Zedong called *contradictions*, always already necessary to bring about revolution.[45] But still, revolution was never guaranteed.

For Newton, Marxist dialectics had revealed the contradictions not only in the society but within the larger U.S. left. Thus the United States–based (white) Marxists forfeited their capacity to be the vanguard. Operating on Hegel's triad, United States–based Marxists remained stuck in a dialectic of Western supremacy. Put into Hegelian terms, United States–based white Marxism could be simplified as a three-part plan: a thesis or the presumed moment of fixity (Western capitalism); an antithesis or negative moment of contradiction to challenge the thesis (Western proletariat); lastly a synthesis, or "the harmonizing of the antithesis," leading back to a new thesis (Western communism).[46] For Marx, Hegel's dialectic was important but idealist, as he was unaware of the material relations of capitalism. Similarly, Newton felt many Marxists did not recognize the contradictions of being pro-white, pro-Western Hegelians. While dressed in anticapital garb, a weddedness to Western chauvinism ensured that for many, the Marxist revolution was nothing more than idealism. As Robin Kelley argues, for many white Marxists the end of capitalism meant the end of the exploitation of the white worker, not necessarily the end of racism, sexism, or homophobia.[47] In fact, some Marxists felt that racism, sexism, and homophobia were distractions from capitalism's real problems. For Newton, such a position was absurd, and not in keeping with Marx and Engels themselves.

Newton's engagement with Marxist dialectics would not have been abnormal for mid-twentieth-century Black intellectuals. Black radical and decolonial thought throughout the mid-twentieth century deeply engaged with Marxism as one element necessary to destroy white supremacy and imperialism worldwide. In *Notes on Dialectics*, for example, C.L.R. James argued that Marxist dialectics, pulled from G.W.F. Hegel's *Logic*, were necessary to understand the contradictions of the Communist Internationals, leading to the historical shifts from the First International to the Fourth International.[48] In Walter Rodney's Russian Revolution lectures, he argued that Marxist dialectics flipped Hegelian, bourgeois idealism: materialism was now the basis of historical change.[49] Carole Boyce Davies argued that in the twentieth century, Claudia Jones would recognize the contradictions in Western, white Marxism, as the "particular neglect of black women," ultimately leading "to the obstruction of the universal (anti-imperialism and class struggle)."[50] For Jones, revolution could not be fulfilled without recognizing the contradictions of sexism and racism.

Some Party member's own positions on internal colonialism would be challenged via Marxist dialectics. The African revolutionary Amilcar Cabral, whose visits to the United States electrified Black radicals in the early 1970s, argued that the oppression faced in the United States could not be neatly applied to the oppression faced in African colonization, as the contradictions of capitalism differed based on location (to say nothing about the different forms of colonization in Africa).[51] Like Cabral, Frantz Fanon famously warned Black radicals that Marxism must be "bent" to fit the colonies, which did not mean that Marxism was wrong per se, but that Marxist theory could not neatly apply to the colonies without a critical eye. This was, in part, because the contradictions in the colonies differed from those in Europe. Unlike Europe's proletariat, Fanon argued that the Black, colonial proletariat were often the most privileged group with the most to lose, making their revolutionary potential not as likely as the lumpen proletariat, or the criminal, underemployed class in the colonies. While Marx argued in *The Eighteenth Brumaire of Louis Bonaparte* that the lumpen proletariat had little to no revolutionary potential, Fanon argued the opposite in *The Wretched of the Earth*—that the lumpen proletariat and the peasantry may be the most revolutionary groups of all in the colonies.[52] Like Lenin argued, Black radicals like Fanon and Cabral showed that the local conditions determined the people's readiness for revolutionary transformation, not a blind-faith reading of Marx's and Engels's nineteenth-century thought.

Influenced by these Pan-African theorizations, what a dialectical approach had taught Newton was that the United States needed a new adversary, a new vanguard, forged out of the local contradictions to reveal new terrain and point toward a new synthesis. This is where he felt that the Party could step in. When Newton called the Party the vanguard of the revolution, he was not promoting a form of U.S. exceptionalism, he did not hold that the United States was uninfluenced by the outside world, or that Black people in the United States were the true leaders in worldwide change.[53] He did not hold that Black people had something inside them racially that made them far more likely to revolt than anyone else. Instead, like the Bolsheviks in Russia for Lenin, Newton meant that because the Party had formed inside of the United States, it was in a good position to unearth the racial-capitalist-imperialist contradictions of the country. The Party would not lead the revolution per se; it was simply the job of the Party to point the way toward revolution. It was the job of "the people," or those oppressed by the United States (of multiple races), to decide what to do with the contradictions that the Party had laid out for them.[54] Newton hoped that the people would join in the larger global revolution.

Importantly, Newton's Marxist approach aligns with the British cultural studies project, emerging around the same time, most closely associated with the work of Stuart Hall. This is because, like Hall, Newton essentially argued that there was no guarantee that his version of the Party would spell the end of capitalism.[55] It was simply the Party's job to point out the capitalist contradictions so that the people could make their own decisions on how to best deal with such contradictions. But importantly, revolution was not guaranteed.

In Newton's Boston College speech, he argued that the Party arrived at their final position of intercommunalism/the global village through the Marxist method of dialectical materialism. In addition, he argued that dialectical materialism necessarily revealed the Party's own contradictions—contradictions that, if not addressed, could prevent revolution. Thinking through nationalism, dispersed colonialism, and internationalism, Newton realized that the Party had missed a *technological analysis*, essential to understand the new contradictions of the U.S. empire. The most important addition Newton adds to Black media philosophy was this: that the Party could not be fully Black nationalists, a dispersed colony, or internationalists in a world "in which a ruling circle, a small group of people" did not care about nations but focused only on the control of "all other people by using their technology," despite physical distance.[56] Newton had come to understand that electronic media created what Lynn Spigel called the "double fantasy of telepresence and tele-absence at the same time," or the feeling of being physically present and absent at the same time.[57] In short, right as white people were physically leaving inner cities (suburbanization), electronic media increased their concepts of dis/embodiedness, meaning television, radio, and other technologies produced the feelings of presence/absence.[58]

Newton understood the particulars of his technological conjuncture. Although many white suburbanites had just left behind the inner cities to move away from poor Black and brown populations, they could now watch their former inner-city homes burn in Black street rebellions of the mid-twentieth century, always from afar and presumably disconnected from the downtown fires. Of course, there was a related movement at this time: white people were not only leaving the United States inner cities but were also increasingly leaving various parts of Asia, Africa, and the Americas. The larger global decolonial and antiracist projects coincided with shifts in highly mediated conceptions of dis/embodiment. Newton's reactionary intercommunalism implied, and I argue, that Western imperialism was technologically changing. Right as colonizers physically left the colonies (as well as inner cities), their media were also ensuring that they never had plans of leaving at all, only creating new dis/embodied revenue streams by leaving behind products for sale in their stead. There may be white flight, deindustrialization, and decolonization, but that did not mean that there would not be new, increasingly disembodied modes of extracting profit from Black and brown people, worldwide. The global village would point toward new ways of both entering Black and brown people's lives and selling to them, worldwide.

Importantly for Black media philosophy, increased feelings of a white lack of blame in the misfortunes of Black people, whether in the ghettoes or the colonies, also coincided with the dis/embodiedness associated with electronic media. Here we can see the contradictions evident in McLuhan's argument that the global (reactionary) village may bring the world closer together via destroying nationalism. If television broadcasting was representative of the suburbs, itself a technological product that marked a physical distancing of white from Black people,

I argue the suburbs were also a physical representative of a distancing of white culpability in Black people's mid-twentieth-century suffering—economically, socially, and politically.[59] Put differently, the global village pointed not toward a new form of racism but constituted a continuance of an "insidious form of racism, the point of which is to forever unburden oneself of all guilt."

If you never see Black people, outside of a television screen because they do not live in your suburbs, what role in their oppression could you possible play? Of course, this is not to say that electronic media produced white people's feeling of a lack of blame in Black problems. It is to say, *à la* Raymond Williams, that electronic media and their capacity to make people feel both *private* (home) and *mobile* (capable of electronically seeing the world from home), reentrenched white feelings of little to no role in Black problems, an argument that predated the proliferation of electronic media. Beyond just McLuhan, Newton shares much with the media philosophy that follows him. For Williams and Spigel, McLuhan's global village less addressed sensorial effects of television and more the entertainment needs of suburbanites. Yet Newton goes further than Williams and Spigel, suggesting that the global village was also a space in which to watch the perceived dangers of Black inner-city rebellion (and decolonial struggle), without white people physically being there. For Williams, television was a medium that extended its viewers from the suburban home (private) to the outside world (mobile); this he called "mobile privatization," which was no "effect" of television, but reflective of capitalism's transformations, serving "an at-once mobile and home-centred way of living: a form of mobile privatization." In a similar way, Newton argued that the global village represented the necessities of capitalism, which also allowed some to move and stay private simultaneously. But Newton also argued that the global village, this space of new relations of mobility and privacy, must have been a very white space.

In this light, Newton was closer to Spigel's argument than Williams's, as Spigel argues that what was required for the white TV watchers was a physical movement away from Black people and into suburbia.[60] Even still, I argue that Newton points to a related but even more radical step than Spigel's: what also emerged was a media economy that privately transported its viewers to see anticolonial/antiracist struggle and racial violence, always from afar, participating in both in the process. This was a media economy that could distance its viewers away from the racist acts broadcasted nationwide and/or distance viewers away from feeling any empathy for the Black people who faced those acts at the same time. Television was but one new medium at the time that served this function, allowing viewers to remain both involved and disconnected from the harms of innercity, Black life and decolonial politics. Under the global village, Black people continued to be a disembodied mass (Black bodies, the Negro) for many white people, rarely seen or heard, unless rioting or marching in inner cities or rebelling in the colonies on TV. Under such conditions we can see a continual disavowal of white culpability in Black and brown lives, a disavowal not new but one increasingly electronically transmitted via reminders of the dangerous, randomly rioting inner cities and decolonizing world. Thus Black conditions were deemed as the fault of Black people destroying *their own homes*, replicating a social Darwinian, racist argument that Black people had irrational, desirous natures if left alone in their natural habitat (the ghetto), and white people required a mediated distance from Black people.

In many ways Newton's global village is more useful than McLuhan's. According to McLuhan, the global village was representative of *our* central nervous system, as it "not only extended a single sense of function as the old mechanical media did," but externalized *our* senses in far more participatory ways, transforming aspects of *our* social/psychic existence.[61] However, less a reflection of *our* central nervous system, the global village for Newton was a supporter of the demands of racial capitalism, concerned with white masculine involvement and participation in transnational capitalist markets. Like McLuhan's global village, which distributed information throughout the body, racial violence was being redistributed throughout Western society to now uphold white supremacist-capitalist-patriarchal worlds, without technically being the exact same violences that had previously upheld the Western concept of the Negro. Increasingly actions and policies that may not seem racist on the surface had racist implications.

In the United States, at least, with a slow but increasing move away from openly racist legal and extralegal structures of Black Codes, Jim Crow, and lynching came increases in redlining, mass incarceration, defunding of programs, ghettoization, hyperpolicing, and environmental destruction, often not presented as racist but necessary for Western man's continued extension. Rather than decrease after slavery, racial violence proliferated for Black people in ways that were denied as racist altogether, always with an eye toward financial profit.[62] Reactionary intercommunalism, the global village, was a theory of the technological reentrenchment of racism as inseparable from capitalism in the mid-twentieth century, so deep that it could never fully be overturned via new civil rights legislation.

The new shifts in man, marked by new movements into/out of the colonies and inner cities, represented the final ideological position of the Party—intercommunalism, meaning "the total technologizing of monopoly capital beyond the mere brute force of imperialism."[63] This is not to say that electronic media never organized colonialism prior to the mid-twentieth century, of course (the telegraph was a central medium for colonial organization in the Americas and far beyond, during the nineteenth century).[64] Instead, it is to say that Newton argued that there was a new media economy that would presumably dis/embody colonialism for good while never fully ending colonialism. Thus there would be new ways to enter the colonies and the inner cities, via technological developments. This would be a moment of minority absorption for Roderick Ferguson, whereby the U.S. state, capitalism, and the academy would collide to make a world where Black and brown people are defined as equal, only via the market.[65] This was a global village (Newton's intercommunalism) that connected to the shifting demands of capital, changing conceptions of nationalism, fear of decolonization and rebellion efforts in the mid-twentieth century, and white denial of blame for those same revolts.

Newton argued that the U.S. imperialists ironically realized that the best way to govern the colonies was to ultimately stop colonialism in some places such as Vietnam and Algeria and replace it with the free market; this is because the end of colonialism, in a heightened Cold War era, assumed a flood of new media would enter the colonies in the stead of the former colonizer. Today, we see similar arguments under critique by scholars like Ruha Benjamin and Simone Browne in relation to artificial intelligence (AI): the colonizer is presumably absent from the technology left in his stead (chapter 4).[66] And importantly, the relations Benjamin and Browne outline can be traced back to these midcentury shifts in capitalism, to the presumed dis/embodiedness of the colonizer via dying colonial regimes and the expansion of the market. The content of the media mattered little under such a media economy; what mattered most was the presumed freedom to buy and sell globalized media, despite geographic location.

But just as important, and in ways McLuhan would not engage (but Williams and Spigel might), Newton argued that capitalism lay the foundation for the transforming global village. In short, Newton's global village spoke not only to suburbanization but also a rising, urgent, capitalist, natural resource scarcity in the West during the 1970s: the increasing demand for dis/embodied forms of media coincided with the oil crisis, a crisis that financially hindered Western physical movement, heightening the need for new forms of dis/embodiedness. Thus the shifting politics of mobility—long of interest for media scholars and our emphasis on time and space—would also be a central factor for thinking about the new technocratic man.

## ENERGY, DIS/EMBODIEDNESS, AND THE NEW ("TECHNOCRATIC") MAN

Newton tested his intercommunal theory on multiple Black Panther Party members. One of those important Party members was Elaine Brown, often called the songstress of the Party because of her singing and ability to write revolutionary music. Brown joined the Party in 1968, two years after the Party was founded. In 1974 she became the first woman to chair the Party. Newton named Brown the new chair while on the run for murder charges, a sign of his own diminishing mental health and sexist violence. The decision did not sit well with many of the men in the Party who held on to their sexist and reactionary politics. While also being romantically involved with Newton, Brown was a person Newton trusted to strategize with. In her autobiography, *A Taste of Power*, Brown recalled that Newton's first explanation of intercommunalism to her was linked to a moment in which he showed her a magazine advertisement. "'It's an ad for Ford cars,'" Brown said, largely unimpressed.

But for Newton the magazine held more than an advertisement for Ford motor cars; the ad was a new transnational position on capitalism as a whole. The advertisement continued: "'We at Ford International fly the American flag...we say, what flag do *you* fly?'" According to Newton, this advertisement was similar to a Coca-Cola ad: "'I'd love to buy the world a Coke.'" During his demonstration, and unable to contain his own excitement, Newton finally asked and answered the question he posed to Brown: "'What does it [Ford's and Coca-Cola's ads] mean?... It means that the U.S. capitalists have taken a turn, a right turn. And I think it's affecting the economic structure of the entire world. We're in a brand new game.'"[67] From these advertisements Newton explained the basis of his reactionary intercommunalism, the new stage of global, technological capitalism that he felt all revolutionaries needed to understand in order to fight against it. Brown described Newton's words as such:

"The American way of life—capitalism—is no longer threatened by Communism. Soviet inroads into the undeveloped Third World are irrelevant. The U.S. capitalists are threatened by a limitation of marketplaces. They not only *need* to sell the whole world a Coke, they're moving to do it.…That's why Ford can ask what flag do you fly. It's not important. When they control your market, they'll have the rest. If you want to be 'black and proud,' they put Negroes in advertising campaigns and have all the Negroes fighting for the right to drink Coke over Pepsi. For the Chinese they throw up Bank of America buildings that look like pagodas. And if you fly a flag with a hammer and sickle, they'll slap it on the dashboard of a Ford and control the Communist communities—that the Communists themselves can't accommodate."[68]

Brown's retelling of Newton's description of intercommunalism, and its sought-after markets, mirrors what we now call transnational capitalism. But it was not just transnational capitalism that was important for Newton; it was also the media that transnational capitalists used to push forward their agenda of Coca-Cola and Ford to new markets. Magazine ads, television, airplanes, and radio are all what Newton called intercommunal technologies of the global village, even as they included and exceeded the electronic media McLuhan associated with the global village.

Unlike McLuhan's, Newton's global village held no utopian promises.[69] In fact, the global village might further the new *technocratic man*, which would devastate people of all races. Newton's technocratic man contradicted Michel Foucault's arguments around the same time that man, "assignable in his corporeal, labouring, and speaking existence," had finally met his end.[70] Instead, for Newton, man used technologies to remake himself into a world citizen, as intercommunal. Newton marked technocratic man as the beginnings of a technocracy, where technology was increasingly automating to a new level where the proletariat was not only being replaced by machines but dying as a result of it. According to Newton, this level of automation led to a new level of human consciousness, dependent on alternative concepts of participation and freedom that were reducible to techno-market relations. For this reason, Newton contended that Marx's disdain for the lumpen proletariat—the unorganized, unemployables of society—was highly misplaced. As Newton stated in 1970, the technocracy ensured that the proletariat "will definitely be on the decline because they will be unemployables and therefore swell the ranks of the lumpen."[71] Under technocratic man's reign, the proletariat's precarity will make everyone open to lumpenization, or the capacity to become Marx's lumpen proletariat. The end goal of technocratic man, for Newton, was a new level of automation, leading more and more people into unemployability and expanding capitalism's crisis.

For Newton, the new technocratic man held no universal applicability but was raced, classed, and gendered from the start due to the expropriation of resources (people/raw materials, etc.). In short, man was not Newton, but McLuhan and Darwin; man measured the evolutionary capacity of humans based on his own ability to manipulate his ecosystem, always different and more technologically advanced than tribal populations. Indeed, the tribal groups were classified as *tribal* in much of Western, social Darwinist discourses of the mid-twentieth century because they were open to expropriation, just like the raw materials that make up our media technologies to this day. For Newton, all "technological advancements have been gained through *expropriation from the people*, including slavery proper but also chattel slavery followed by wage slavery," and due to "the expropriation of the world," the reactionary intercommunalist of the United States "dominate world markets."[72] Newton was spot-on in his argument that the United States was a new world empire, and part of the new transnational position the United States would take was based on the changes in capitalism that Newton's dialectical materialism was trying to predict.

Again, here Newton is politically closer to Raymond Williams's position on media than McLuhan's: changes in society were not the product of media transformations but capitalism's, which was of course connected to media. But Newton saw something Williams did not: Newton realized that by the 1970s the United States's capacity to geographically move around the world was being threatened, and the technocrat required not a new form of electronic movement per se, but the increasing proliferation of dis/embodied electronic movement. Newton was starting to see that capitalism's overreliance on oil for transportation was a central factor in the expansion of technocratic man's electronic reach, in the need to reach new markets. In short, rather than only physically touch down inside a space, Newton suggests that technocratic man's obsession with dis/embodiedness under a new era of capitalism is inspired by the 1970s energy crisis, making dis/embodied, semicentralized media increasingly important for neocolonialism.

By the end of World War II, the United States took the place Britain once occupied on the global economic stage in the nineteenth century. Part of the United States's rise to economic power involved not only the postwar destruction in Europe and the rise of consumerism and pop culture that Stuart Hall studied, but the establishment of the 1944

Bretton Woods system, which pegged world currencies to the U.S. dollar and gold standard.[73] Coming out of World War II and attempting to rebuild themselves, the Bretton Woods system allowed largely European and Asian economies to retain the value of their currencies, all under the assumption that the United States dollar could always be converted into gold. In effect, Bretton Woods globalized the U.S. dollar. It also led the United States to make ironic, contextual calls for European nations to decolonize, not due to benevolence but as an attempt to open "numerous markets for American goods and services."[74] By the 1960s, this system effectively situated much of the world's oil prices on the U.S. dollar.

For Newton, such a system situated the United States on a world stage that had not existed before *(the* empire), and the country required maintenance of its economic powers in the midst of the end of Bretton Woods, the conjuncture Newton theorized from in 1971—a time that was essential for technocratic man. President Nixon removed the United States from the gold standard in 1971 because too many countries were questioning whether gold actually backed the U.S. dollar and were calling for proof. This signified economic vulnerability in the United States, exacerbated by deindustrialization, increased unemployment, and inflation, and such economic vulnerabilities were fully on display in the early 1970s with the U.S. dependency on foreign oil. Coming to a full head in 1973, when Egypt and Syria using Soviet weapons attacked Israel as a settler-colonial state, the United States–backed Israel, airlifting supplies to Israel so that it could defend itself against Egypt and Syria (i.e., the Soviet incursion). In response, the Organization of the Petroleum Exporting Countries (OPEC) placed an embargo on oil sales to all states that supported Israel, including the largest backer of Israel, the United States.[75] This would be known as the energy crisis, a precursor to today's climate crisis.

For my purposes, the energy crisis would also contribute to a significant rethinking of physical movement, especially because oil and food prices skyrocketed in the United States. Now movement would have to rely less and less on oil—that is, physically being in a place—and more on dis/embodied electronic forms of mediation. Under such a logic one could sell a product any and everywhere. This, Newton argued, would be the conundrum technocratic man examined: in a world of restricted physical movement, how does the United States move into colonies in new ways? For Newton, the answer involved not only planes and vehicles but media such as the television, radio, and more—all of which were designed to turn Black and colonized people into consumers.

Furthermore, with the embargo from OPEC, Newton would reject the idea that all humans, as well as Black people, were at fault for the 1970s energy crisis. Such arguments ignored both that the United States was a major exporter of oil from the OPEC and the longer history of conflating Black people with nature, which could be extracted for capitalism's excess in similar ways as oil was being extracted.

In Newton's 1974 "Dialectics of Nature" essay, written right after the start of the embargo, he critiqued the popular energy crisis discourses that considered "underdeveloped nations" "as objects of blame for the whole mess" of the current energy crisis.[76] Newton argued these discourses did not focus on the true problem: capitalism. In the historical articulation of some people as close to nature (which is central to understand the Negro as a medium), and the contradictions of the energy crisis, "Dialectics of Nature" held that we will soon reach a world in which even white people will suffer in ways similar to what the Western colonial project relegated largely for Black and brown people (lumpenization):

> Reactionary intercommunalism perceiving the interrelationship of all natural phenomena, including all human beings, seizes upon the phenomena in an attempt to distort the balance in its favor. This exploitation has led to enormous profits and power in the short run. But in a split second, historically, the superindustrial engines of the imperialist, reactionary intercommunalists have come to grief, and even the populations of the Anglo-American Empire itself are in the process of being "nativized" and pauperized in the name of "energy crisis." This crisis is, however, one of capital, not one of energy.[77]

For Newton, the proof of the death of nationalism lies not in critiques of the state but in the promotion of capitalism as an inherent good. It followed, then, that colonialism had to change from its former state, to make Black people *free*, via the purchasing of products. In the process, the precarity once relegated largely to Black people would become the precarity of all, based on purchasing power, further proliferating liberal conflations of the capitalist market with freedom and democracy and the potential to decrease revolts against oppression.

Despite the fact that the United States was suffering from the energy crisis, Newton feared this obsession with purchasing power, rather than redistribution, led to a technocracy, in which a new form of Western human consciousness emerged. In other words, the energy crisis of the 1970s would not only lay the foundation for our current climate crisis, via the need to extract oil at any and all costs; the energy crisis also further instantiated a Western media obsession with moving without moving at all. In many ways the energy crisis signified a need to traverse space in ways that were increasingly unfeasible via the OPEC's raised oil prices, and the electronic media (or more accurately, the mobile private media) would be central to the capitalism Newton critiqued as reactionary intercommunalism (i.e., the global village). The United States had to figure out: How do we move in ways not reliant on geographic, oil-guzzling traversal?

Of course, my argument is not that electronic media were a response or reaction to the energy crisis of the mid-twentieth century. What we call electronic media date back at least to the early nineteenth century. I am also not arguing that the oil crisis is the determining impetus for the West leaving the colonies. Decolonization occurred well before the oil crisis, and in many cases was sparked by the colonized people's forced take down of their colonizers. And of course, the Vietnam War was raging for years *after* the energy crisis, suggesting that physical movement did not disappear due to rising oil prices. However, what I am interested in is illustrating that the technocratic technologies became increasingly important in a world where physical presence was less necessary to increase profit, meaning the energy crisis coincided with an increasing Western interest in making money without physically being in place. Electronic media helped facilitate a concern with how to leave and remain present at the same time. Thus the seemingly benevolent positions of the United States to the plight of oppressed, colonized people throughout the world cannot be disarticulated from an increasing concern with the rising cost of physically getting to the colonies, and an explosion in media to sell capitalism to those colonies, whether or not white people physically occupied the territory any more.

The newest employables under such a technocracy were the technocrats, a new man for Newton who, if capitalists were not careful, would replace capitalism all together with something worse. In ways that forecast McKenzie Wark's book *Capital Is Dead*, the technocrats were not the owners but the electrical engineers and computer scientists that Newton acknowledged in his Boston College speech, particularly those at "MIT [Massachusetts Institute of Technology] over the way."[78] As Wark argues, there is still the capitalist class that owns everything, from the land under our feet to the factories, "but maybe now there's another kind of ruling class as well—one that owns neither of those things but instead owns the vectors along which information is gathered and used."[79] Although Wark is talking about information economies (which I discuss in chapter 4), and Newton is talking about electronic media,

Newton points toward a similarity that is taken for granted in contemporary media philosophy: that the colonizer's own physical traversal of geographic space is increasingly unimportant as circulation and transmission of information for absurd profit exceeds national boundaries.

Newton also argued it was the growing technocrats who were increasingly transnationalizing capitalism in ways that remain prevalent—so much so that they would change the entire structure of capitalist labor and nationalistic relationships. In his 1970 speech at Boston College, Newton argued that technocrats speak to a wholly new phase of capitalism—the global village, run not quite by the bourgeoisie.[80] Newton continued, at some point the technocrat may would join the bourgeoisie, with or without any ownership of the land, and more important, both would seek to transnationalize their profit at the expense of any benefit to the larger population of the United States. Like McLuhan before him, Newton argued this transnationalization made the global (intercommunal) village an inherently antinationalistic project: profit exceeded all national allegiance and physical presence. The lack of a national allegiance, and its relation to controlling the colonies, also ensured that the colonies no longer required physical occupation but technological occupation. Increasingly in a world of rising oil prices, man distanced himself from colonialism, so as he could benefit from neocolonial markets—only now with Black and brown faces in charge, rather than white ones.

In the wake of Nixon's Black capitalism push, a 1968 news story by Fred Nolan in the Party's newspaper, what was then called *The Black Panther: Black Community News Service*, speaks to a similar concern that Newton had about opening markets to everyone. In particular, it noted that Nixon used the Black bourgeoisie to trick the larger Black masses: "now tricky dicky Nixon" had been promoting the Black bourgeoisie to lead Black capitalism, unaware that "capitalism is one of the major reasons we have to go through these revolutionary changes. The truth is, just because you have a black hand picking your pockets, doesn't make the exploitation stop any quicker than it did with a white hand."[81] With the understanding that technocratic man was running out of natural resources, technocratic man now required expansion of the market, further displacing any need for white physical presence in the ghettoes or colonies.

In Newton's 1972 "The Technology Question," he similarly argued that Vietnam was not being attacked for its land or resources, like previous colonial endeavors, but so that the United States could sell to it:

If national liberation wars are just strategies to mobilize the unconscious peasants or workers, I would agree with that....However, if the people are laboring under fantasies that they will be liberated through troop or arms withdrawal with the U.S. reactionary ruling circle staying intact, then they are living in romantic finalism. By their own conclusion, they will condemn their very liberty, because the United States does not need their territory. That is not the question. The people of the oppressed territories might fight on the land question and die over the land question. But for the United States, it is the technology question, and the consumption of the goods that the technology produces![82]

While the United States was increasingly worried about oil prices, Newton suggested that there was more than one way to enter a colony. There were new extensions that no longer relied strictly on the physical conceptions of the nation, but movement into the colonies from the privacy of a seller's own home. Now, in a world where the West was trying to rethink itself due to rising oil prices, you could profit in new ways from the colonies without ever physically going there. Civil rights and the end of colonial rule were not benevolent gifts from Western nations, but consistent with the shifting relations of the larger capitalist, technocratic global village.

While McLuhan considered the global village an environment where hierarchies may disappear, Newton's global village required capitalist and racist violence. The global village was reactionary, it extended man's own developmental image back at him. For Newton, the ruling circle was ahead of the game, maintaining itself via intervening in the new markets. Reactionary intercommunalism was no democratic process but a specialized global village that created differential engagements with capitalism. Reactionary intercommunalism is McLuhan's global village; only for Newton, peaceful coexistence was not guaranteed. There was only "peaceful co-optation" to produce new markets.[83] For Newton, the global village lacked technological or economic determination. Like everything, it was in dialectical relation with the necessary contradictions of capitalism, decolonization, and Black radicalism. Rather than a negative blight on man's record, the mid-twentieth-century projects of decolonization, race riots, energy crisis, and class rebellion could now be capitalized on via the technocracy, making decolonialism, rebellion, and antiracism potentially profitable. For the reactionary intercommunalist, technocrat, or the global villager, the nation was of decreasing importance compared to the ultimate conflation of capitalist markets with (Western) human freedom. Yet this was not all. For Newton, the technocrats arrogance opened a way forward. It was time for the oppressed people of the world to realize the openings created by intercommunalism. Indeed, it was time to rush the global village, not to become capitalists, but to take it over for the global, Black revolution, to create a new form of revolutionary consciousness.

## MAKING BLACKNESS IN A REVOLUTIONARY WORLD; OR, ALGIERS IN OAKLAND, AND VICE VERSA

Newton did not view intercommunalism as an end but as a beginning. As Cabral noted, Black and brown people of the world had been impacted by similar yet different forms of racial violence; but that violence was not all-encompassing, it was not a determining factor on what or who they could be. Despite such violence, Black people throughout the world began producing a political form of Blackness, one not based on the colonizer's classifications (the Negro) but on the ability to create new modes of comradery throughout the world. One major influence on the Party, Malcolm X, distinguished between what he called the "Negro revolution" and the "Black revolution." In his classic 1963 speech, "Message to the Grassroots," Malcolm X argued that the Negro revolution (the petit bourgeoisie) was too afraid to bleed, while the Black revolution was global, far beyond the United States's understanding of the Negro, and it sought to destroy all forms of Western colonial rule.[84]

Newton similarly argued that such lines between Black and Negro could be drawn because the reactionary intercommunalists not only relied on their technologies for profitable ends but often latched onto the Black and brown petit bourgeoisie at home and abroad, always at the expense of the majority of Black and brown people in the world. Blackness was no space of death, for Newton, but purposefully a new life that the white world could not understand. We should really consider this in our contemporary context of theorizations of Blackness as social death, which would have made little sense to Newton. From South Africa to the United States, in the 1960s and 1970s, Blackness was being put forth as a new stage of humanness, one that could not be read as synonymous with the Negro (medium), or white definitions of what Black people were. Instead, Blackness was a new globalized stage of humanity.

Thus with this political conception of Blackness came the development of new, alternative epistemological projects, of new ways to think about oneself and the world, both in and outside of the university. In other words, Newton was a part of a cohort of Black radicals throughout the world who were pushing for the redevelopment of what constituted knowledge. The Party sought to engage in such an epistemological intervention at the level of "the block," as Newton often called the ghetto, via the Party's important social programs (free ambulance, free breakfasts, free taxis, free education, etc.), which fundamentally changed the discourse on what poor Black people in Oakland (and throughout the United States) know and can do for themselves as needed.[85] At the university level the Party would also be involved in one of the more important twentieth-century epistemological ruptures: Black studies. The Party's role in Black studies can be seen as early as the mid-1960s, with Newton's and Seale's participation in Merritt College's Black student movement.[86] At San Francisco State University, Party members were also important contributors to the development and expansion of the first Black studies department in 1968. San Francisco State University students like George Murray, who participated in the campus protests and would become the Party's minister of education, did not see the work of the larger Party outside the university as separate from Black studies.[87]

For the Party, Black studies was no mere academic discipline, on par with English or communication studies, but a route toward the production of a new form of consciousness, one that may implement a revolutionary Black praxis throughout the world. Prior to his killing on the University of California–Los Angeles's campus in 1969, Party member John Huggins stated: "When we say a black studies program we're dealing with real things—with the survival of a race of people who have been brought to this country, brutalized and miseducated," but also Huggins called "for all Black students, Mexican American students and white students to unite, because you don't have any power either and are being used by the people who oppress you."[88] For Huggins, Black studies created new relations across racial and nationalist lines, potentially pointing to the formation of a new consciousness, not reducible to U.S. Black people, even as we were the target audience at U.S. universities. And we can say that the fear of such a revolutionary Black epistemology was more than merely symbolic, as it ultimately led to the killing of Huggins and Alprentice "Bunchy" Carter on UCLA's campus, killings that were inflamed both the FBI's violent counterintelligence program and by differing approaches the Party took to Black studies versus the approach by other Black radical organizations in Los Angeles.

While technocratic man's intercommunalism was an outward expansion, pointing toward the transnationalization of the capitalist market,

Newton asked, Why should the technocrat have a monopoly on movement? Revolutionary intercommunalism would be a Black studies theory in an increasingly mediated, dis/embodied, technological world. Arguably, intercommunal media technologies would lead to the quicker proliferation of a globalized Black consciousness, which suggests no neat separation between the emergence of Black studies and the distribution of new, electronic media of the mid-twentieth century. Put differently, Newton sought to theorize *how* to globalize Black consciousness, *how* to turn the technologies of the reactionary intercommunalists against the colonizer and toward Black revolution. Despite its name, the Black revolution was not about a Black-race-only movement, with the United States as its central focus. Instead, the Black revolution spoke to a *perspective* that sought to destroy colonial, racist, capitalist relations, linking Black people in the United States with exploited people, of all colors, throughout the world. Intercommunalism was not merely a theory for the university (or even for the university at all); instead, it was designed to mediate the relations between the block, colonies, university, and factories, of which Black studies would play a crucial role. But arguably, another highly crucial part, that which materialized the connections between the block, the colonies, and the university, would be played by the media of Newton's revolutionary global village.

Revolutionary intercommunalism was a full reorganization of the reactionary intercommunal world system, one that not only transformed epistemologies but reproduced the colonies as in solidarity with the ghettoes, and vice versa. For example, while connections were made with the North Vietnamese, the North Koreans, the Mozambicans, and Palestinians, maybe nowhere was the Party more active than in Algeria. Colonized by the French in 1830, the North African territory of Algeria would be held up as representative of the French's "civilizing" gift in the Third World. More than one hundred years later, Algeria remained a French colony, facing apartheid-like conditions and violence from the occupying force in the name of Algerian development. In the wake of World War II, and French arguments that they fought to free the Jewish people from Nazi Germany, Algerians protested for their own freedom, arguing that the Jewish genocide in Europe was linked to French brutality in Algeria. In other words, the Algerians asked, How were the French any different from the Nazis? Rather than agreeing with the Algerian protestors, the French gunned them down in the streets of the city of Sétif on May 8, 1945, just a day after the Germans surrendered to the Allied forces. An estimated forty-five thousand Algerians were massacred over several days of French attempts to quell nationalist freedom dreams. These events would act as one spark for the later Algerian Revolution, which officially began in 1954.[89]

Importantly for this book, the Algerians would eventually defeat the French in 1957, inspiring the 1966 film, *The Battle of Algiers*. The film and the actions of the Algerian people would also inspire antiracist and anticolonial forces throughout the world. The Black Panther Party drew major inspiration from the Algerians, especially their important film. Although the Algerians were not Black, in the U.S. sense of the Negro, *The Battle of Algiers* was required viewing material for those who wanted to join the Party, and Algeria would eventually become the base of the Party's international chapter.[90] Furthermore, the film would inspire the push for Black studies at San Francisco State, where the first Black studies department was founded. In other words, the film spread a global consciousness, one that reorganized the world and its epistemological order on the side of the oppressed, what was called a Black perspective, not based on racial inheritance but political struggle.

By August 1969, Algiers would become an important and frequent topic in the Party's newspaper, *The Black Panther*. The timing of this aligns with the Party's former Minister of Information Eldridge Cleaver's flight from the United States in 1968 to eventually find asylum in Algiers. In what Cleaver viewed as an attempted retaliation for the assassination of Martin Luther King Jr. in April 1968, he was involved in a shootout with Oakland police, which left two police officers wounded and one Party member, "Little" Bobby Hutton, killed by police.[91] Charged with the attempted murder of an officer, Cleaver fled to Cuba then Algeria, where he established the international office of the Party. In August of 1969, the Party's paper featured both a reprinted interview from "Free Palestine" of a "representative of the Palestine National Liberation Movement" and the story "Eldridge Warmly Recieved [sic] by the People of Algiers." The newspaper highlighted the transnational, decolonial concerns of the Party (which Newton later called intercommunalism), as itself a medium that kept the Black community up to date on global decolonial concerns, that brought Algeria to Oakland.

Cleaver's news story begins with: "The passionately anti-Israeli Young Arabs of Algiers cheered new heros [sic] today: members of the American Black Panther Party."[92] Cleaver, one of many figures who disagreed with intercommunalism, also reflected a central Party position at the heart of Newton's intercommunalism.[93] The position was that Black people in the United States were not in mere solidarity with oppressed Arab peoples in Africa and Asia; though from very different backgrounds, with unique concerns, the problems of Black people in the United States *were* the problems of the world's colonized peoples, as all were suffering from different iterations of Western racism, increasingly discoverable via the expropriation of intercommunal technologies. This was not a simple conflation of U.S. police brutality in Oakland with French occupation in Algeria; it was, instead, a recognition that the U.S. military not only put down innercity riots, but also funded Western powers against decolonial efforts.[94] This was a call for a global Black consciousness against Empire, as per Joshua Bloom and Waldo Martin Jr., but the crucial thing to remember is that such a consciousness was mediated by the expropriation of the reactionary's technologies—that which the reactionary intercommunalists hoped would solely be used by the Black and brown petit bourgeoisie to expand bottom lines.

The important concern here is the technological emphasis that Newton gave to revolutionary Black consciousness. Newton also asked, What *mediated* the Party's theoretical position, that which lay the groundwork for the Party to agree that the fight against imperialism and colonialism in Algeria was the fight against U.S. militarism and brutality at home? Newton would add that this articulation between the colonizer and the U.S. police (as well as the fight against both) was solidified through an intercommunal, media technological economy. In ways that McLuhan might disagree with, Newton argued that Black studies, *The Battle of Algiers*, *The Black Panther*, and television (or both electronic *and* nonelectronic forms of mediation) could facilitate the creation of the global village as a radical, interconnected political consciousness, pointing toward the revolutionary transformation of the world.

While electronic media were the dominant form of media in McLuhan's global village, they were but one form of media under Newton's: television broadcasts of the Vietnam War and Algerian radio waves were important for the global village; just as *The Black Panther* newspaper in Oakland, the Black studies movement, and the circulation of the film *The Battle of Algiers*. All could be ammunition against the reactionary forces throughout the world. This addition of both newspaper and film to Newton's global village may seem trivial, but it is not for McLuhan and his philosophy. For McLuhan, film was the *antithesis* of the global village, as the global village involved what he called "cool media," which "contrast with the film shot."[95] Cool, electronic media forms, were always in "low definition," or media of which "little information was given," and so much has to be filled in by the listeners/

watchers.[96] McLuhan argued that the low degree of information forced electronic media users into a far more participatory and involved form of engagement, representative of the global village as a new media economy. Alternatively, "hot media," such as film, extended only one sense (the eye, for McLuhan), which allowed for "less participation than a cool [medium], as a lecture makes for less participation than a seminar, and a book for less than dialogue."[97] While the effects of cool media occurred at the sensorial level, they would eventually lead outside the human senses and into our daily lives, creating new modes of consciousness and involvement with people from different parts of the world, which could potentially end various forms of discrimination.

While McLuhan was cognizant of electronic media's influence on white leftist movements of the 1960s, he may never have paid much attention to the Party's interests in underground newspapers and films like *The Battle of Algiers*.[98] As traditionally hot media, film and print media were creating forms of participation and involvement that McLuhan associated with cool media—a participation and involvement that has been part of Black and decolonial radical imaginations, at least since the Haitian Revolution and even to this day.[99] The *Battle of Algiers* was less a hot medium for the Party and more what Kara Keeling called a "cinematic reality" or "synergistic relationship between living organisms and the technologies, economies, and social relations they participate in producing, reproducing, and shaping."[100] In other words, rather than allowing less participation, *The Battle of Algiers* existed in the context of Newton's global village, where anticolonial, participatory, involved struggle trumped the assumed effects of mechanical, hot, nonparticipatory media for McLuhan. This was a time of Black self-making in the face of Western aggression and attempts to reduce Black people to items—what I have called media. The film was one way of creating a sense of Algiers *in* Oakland, or participation and involvement of different people fighting similar brands of Western imperialism, but from afar.[101]

The form of Black consciousness that the Black Panther Party pointed toward was *not* reducible to the lives of Black people in the United States. It was a project of new worldmaking, whereby a new form of consciousness was being forged in and by a world of increasing speeds and electronic transmission of information. For Newton, *The Battle of Algiers* was no mere hot medium; via this film, and other media forms, Algeria entered Black consciousness in the United States, expanding potentialities for liberation.[102] Media could move the achievements of

Algeria to Oakland, and vice versa. In part, this suggests that the trajectory of Black studies and concerns of a global Black consciousness would be very different without the media relations of the global village that Newton theorized. In Newton's global village—one of film, radio, television, and computers—the grounds on which Black people engaged in Black radicalism shifted, no longer (if ever) based on a U.S. exceptionalism or a nationalistic project but wholly intercommunal, at increasing speeds of transmission, toward the destruction of the reactionaries.

All of this is to say that media technologies were not only in the hands of the white technocrats but were expropriated by Black radicals for antiracist and anticapitalist goals, or what Williams called "alternative uses."[103] As Elaine Brown remembered, Newton expressed hope in the struggle against technocratic man, as Newton felt the Party could use technocratic man's media against technocratic man. For Brown this meant reactionary intercommunalism was simultaneously, and ironically, future-oriented, while lacking imagination: the reactionaries had deemed the future as financially set, measurable, and predictable—even as they heavily relied on speculation. In the process, reactionary intercommunal arrogance in the face of uncertainty also opened space for a more revolutionary intercommunal moment and future not yet materialized, and Newton's understanding of the Party, as the vanguard, was in the best position to bring it about. Brown quoted Newton as saying:

> "There's only *one* machinery to seize, the toppling of which makes way for an egalitarian redistribution of the wealth of the whole world—true communism. And there are only two classes: the billions of us and the few of them. Whatever the differences in the levels of oppression, from the industrial and technological workers of the impoverished Third World millions, the majority of the world's people have become *one* class of dominated people. In other words, we have a setup for global revolution: revolutionary intercommunalism."[104]

Newton's description of the transnational approach of corporations like Ford and Coca-Cola opened room for the Party to be transnational as well. Newton's was not a call for Black people to become capitalist, but a call for the unification of Black people in the United States with people around the world who were critical of Western imperialism, a call made possible in differing ways based on the changing media economy. In short, while McLuhan's global village brought together the United States with the French, Newton's global village brought together the United States's ghettoes with what Frantz Fanon called the Algerian native sector.[105] As Lewis Gordon argues, Fanon would also see the value in media, as Fanon theorized both the newspaper and the radio as weapons against colonization.[106] Ironically, via the circulation of the intercommunal technologies, in the name of capitalism-as-freedom, the reactionary intercommunalists created a new Frankensteinian monster: they increasingly opened up the space for new solidarities to be formed *against themselves*, and at quicker and quicker electronic paces.

What articulated U.S. Black people's fight against the West with the fight in the Caribbean, or Africa, or Asia was the technologies provided by reactionaries and the ability of those technologies to mediate shared critiques of Western imperialism. Channeling McLuhan's *Understanding Media*, in his "On the Relevance of the Church," Newton suggested that there were few differences between the television and the airplane: "We say that [the Party is] the *contradiction* to the reactionary Western values," but still, "technology is too far advanced for us to isolate ourselves in any geographical location—the jet can get there too fast and so can the early-bird TV set—so what we have to do is share the control of these devices."[107] As different yet similar extensions of man, televisions and airplanes could work against man as well. Newton felt we needed to study these presumably different yet similar technological relations. He made few if any distinctions between the technologies of what he called the global village, as all enriched the reactionaries and could alternatively be used to bring a global lumpen proletariat, anti-colonial people together. Through the television and airplane, reactionary intercommunalists mobilized the world, and unintentionally placed their enemies in new intercommunal, revolutionary communicative relations with one another.

## DREAMS OF REVOLUTIONARY INTERCOMMUNALISM 2.0

The Western, social Darwinian approach to nature was a central facet of reactionary intercommunalism, or McLuhan's global village. For Newton reactionary intercommunalism was a necessary step toward not only continuing man's presumably inevitable technological update; such intercommunalism was also designed to continue to enrich one population of the world over others. Intercommunalism was concerned with the creation of a new global village that was not that new at all—much of the methods of enrichment remained in the control of Western man. Within the search for new markets we see a further Darwinian conflation of capitalist, free-market economies with (Western) human evolution and social development.[108]

Yet there were always critiques of Western man, especially from those whose bodies have often served his media function. Revolutionary intercommunalism, or Newton's global village, is but representative of one of those critiques. Newton and Party members illustrate that, if the Negro is a medium, then this does not mean that white people's construct of Black people is fixed. The proximity of the Negro to social Darwinian constructs of nature have led many Black people, such as Newton, toward far more critical conversations about what constitutes nature and man in the first place. Racial Blackness holds an "ecological" concern, as an "embodiment of ongoing dispossession" and "rendered as the promiscuous interplay between harvested flesh and land."[109] Yet critiques of the relationship between the Negro and nature also assume a media philosophy that this book illustrates: if media are a product of the extraction of raw materials, the "harvested flesh and land," then the Negro calls into question what constitutes media. The truly important question lies at the intersections of these Black studies, cultural studies, and media philosophy concerns: What would it look like for the Negro to throw off what Fanon called the "livery [which is to say the *media* for me] the white man has fabricated" for us?[110]

Whether it was McLuhan's or Newton's, the global village never eradicated Western hierarchies or nationalisms. Indeed, the Western hierarchies worthy of challenging for Newton were largely limited to race, colonialism, and class, with little emphasis on patriarchy, gender, and sexuality. We should leave behind the lack of critical examination of patriarchy, gender, and sexuality with Newton. What we can take from the Party and Newton is a healthy skepticism of any guarantee of revolutionary potential in media technologies, which again is to pick up Stuart Hall. Because media relations were not reducible to sensorial effects, there were no guarantees in the global village, as media could be used to challenge or support capitalism. Newton thought that revolution was possible precisely because the reactionary intercommunalists were amid some of their biggest shifts. There was no guarantee that the reactionaries could be fully stopped. However, in their arrogance, they potentially brought together Jamaica, Mozambique, Palestine, Algeria, and the Black ghetto in the United States into a collective front that may end imperialism.

In an increasingly web-mediated society, we would do well to remember the lack of guarantees in technologies that Newton forefronts in intercommunalism. Newton suggested that technology, and particularly those aligned with the global village, could be revolutionary in the same way that many argue YouTube is today.[111] But Newton also thought that the revolutionary potential lay not in increased representations of Black people on the screens or airwaves but in the increased communicative capacities that were left unintentionally opened by the reactionary intercommunalists. Were Newton still alive today, his critiques of capitalism may have led him to see something that he had predicted with reactionary intercommunalism: long before today's widespread commercialization of the web, for a large portion of Black and brown people in the United States critical of the transnational capitalists, there is a disproportionate requirement to engage in the same processes of transnational capitalism that are under critique.

The web is today largely a world of likes, shares, and adds that can spread *The Battle of Algiers*, *The Black Panther*, or Black studies (or snapshots of each, brushing over their nuance) as merely information for excessive profits for those who do not care about, or may be hostile to, radical politics. In other words, as Wark has warned, radical politics are now presented as *just information*, circulatable within, alongside of, and without the politics of their origination.[112] It is here that we can see why Karl Marx remains a top seller on Amazon.[113] Under such a context we cannot assume that technologies hold a transparency, or that they reveal a truth that everyone can recognize, as Newton warned us against. Instead, we may be dealing with the full maturation of the reactionary intercommunalists that Newton's dialectical method predicted in the early 1970s, fully materialized via the web, that digital space that media philosopher Paul Levinson argues McLuhan also truly predicted when he theorized the global village.[114] I will take a page from Levinson: Newton's global village foresaw the web as one space with no guaranteed radical potential but toward the excessive enrichment of today's corporations, like Facebook, Amazon, and more—all of which exist far beyond any national boundaries. This would situate Black studies, as per Newton's and the Party's theorizations of it, at the forefront of contemporary media philosophy.

Electronic media, per McLuhan, were not necessary for Black people in the United States to care about what was happening to people in Vietnam; the web is not necessary now for Black people in the United States to care about what is happening to people in Palestine. Instead, what we can say is that reactionary intercommunal technological attempts to expand capitalist markets, no matter national affiliation, have ended up expanding much more than just markets. Intercommunalism, as a completely unstudied iteration of media philosophy, opened space to see the interconnected forms of oppression that people were suffering, and continue to suffer, throughout the world. Furthermore, intercommunalism made it clear that there were consistent perpetrators of that oppression.

Newton theorized how all global concerns became local, and vice versa. Of course, he was not alone in this. Along with multiple radical groups and decolonial projects throughout the world in the mid-twentieth century, Newton was able to articulate the forms of oppression in the United States to Western imperialistic approaches to Black and brown people throughout the world. However, I add that Newton was able to do so while cognizant of the media economy that has been largely overlooked in the studies of him. Part of Newton's political approach cannot be separated from the media economy that he engaged in, whereby TV, radio, film, newspapers, and more all worked toward the creation of the global village—one in which radical and reactionary intercommunal responses were both potentially possible. It would be such a global village that would lay the foundation for today's web-mediated world, the subject of the next chapter.

CHAPTER 4

# Black "Matter" Lives: Michael Brown and Digital Afterlives

Wilson later testified that Brown "looked like a demon"
on the day the confrontation and killing occurred. In other
words, he was not afforded the status of human—not because
of what he had done but because of who he was. He was not
just a husky teenager with a cocky attitude. He was not a kid
who loved video games or had struggled in high school; he
was not a son whose mother had struggled to put food on
the table and was planning to go to college. He was not an
unarmed local kid simply refusing to follow instructions. He
was a "demon."

—Barbara Ransby

On August 9, 2014, a white police officer named Darren Wilson infamously shot and killed an unarmed Black teenager named Michael
Brown Jr. in Ferguson, Missouri—a largely Black community on the
outskirts of a highly gentrified Saint Louis. Brown was walking home
with his friend Dorian Johnson from a local corner store in which
Brown had just allegedly committed larceny. In their attempt to cross a
busy street on the way home, Brown and Johnson were stuck walking
in the middle of the street until the cars driving toward them passed by.
While Johnson and Brown were jaywalking, Wilson drove by them in
his police sports utility vehicle (SUV). Wilson reported that he slowed
down and nicely asked the two pedestrians to get out of the street and
onto the sidewalk. Alternatively, Johnson said that Brown and he were
told to "get the fuck" on the sidewalk by Wilson. Wilson denies saying this to the two teenagers. Whatever Wilson's response was, Johnson

answered, "We're almost home." Johnson reported that Wilson then angrily snapped back, "What did you say?"

Following the disputed verbal exchange, Wilson backed up his vehicle to confront the teenagers, almost hitting them with the SUV in the process. Witnesses reported that there was some sort of physical altercation between Brown and Wilson, while Wilson was still in his police vehicle. Some reported that Brown punched Wilson; and others argued that Brown did not punch Wilson but was being pulled into the car by Wilson. Wilson fired two shots at Brown from inside the police vehicle, one grazing Brown's thumb. This caused Brown to turn and flee from Wilson and the vehicle. Wilson exited his vehicle and pursued Brown on foot, allegedly ordering Brown to stop running. Some say that because Wilson was firing at Brown's back, Brown turned around with hands raised, which would become the symbolic gesture of the "Hands Up, Don't Shoot" movement that would follow. Others say that Wilson was not firing at Brown's back, and that Brown turned around with his hands lowered, almost in a three-point football stance, before charging at Wilson, as if he sought to tackle the officer to the ground. The latter account matches Wilson's own: he argued that it was Brown who was the aggressor, charging at him and forcing him to fire ten more rounds at the unarmed teen. Brown was hit by six additional rounds from Wilson's gun.[1] Afterward, Brown's lifeless body was left in the middle of the street for more than four hours, incensing a largely Black Ferguson crowd that gathered as onlookers. Despite the community's anger, Wilson would neither be indicted on state charges by the grand jury in Saint Louis, nor would he face federal charges for violating Brown's civil rights.[2]

The hashtag "Black Lives Matter" (#BLM) emerged online after the 2012 killing of another unarmed Black teenager named Trayvon Martin by a neighborhood watch volunteer in Sanford, Florida.[3] But it was Brown's 2014 killing that caused #BLM to further unite offline into multiple activist groups, such as arguably the most well-known coalition, the Movement for Black Lives, which includes multiple local and national activist organizations.[4] In her book *You Can't Stop the Revolution*, Andrea Boyles argues that 2014 Ferguson (or rather "post-Ferguson") was an important time-space to understand contemporary forms of activism in Black communities, laying the foundation for a new "profound push for black liberation that countless populations" continue to organize behind today.[5] Likewise, from the important histories of the Movement for Black Lives, like Barbara Ransby's *Making*

*All Black Lives Matter*, we know that Ferguson was a crucial moment, as it was then "that the slogan Black Lives Matter migrated from the virtual world of social media to the real politics of the street."[6] Ransby reminds us that Ferguson signaled a patent rejection of hierarchical, het-ero-patriarchal politics, pushing forward a Black, queer feminist ethic. This ethic was led by three Black women—Alicia Garza, Opal Tometi, and Patrisse Khan-Cullors—who are largely agreed to be central to the movement's naming and current political power. In each of these impor-tant takes, the organizations inspired by the words Black Lives Matter have clearly entered into the minds of people throughout various parts of the world. Likewise, the #BLM has been able to enter the minds and social media accounts of people who both do and do not have connec-tions to grassroots political mobilization.

Much of the critical research on Brown, #BLM, and the political mobilization inspired by #BLM largely veers into two important schol-arly discourses. The first area of study connects Brown and #BLM to the longer history of racial violence (enslavement, Jim Crow, lynching, white flight, the war on drugs, etc.).[7] It argues this history was necessary for the development of the Movement for Black Lives, especially its *of-fline* formations. Indeed, this first area of study largely ignores the digi-tal. The second area of study does not ignore racial violence but con-nects it to mining the Internet for tweets and more on Brown's killing (as well as the killing of other people), which is to say *online* content.[8] In other words, this second area of study largely stays at the level of online representations. While both discourses are important, I draw attention toward something largely absent from them: What is the relationship between these two contemporary areas of scholarship and the *form* (not content) of the larger digital media economy?

The important offline questions that are asked by scholars like Ransby, Keeanga-Yamahtta Taylor, and Christopher Lebron, and the just as important online questions asked by Deen Freelon, Charlton McIlwain, and Meredith Clark, may be different. However, as I have argued elsewhere, both questions are chiefly concerned with asking whether or not "Black lives, as human lives, should *matter* enough to convict white people of the murder of unarmed Black people."[9] In both discourses the *matter* of #BLM is largely centered around the dictionary definition of the verb *to matter*, meaning "to be of importance or have significance." To say that "Black lives matter" here is to say that we, as Black people, have importance or significance for the dominant societ-ies that we find ourselves in. This amounts to asking something like: "Is

Brown deserving of recognition as *not* killable by Wilson or the white, Missouri establishment?" And if Black lives are not valued as recognizable, then "Why do Black lives not matter?" becomes the second assumed question of both of these discourses, even if unasked.

As I have illustrated throughout this book, the idea of mattering in these dominant discourses is not incorrect, but what I point to in this chapter remains different from what is currently offered in much of the #BLM research: #BLM and Brown make us ask, "Why do Black bodies *equal* matter?" In other words, why is the Negro *matter* under the dominant Western and white frameworks that have difficulty seeing Black people in our own humanity? Rather than a verb, I reframe the matter that #BLM points toward as the noun, one vital to understand for the Western self-concepts of humanness.[10] As Jane Bennett argues, matter is often deemed a "dead object," pulled from nature, in both Western scientific and philosophical inquiry.[11] For Bennett one of the problems with arguments that matter is dead is that they are so often coupled with Western anthropocentric assumptions that humans are agential and self-determined. A similar logic organized the white construct of the Negro, as chattel, as the captive Black body distinct from the dynamism of Black people. Here the Negro is situated as "absent self-determination" in ways that so often mirror Western conceptions of matter.[12] The dominant discourses on #BLM assume that Wilson, the police force, the Federal Bureau of Investigations, and the Missouri establishment, both on and offline, saw Brown as a *life* in his final moments, and not merely as the Negro. The better questions are: Why do Black bodies = matter? Why do Black bodies ≠ Black lives? If the Negro = matter, then Western recognition, as it currently operates, does not neatly apply to us as Black people. As such, the problem may be less, Do Black lives matter (verb)? and more so that Black bodies matter (noun) way too much.

Of course, we are *all* matter in the scientific sense. But what I argue we see with the Negro and matter is something that W.E.B. Du Bois pointed us toward in *Darkwater: Voices from within the Veil* while talking to a white friend about racism. Du Bois admitted, racist acts were not something that happened to him every day, but they *could* happen at any moment. And if racist acts did happen, Du Bois realized that his prestige as a scholar in 1920 when his book was first published, or as a member of the Black middle class would matter for not. Du Bois did not argue that he was a slave in those moments of racism (indeed, he pushed back against such ideas, not fully critiquing those Black people who "knew the lash," or were once enslaved, unlike himself). Instead, in such moments Du Bois understood that he could be either shunned by white people from publishing his work or worse—at the height of lynching, he could be reduced by white mobs to ash and matter.[13] Likewise, although recent police killings of Black people differ from Du Bois's 1920s, just as they differ from Black enslavement a century prior to *Darkwater*, they do illustrate that while such racism may not happen every day, it can happen to any Black person, at a moment's notice. In short, one's class status may provide them with an opportunity to be stopped less by police, but even still, with just one stop, everything could end in the blink of an eye. Like Du Bois told us a century ago, this is something that we are aware of as a possibility every time we step outside.

Another important difference must be acknowledged between Du Bois's 1920s and the "post-Ferguson" moment. This historical relation of Brown's body to matter does not disappear online but continues on in new digital ways. For example, today's Internet users have the ability to watch Brown be killed over and over again online... well, almost. Not long after Brown was killed, digital animations of Brown's final moments began circulating on social media platforms like YouTube, Twitter, and Facebook. In spite of (or maybe because of) the absence of footage of Brown's killing, the disturbing digital animations of Brown's killing appeared online, suggesting that there was a new market for circulating Black death.[14] You do not have to be in a set location to see Brown's killing; it is now available on your laptops, cell phones, and other mobile devices, nearly instantaneously, collecting information about users who watch the videos and monetizing that information for platforms like YouTube, Twitter, and Facebook.[15] In the midst of being digitally killed online, Brown's Black body is repeatedly technologically recaptured, receiving likes, dislikes, comments, and advertising dollars even to this day. Brown's digital animation is one of the clearer reinventions of the Negro online one can find: Brown's digital recreation is literally not about his life at all but a product of a long history of the Western fabrication of racial, social evolutionary inferiority, only now on digital media devices.[16]

Finding the digital animations is easy. They show up in YouTube searches using the words "Mike Brown." The animations struck me as odder than the news stories, blogs, and videos that I found, not because they diverged from these dominant narratives but because they disproportionately back them up. Indeed, the digital animations are creations that are presented as if they factually document the killing of Brown in ways that a lay audience would miss. Of course, the content of these animations is important but the form through which that content is expressed also requires attention: racial violence continues but now circulated online, repackaged for anyone who has Internet access. Maybe a better way to say this is to paraphrase Kara Keeling: the analogue remains in the digital.[17] Brown's digital killing is similar to the long history of mediations of racial violence via photography, lynching postcards, or television; but also very different as each of these mediations today can be easily found as information online on the same device. It is as though by going online, racial violence has gone further unthought and normalized as merely circulatable information among multiple other forms of information.

Many digital animators purport to transparently reveal the "facts" of what really happened to Brown, promising disembodied, truthful representations. But there also remain political, offline assumptions about whose testimony is transparent enough to even make an appearance in the digital animations, speaking to a long history of digital studies critique.[18] Following Wilson's testimony of events, many digital animators concern themselves with the exoneration the police officer, upholding Western discourses that have associated transparency with the same lawful figure overrepresented as human: white, heterosexual, cisgender men.[19] The content of the animations is the court testimony of Wilson, meaning that the animations are specifically concerned with aligning themselves, after the fact, with the grand jury that found that Wilson was not at fault for Brown's killing. Transparency, then, aligns with Wilson, even as we are promised that digital media provide the transparency. Despite a plethora of court testimonies that can contradict Wilson's account, the digital animations situate Wilson's testimony, and those who back him up, as the statements capable of transparent, digital revelation of facts. In short, Wilson is positioned as in line with a long history of Western man, capable of artificial selection and self-determined control over all situations; but Brown and Johnson appear closer to matter, always already Black bodies (at least for dominant Western frameworks), those entities selected by man and incapable of challenging him. The relations that have permeated post–European Enlightenment thought exist online today.

This is not a chapter about Michael Brown, the unarmed teenager who lost his life, walking home from a store per se. It is not a chapter about Black Lives Matter. It is also not a chapter about the continuation of the fight that Black people engage in as we are threatened for existing under white supremacy. It is a chapter about how racial Blackness (the Negro, captive Black bodies) continues under an increasingly popular logic that racism is dying—all of which I argue can be articulated to the larger transformations of the media economy. It is a chapter on the Western fabrication of the Negro that circulates in new ways based on the changing digital media economy. In other words, this chapter is about the restoration of Brown's life in the call for scholars to pay closer attention to the flippancy with which his body has been recreated online, far beyond any form of life that Michael Brown (and many others who have been hashtagged) had during his too short time on this planet.

## DIGITAL STUDIES AND THE RESURGENCE OF TRANSPARENCY

At the time of this writing, there were fewer than a dozen digital animations of Brown's killing on YouTube alone (although there are other digital animations of other Black people who have been recently killed). Depending on their level of controversy, the animations of Brown are constantly taken down and re-uploaded, under different user accounts. If they are taken down, it is often because they are flagged as inappropriate by users who must do the work of flagging the animations for the larger platform. The animations come in image and video form, and they are utilized mostly for personal entertainment but also for local and national news media outlets to illustrate what "really happened." For years, digital animations have even been promoted by some digital animators as suitable for court purposes (though rarely, if ever, are they admitted into the courts, because they are considered as outside evidence).

Brown's digital killing is not the first example of a digitally animated crime scene, but it does provide an important lens to think about race, gender, digital media, and matter.[20] Here we can see components of what Lisa Nakamura turned our attention to with the circulation of online video games: the history of racial violence goes nowhere via online settings but carries over in new digital ways.[21] That racial violence is not immaterial because it is online; instead, another materiality emerges, via a new digital economy where commodities no longer have to signify a physicality of property, but the buying and selling of the information that we willfully place online about ourselves (or rather the buying and selling of our digitalized selves).

The quantity of animations of Brown's killing is not really at issue, as much as the form of the digital animations. The larger digital media economy is one of increasing proliferation of information, in which the circulation of more and more information is equated with a capacity to locate truth. Information, like communication, is a twentieth-century creation, largely concerned with the scientific location of knowledge, deemed distinct from rhetoric and propaganda, which were rebranded as biased forms of knowledge in the late nineteenth and early twentieth centuries.[22] Terms like communication, information, and media came to organize the twentieth-century development of information theory, important to computer science today.[23] This increasingly situated computers and digital communication as potentially capable of revealing some human-less, unbiased, transparent, neutral data. In the wake of Alan Turing's machine—one of the central gatherers of information toward breaking the Nazi's Enigma code during World War II—the digital is increasingly equated with the promised delivery of transparency by the end of the twentieth century. This scientific approach to communication and information bled outside of computational calculations, giving birth to arguments that human communication, too, could be quantified and scientifically analyzed—sparking the mid-twentieth-century development of social scientific elements of the discipline of communication.

On the one hand, we know that Brown's physical killing is material, rooted in the Negro's relation to matter (that which made the teenager killable in the first place); on the other hand, Brown's digital killing is also material because it is coupled with the history of predictive technologies, which are concerned with extracting surplus information out of everyone online, as if doing so provides a transparency impossible in the hands of humans. This form of extraction of course benefits someone (particularly platform owners), similar to yet different from the way that the buying and selling of Brown's ancestors profited someone.[24] The form of the economic has changed, and that change is inseparable from the related change in the media economy. Just as Safiya Noble has shown that Google's algorithm is structured off largely white, male subject positions, most of the digital animations of Brown's killing remain disproportionately slanted toward Wilson's court testimony of events—which suggests that the transparency of the digital media economy is based on some, not all, humans.[25]

For example, the image in figure 2 is from the Colorado Justice Project—an organization that largely makes digital forensic animations based on social scientific, behavioralist logics of criminology. The Colorado Justice Project argued Wilson, not Brown, was the one who

FIGURE 2. Digital animation of Michael Brown charging Darren Wilson. See the Colorado Justice Project, "Michael Brown Full Sequence," YouTube, December 14, 2014, www.youtube.com/watch?v=eBcBQoHNjQE (accessed October 22, 2017).

deserved justice in the wake of Brown's killing. In the figure the viewer is visually on Wilson's side. On their website, the Colorado Justice Project argues that Brown was responsible for his own death, and their animation presumably shows this.[26] The Colorado Justice Project's animation assumes that Wilson provides some transparent narrative of what happened between Brown and him. Furthermore, they argue that, due to such transparency, circulating their digital animation on the local Ferguson news stations could have prevented the Ferguson population from rebelling after prosecuting attorney Robert McCulloch decided not to indict Wilson for murder charges in Brown's 2014 killing. In their opinion, Black anger could have been easily quelled simply by circulation of their digital animation.

The Colorado Justice Project's digital argument is not new. As noted in this book's introduction, communications and area studies were centered around a similar logic: that Black and brown people's rightful anger could be quelled by the circulation of better information about the West. Likewise, such scholars as Simone Browne, Shoshana Magnet, and Ruha Benjamin all argue against dominant assumptions that human biases are stopped via digital media.[27] Browne refers to this presumed neutrality, which holds racial implications, as "digital epidermalization," where human-manufactured digitized code is presented as a process of identification that enables the (Black) body to function as evidence.[28] Likewise, the Colorado Justice Project is one example of representing Brown's Black body as evidence for his own killing.

Part of the transparency, or presumed neutrality, for Nicole Starosielski, relates to the assumptions that power relations were once far more centralized, but digital media are largely *decentralized* today. The decentralization argument goes somewhat like this: whereas previous media outlets, like television and radio, once centralized content from a few channels to produce what its watchers see and hear, social media displaces this model, making the user-turned-producer. This is not to say that the web produced this relation, but that it capitalizes off of a larger decentralization of capitalism that was already happening in the mid-twentieth century (see chapter 3). Decentralization combines with the arguments that there was an increase in information and thus an ability to produce transparent content. Western, liberal humanist discourses are celebrated here, as we are now all capable of being users/producers of the content, rather than just having content produced for us. In short, "we are all the same" under this logic. We are no longer passive voyeurs of television, for example, but we can be "prosumers" of online, web content.[29]

Contrary to decentralization, Starosielski argues that our information economy is infrastructural, which is to say that it is "*semicentralized* rather than distributed; territorially entrenched rather than deterritorialized; precarious rather than resilient; and rural and aquatic rather than urban."[30] For Starosielski, the turn to decentralization speaks to the larger human incapacity to recognize how centralized power relations remain the foundation for new media economies. In the process, previous Western human power relations (such as transparency) can seep into the logics of contemporary media.[31] Denise Ferreira da Silva uses a term that is helpful for theorizing our contemporary digital economy: the "transparency thesis." For da Silva, post-Enlightenment Western Europeans believed that they were uniquely capable of the transparent representation of facts, which simultaneously demanded "obliteration of the others of Europe," or the Black and brown people enslaved and colonized, as these others were deemed incapable of being represented under Western concepts of humanness.[32] To be transparent was to be uniquely human, and despite holes in the transparency thesis, Western discourses have been obsessed with continual attempts to reproduce Western monopolies over humanness—which equate to keeping transparency alive.[33] Transparency transforms to fit the needs of contemporary capitalist society, meaning that it has recently gone online. Transparency and neutrality no longer lie in the hands of man per se, but, as Neda Atanasoski and Kalindi Vora argue, in the technological affirmation of the "particular notion of human freedom, leisure, and happiness emerging from imperial modes of liberal governance."[34]

Today, digital technologies presumably free humans from the burden of their old mistakes, their faulty memories, their racist, sexist, homophobic, and transphobic dispositions.[35] It would be such thinking that Ruha Benjamin calls the "New Jim Crow," as new technologies reflect existing inequalities but are still promoted as progressive.[36] Maybe most appropriate, Achille Mbembe argues that the digital media economy is increasingly subordinating a former enlightened, reasoned subject to a new electronic/digital form of reason, found inside the digital machine.[37] Many allege that information technologies are the transparent ones now, and not Western man. However, because our contemporary economy is structured by Western man's previous power (his infrastructures), we must question the full displacement of his transparency, particularly as similar liberal human concepts of equality and transparency were simply placed into digital machines, not discredited.[38]

Digital transparency is now supposedly replacing man's transparency. The conjuncture in which this happened should not be overlooked: Turing's breakthrough with cracking the Enigma code did not occur outside the context of Black radical, decolonial, and revolutionary politics of the mid-twentieth century. As I noted in chapter 3, Black and decolonial movements throughout the world were not only physically kicking out the colonizer but challenging his entire project of knowledge. Throughout the world, both Black and decolonial thought made the argument that Western man was not the epitome of the human, but was only one human, highly situated in time and space, as white, male, capitalist, and Western. And, as we can see, there was also a central technological shift under way at the same time of the decolonial challenge to Western man: the swing toward media economies of digitalization as a fix to (Western, white) human biases.

The transformation from a militarized monopoly over computers to today's mobile devices—the computers that we take for granted in our back pockets—coincided with promises of decentered, dis/embodied new forms of transparency, found inside McLuhan's global village. Digital media conveniently appear right at the time when radical, worldwide political movements were gaining traction and casting doubt on Western man's transparency and legitimacy. As Tara McPherson argues, "the very structures of digital computation develop at least in part to cordon off race and to contain it."[39] Right as voices ramp up via feminist, queer, Black, and decolonial movements to challenge man's infrastructures, we see the increasing rise of a digital transparency, linked to the promises of fixing man's problems.[40]

Digital media presume to remove man, while in fact reinforcing his own raced and gendered power dynamics, only in new form. If man is too racist, too sexist, too homophobic, or too transphobic to be fully trusted, we are promised that we should trust his transparent media at our borders, airports, and especially on our mobile devices and social media accounts, with our consensual agreement to be surveilled. Man now places his former human transparency into digital media, which is to say they function to assist him with his own maintenance, they keep his features of transparency alive well into our present. In such a world, Darren Wilson is no neutral classifier but connected to a history that always assumes his transparency before he acts.

Many digital animators, in their trust of the law and scientific crime analyses, abide by assumptions that police can be trusted over Black witnesses, continuing Western transparency in both old and new form. Benjamin notes that it may seem trivial to make distinctions between the inability of digital soap dispensers to recognize the darker skin tones and racial crime algorithms, but it is not.[41] Likewise, while digital animations cannot be said to be the same as face recognition technologies, or fingerprint scanners, they all exist within a contemporary digital media economy in which digitalization equals transparent, human-less revelation—all of which are deemed inherent goods, or proof of human development beyond individualized racism.

The construct of man transforms with changing media; this is no surprise as, I have argued, media hold epistemological implications. Man's presumably individual racism is now replaced (or better yet, further supported) by presumably neutral and decentralized information technologies.[42] Alternatively, I hold that information does not produce a race-neutrality, but it backs up changes in capitalism, which requires racism to appear to be solved, via presumably neutral information processing. Part of this requirement cannot be read as separate from the Cold War and the attempt to open up markets to Black and brown people, all based on a long-held fear that Black and brown people are attracted to socialism because of Western racism (chapter 3). In this light, the digital information machine steps in for the gestapo, with the argument that these machines are just revealing what has always already been there. The gestapo does not disappear but goes into the machine. Man goes nowhere but is rearticulated in informational form. This is not to argue that the digital animations "got off" Wilson from the murder charges (of course, the animations were not used in the courtroom). Instead, it is to argue that these digital animations are part of a larger media economy in which transparency goes online, while still holding similar, semicentralized power relations: the anthropocentric replication of the Western human over other humans, of man over matter, of (white) life over (Black) bodies, of man over commodities.

## COMMODIFIED NEW MEDIA LOGICS

Few would argue that a Black enslaved person on an auction block in the nineteenth century is the same as information on that enslaved person online today. However, there remain arguments that #BLM is just a new iteration of an older fight, with little interrogation of how that fight shifts with the shifting media economy.[43] Per the digital animations, but also his own social media presence, Brown existed within a different media context from that of an enslaved person in the nineteenth century: a digital information economy, where information is theorized as both a mathematical pattern of organization and as a commodity.[44] While information has long held a commodity relation, that commodity relation transforms via the new, information machines—as information is gathered quicker and easier, as big data is mined through and made transformable into massive profit. The Negro has never fully lost the original commodity relation under white supremacy, as representable via Jim Crow, mass incarceration, the war on drugs, ghettoization, and gentrification. Yet as McKenzie Wark argues, the "commodity form is not eternal."[45] The transformation of the commodity in the West has impacted concepts of Blackness, property ownership, and humanness.

Some refer to this as the "information society," meaning that we live in a new media economy where information is considered as something that we all have equally.[46] Information is the important commodity now, circulated based on new modes of measuring of our likes, adds, and shares on social media. Under such an economy the Negro's commodification today means something different than it did in the nineteenth century. For example, we can do online Google searches to learn more about Black enslaved people today. But that is not all: our information in the form of that same online Google search can then be tracked and sold by Google based on our Gmail accounts, to say nothing of the search results we may get, which, as Noble has shown, are organized not by reliable information but advertising dollars to increase Google's bottom line.[47]

Furthermore, in some cases we can be targeted to purchase a Black enslaved person's book on Amazon based on those searches (to say nothing about our capacity to rewrite their stories on Wikipedia). In such an economy, commodification and profit lie in the information created by the user, not just the circulation of the Black body. And, as has been critiqued, discourses also begin to flow about the democratic potential of such circulation, as, theoretically, we can all buy, sell, and make this content, rather than just have it made for us.[48] In short, such discourses that conflate democracy with the market are structured by what Cedric Robinson called a "capitalist democracy," where the market and competition are presented as the political equalizers for social ills.[49] We can see similarities between the informational media economy and what Huey Newton feared in the mid-twentieth century as a reactionary global village (chapter 3): Black and brown revolution is being conflated not with decolonial and radical political struggle but with the enrichment of a small Black and brown petit bourgeoisie.

We have not fully moved away from the inferiorization of the Negro, but we have moved closer toward a society that seeks to deny the continued importance of the inferiorization of the Negro to its function. What some have called a postrace society is actually the marker of transforming commodity relations, of which platforms do not determine but do capitalize on. The democratic potential associated with the digital information economy displaces the idea that the commodification of the Negro is different from the commodification of anything else. In other words, if we are all commodified online now, then the commodification of the Negro must not be worse than anyone else's. Indeed, as slavery is presented particularly by right-wing groups as in the past, with no contemporary relevance, then the commodification of the Negro does not really matter at all under contemporary right-wing, online discourses. It is here that *#AllLivesMatter*, that #BLM is presented as taking away from the idea that white people suffer too. Inseparable from the violent afterlives of slavery (of which #BLM is a response to) and open to discourses of freedom in the digital informational media economy (which states that commodification is really just part of everyday life), the Negro today lies at a unique moment of analogue and digital.

The Negro is contradictorily called forth, when need be (to justify why a Black person was killed by the police, for example), and dismissed, when need be (to shun the idea that those same police killings had anything to do with race, as we are all commodifiable now). This is not the commodification of labor that Marx critiqued per se; it is instead the commodification of the digital constructs of ourselves, gathered via platforms that provide us with the hardware and software for us to operate on, so that we may labor—without ever selling our labor—to the capitalist.[50] Under such conditions Brown's racial Blackness could never serve the exact same function for Wilson in 2014 as it might have for a slave catcher chasing after a Black enslaved person during the early nineteenth century; Brown's racial Blackness could not even serve the same function for Du Bois's 1920s. Unlike the legal status of enslavement or Jim Crow, today's discourses suggest that everyone is open to very different forms of commodification under informational capitalism, which seeks to make everyone with access to the Internet a prosumer/commodity.

Information must be troubled when considering what the Black body has signified throughout U.S. history: measurable data and matter (via slave breeding and pricing of slaves based on their physical characteristics) and commodification, well before an online presence.[51] If information is the commodity, then Brown's racial Blackness was and continues to be multiply commodifiable: both property via an afterlife of slavery (or the reduction of Brown to nothing more than a Negro, to matter, by and for another) and as information via the circulation of his digital animations. Before Brown's Black body can be captured online in the digital animations, it carried with it another commodity form: the Negro, which troubled Brown's relationship to some universal humanity as it is imagined in the West. Mirroring what Andre Brock referred to as "double commodification," Brown was killed via the violent relation of the Negro (or racial commodification, no longer reducible to the plantation, but increasingly a product of policing, ghettoization, and gentrification) and his killing was justified as race-neutral in a new context in which everyone is commodifiable online (informational).[52] When all can purchase commodities and become commodifiable, there is an increasing demand to deny the centrality of the Negro's commodification toward societal development. When everyone is commodifiable, no one is.

There are at least two ways that Brown's Black-body-as-medium has operated within contemporary information economies: (1) Brown was made a "demon," or his Black body was informationalized as a signifier of Wilson's race-neutrality (content); and (2) Brown was also "ungendered," or his Black-body-as-medium functioned for Wilson's use, as per the history of racial commodification (form), or matter. I am less interested in making the distinction between Brown online (content) versus off (form) and more interested in the way that media economies inform and are informed by the different types of commodification Brown faced. Brown's online commodification was never separate from a history of racism but informed by his connection to such violence. Unlike many white users, Brown has different relations to commodification: both online (information) and offline (the Negro). This multiple commodifiability serves as something that both sparks the racism that circulates online as well as digital fights against that racism, via #BLM and the organization of antiracist groups online today.

To be multiply commodifiable is to engage in the work of the commodity online that much of the #BLM research ignores: it brings together the maintenance of the Black body's proximity to violence with the information economy's fabrication of the nonracial commodity. Whether it is Brown's physical or digital body, his commodity relation is similar: he is so often deemed reducible to Wilson's property—meaning, as Christina Sharpe argues, Brown is Wilson's "projection," having no reality outside of what Wilson has created for him.[53] Both the law and the digital animations conceal a longer U.S. media function: the inability for the courts to find Wilson at any fault for murder means Brown *matters* less as per the discourses of #BLM (a verb) and more as a multiplicity of his differential Western mattering/commodification, or by and for Wilson (matter as a noun). Similar to the Marxist idea of commodities and Kantian matter, Brown was deemed as that which lacks self-determination, always controlled by man.[54] Brown is made information/property/matter/the commodity of Wilson in both his digital and his physical killing. Wilson remains in control of Brown but in ways that are now promoted as race-neutral. Within an informational economy, Brown can no longer be a "nigger," which is too "racially charged"; instead, he must have been a *demon*.

## HOW TO MAKE A DEMON?

Brown was killed during an important context of information economies, of both professional and amateur user (re)creation. Furthermore, this was a context with semicentralized implications, in which the lines between professional and amateur were always up for debate, but still connected to previous power relations. What this means is that Brown's killing was part of an information economy in which crime scenes have been digitally rendered by digital forensics for nearly thirty years.[55] Brown's killing occurred in the context in which information economies situate users as producers and consumers of content, well beyond the work of digital forensics. No longer was the digital recreation of crime scenes monopolized solely by centralized media outlets or government officials. Now, the digital animations were produced and consumed by users. More specifically, the digital animations step in as surrogates for the users who were not present to witness Brown's killing, but they do so by providing a representation that purports transparency, which is to say human-less credibility.

The digital animation can be crowdsourced from multiple information sources (court documents, television interviews, newspaper and web articles, blogs, Brown's own online presence, etc.), presumably removing all human biases from the digital crime scene in the process, while never decentering previous hierarchies, instead maintaining semi-centralization. In short, the human-lessness is largely fabricated by those with the most access to the Internet—largely Western and largely capitalist figures. Furthermore, the human-lessness of the media economy is a metaphor for race-neutrality. Of course, Wilson was positioned as race-neutral in the digital animations and those same digital animations were presented as assistants for users to witness Wilson's race-neutrality. The digital animators circularly produced what they presume is already there: Wilson's killing of Brown had nothing to do with race and their animations would prove his race-neutrality. They promote the idea that race was not an issue in a digital economy where everyone is open to commodification online.

The digital animators start with the larger assumption of postrace, digital arguments, which Lisa Nakamura argued began in the 1990s: that racism is actually a distraction from the true issue at hand, which in this case, animators presumed, was Brown's natural propensity for crime. The digital animators provide an update of the Negro, now on-line. Brown is fabricated as the Negro, presumably without any human involvement. What better example of Wilson's lack of racism do we have than in his infamous reclassification of Brown as a *demon*, or, for Wilson, a raceless supercriminal who required Wilson's heroic actions before Brown hurt someone. During the *State of Missouri v. Darren Wilson* case, Wilson stated the now-infamous line: "[Brown] looked up at me and had the most intense aggressive face. The only way I can describe it, it looks like a demon, that's how angry he looked."[56]

There is a consistency between Wilson's testimony, Brown's demonization, and the digital animations: Wilson must consistently note that he has no problems with Black people. The demon is an informational-ized rereading of Brown, one that strips away racism as a factor in his

FIGURE 3. Digital animation of Michael Brown attacking Darren Wilson's automobile. See Conservative Daily Review, "Michael Brown Shooting, What Really Happened," YouTube, May 18, 2016, www.youtube.com/watch?v=rKJx9Y9Nbng (accessed October 22, 2017).

final moments. Whereas a white police officer who killed a Black person in the 1920s may have easily called that Black person a "nigger," such justification today is representative of a human bias, deemed as not reflected in Wilson's demon classification. In one screenshot from one of the few cartooned animations on YouTube, after Wilson respectfully and meekly asked Brown to "please walk on the sidewalk," Brown's caricature became enraged and charged at Wilson's driver side door, almost destroying the door with his bare hands (figure 3). Here Brown is animated as the demon—irrationally evil, hyperstrong, and angry. We are promised such a classification is not racial; Brown's killing held no relation to a largely Black area, heavily and violently policed by its largely white police force (Wilson both admits the police were not very well liked by the Ferguson community and also that the police did not care much for that community).[57]

Instead, in this animation Brown's demonic qualities precipitated his death. To cause one's own death is to remove racism as a factor, as Brown could have attacked anyone. Indeed, Wilson argued this when he stated he had to make sure that Brown was off of the street because "he still posed a threat, not only to me, to anybody else that confronted him."[58] Wilson was not only man—as in the Western human, capable of selecting Brown in sociotechnological Darwinian fashion—but he was man in a new media economy centered around the denial of the captive

FIGURE 4. Digital rendering of Michael Brown at a Ferguson market. See Unemployed hr4213, "Ferguson Missouri's Michael Brown THUG-LIFE Robbing and Stealing," YouTube, August 15, 2014, www.youtube.com/watch?v=V6dgGZ63mXA (accessed October 22, 2017).

Black body to his own maintenance. Furthermore, the digital animation suggests an unending tautology: that Wilson's testimony was not unimportant for the digital animators but one of the central factors in the excavation of a transparent, neutral retelling of events, and that the digital animations were somehow proof that Wilson's version of events were transparent and unquestionable.

In another screenshot of an animation from YouTube (figure 4), we can see how Wilson's documented justification for why it was necessary to kill Brown continued to inform other digital animations. With rap music blaring in the background, the words "Sweet Kid My Fucking Ass" and "Fucking Thug" are superimposed on top of video of Brown at a Ferguson market, Sam's Meat Market.[59] The original, brief surveillance footage used in this animation comes from the store's surveillance footage, taken prior to Brown and Johnson crossing paths with Wilson on the street.[60] For everyone from Wilson to the amateur digital animators and local and national news stations, this video infamously functioned as justification for why it was necessary for Wilson to kill Brown in the first place. The twenty-five-second animation is on a loop, repeatedly illustrating the moment that Brown pushes a store clerk. Thus the animation is an unending, decontextualized replication of Black criminality (i.e., the Negro)—it is an informationalization of the charge that Brown committed larceny, which is why Wilson argued he stopped Brown in the first place. The digital animation's over-the-top stereotyping (of Black crime and rap music) functions to support Wilson's initial testimony as transparent, which is to say, the animation supports Wilson's proclamation that Brown was a legitimate, evil threat, or that he was a demon.

Interestingly, while the depiction in this animation is considered amateur, the professional ones follow similar patterns (see the Colorado Justice Project's animation in figure 2): always positioned as neutral, often accompanied by a reporter-style voice, presumably white, calmly explaining the events, privileging Wilson's perspective. The chief difference between the amateur and professional animations is that the professional animations claim to have gathered more data from a variety of sources to compile their animations. Here the demon exceeds court documents and is replicated in Wilson's postcourt appearances as well, which further back the race-neutrality so associated with the animations.[61] The closer Wilson remains to race-neutrality, the more sympathy that he garners. For example, one woman led an online fundraiser to support Wilson's trauma after he killed Brown, eventually raising more than $1 million for him. But her justification for the fund is less about supporting Wilson and more about critiquing all antiracist protests against what she sees as *perceived* racism in police shootings. She notes that her father was shot by a police officer when she was seventeen, and because he "was Caucasian. . . it didn't make it past the nightly news."[62]

According to this woman, Wilson's case was only newsworthy because Brown was a Black teenager, and, as such, it was Wilson who faced actual racial discrimination—something that should not exist anymore. She implied that anyone could be shot by the police, and racism is not a legitimate excuse for organizations to protest police killings. Her discussion of racist police violence resonates with a very common trope repeated on conservative websites and television channels: that it is racist for the people who protest the police killings of unarmed Black people to talk about racism. Here an older relation goes digital: white people are deemed race-neutral, while Black people are deemed the true racists. The CIA argued something similar in its 1948 document, "The Break-up of the Colonial Empires and Its Implications of US Security." Her comments also mark our current context of information, which suggests a flattening out of the commodity relation online, assuming racism is no longer a central organizing principle of U.S. commodification. Although a longer discourse than the twenty-first century, such postracism assumptions are only amplified under the digital economy, one increasingly concerned with the representation of semicentralized power as decentralized. Like the larger digital media economy, the online fundraiser suggests that anyone can face some form of commodification, or push back against it, and it is those who promote #BLM who are ignorant of this realization. Here all lives matter.

What we find in the court cases and postcase interviews matches what we find in most digital animations: Wilson is a nonracist police officer who had to defend himself from a demon, who, no matter Brown's race, had to be stopped before hurting others. It is merely a coincidence that the demon looks like the Negro, or a medium. Cast aside the history of Ferguson as a largely Black community, its relation to Saint Louis's racism, and the histories of aggressively policing Ferguson's Black community members for perceptions that they were more prone to criminality than white people, itself an imagination of the Negro. As long as Wilson couches what happened in race-neutral terms, like the demon, he aligns with the larger media economy. Under such a context the online always informs the offline, and vice versa. Brown is dominantly digitally rendered as a demon, as a figure that presumably has no racist implications, largely because Wilson said so. Wilson and Brown presumably lay on equal footing that fatal day. The digital information economy does not determine this race-neutrality, but it is highly informed by and informs such renderings.

## THE UNGENDERING OF MICHAEL BROWN

The disproportionate forefronting of Wilson's narrative as transparent via digital animations replicates a racial re/establishment of man (McLuhan's) as distinct from nature, only now online. If we stay strictly at the level of media content, Wilson may be read as race-neutral, replicating the contention that everybody is commodifiable under information economies. Yet Brown's Black body, as media form, tells a different story. Wilson's reclassification of Brown as the demon also *ungendered* the teenager, which is to say that in Wilson's owning, desiring, and naming of Brown, Brown's gender functioned not for himself, but by and for Wilson. Hortense Spillers argues that ungendering is the process of commodification that puts the Black body in sexualized/gendered service for white people.[63] For Spillers, gender must be thought about as a colonial construct, meaning that through the Western enslavement of Africans, the Africans were forcibly given the gendered constructs of the world of their white enslavers. Even as the white enslaver's gendered constructs may not have aligned perfectly with Africans' pre-enslavement gendered worldviews, they came to define what Black gender would mean in the West.

For Spillers, this is not a call for a return to an authentic gender, lost via slavery; instead, it is an articulation of how enslavement in the Americas created the captive Black body, which was designed to extend the political and economic well-being of white, Western, capitalist, male worldviews. In the process, enslaved people's new gendered self-constructs became useful in the service of white enslavers: productive of more slaves and the sexual desires of enslavers. Importantly for Spillers, these gendered constructs of the world do not end with the end of racial slavery. Instead, they are replicated in ways that suggest that the captive Black body always remains open for ungendering and regendering when necessary, by and for white people, even after slavery in the United States is deemed illegal and later abolished in 1865.

Brown existed by and for Wilson, especially in the contextual ways in which Wilson attributed gendered constructs to Brown when those constructs best served Wilson. In other words, Brown's materiality always already exceeded his informational representation in the digital animations, to include the longer narrative of the Negro as serving a media function by and for white people. So long as Brown was a demon, not a nigger, Wilson could claim his actions lacked any racist motivation. However, using the same testimony that digital animators argue illustrates Wilson's race-neutrality, I show that Wilson ungendered Brown, rendering Wilson's assumed nonracist activities fully questionable. Again, Wilson uttered this infamous description of Brown to the court: "*he* [Brown] looked up at me and had the most intense aggressive face. The only way I can describe *it*, *it* [Brown] looks like a demon, that's how angry he looked."[64] In Wilson's own words, Brown was an *it*. Of course, we can take this as a slip of the tongue, a mistake on Wilson's part. Or we could read Wilson's words as emerging within the new mediated context of this chapter's focus, where we are promised racism no longer exists and Brown's Black body disproportionately serves a media function by and for Wilson, despite the presumed lack of racism. He "looked up" and "*it* looks like a demon" are the transforming ways that Wilson describes Brown in the same sentence.[65] In the slippage between *he*, *it*, and *demon*, Wilson suggests that Brown is malleable, as per Wilson's own needs. Brown is an it, meaning he is connected to a longer history of colonial concepts such as nature, elements, and matter—the content needed for the nineteenth-century secularized invention of the Negro. This media/matter relation is the racialized foundation that Brown's online presence is built upon.

Gendered concerns are a consistent component of Wilson's statement in the grand jury case, suggesting a fluctuating relationship between Brown being a teenager and an item at the service of Wilson. For Spillers, this gendered fluctuation is consistent with the transforming relationship of commodification that stays with Black bodies well after slavery. In the assumedly transparent narrative of Wilson, Brown's gender functioned but only as Wilson saw fit; another way to say this is that Brown's Black body was a medium, extensive of Wilson's power to police the Ferguson community from trampling over any semblance of civility and white maleness. In Brown's case that trampling came down to talking back to a white police officer. One of the consistent retellings of the killing that Wilson provided was that Brown called him a "pussy." When recounting Wilson's narrative of his own physical struggle with Brown, one Saint Louis County detective repeated words that were consistent with Wilson's own description: "The subject [Brown] then responded with, 'You're too much of a pussy to shoot me.' And that was a quote from Darren Wilson."[66]

In line with Wilson saying that Brown was a demon, to be called a pussy also positions Brown as taunting Wilson, again suggesting that Brown holds some power over Wilson. Even though Wilson's account has been denied by more than one eyewitness, the sexualized/gendered implications of this are deemed as transparently true by everyone from the above Saint Louis County detective, to Wilson's sergeant, to the FBI agent who first interviewed Wilson for the federal case, to the digital animators. Each contends that there was no reason to doubt Wilson's retelling. Despite the transparency being monopolized by the state, many digital animations seem to pick up on this as the space from which the truth of the case emerges, as they depict Brown's hypermasculinity as overpowering both store clerk and Wilson. My goal is neither to prove whether or not Brown called Wilson a pussy, nor is it to argue that Wilson being called a pussy emasculated him, which seems to be Wilson's own argument. Instead, I want to illustrate that Wilson's retelling of his killing of Brown has gendered implications that function by and for himself. In retellings of himself as a pussy, Wilson attributed a hypermasculinity to Brown that existed to justify the killing in hindsight. It also suggested that this was a gendered relation that Brown never defined for himself, but that Wilson had the overarching ability to *give* to Brown. Even without social media, pussy suggests that Wilson owned the gendered grammar of Brown.

Gender, sexuality, and desire consistently permeate Wilson's other statements as well. For example, Wilson obsesses over Brown's size, according to multiple reports. In the grand jury case, Wilson noted that when he first drove up on Brown and Johnson, the first thing he noticed was them walking in the middle of the street, and then "the next thing I noticed was the size of the individuals because either the first one was really small or the second one was really big."[67] During the physical altercation between Brown and Wilson at the police car, Wilson argued in the grand jury case that "when I grabbed him, the only way I can describe it is I felt like a five-year-old holding onto Hulk Hogan...that's just how big he felt and how small I felt just grasping his arm."[68] Wilson's sergeant confirmed this, saying Wilson told him that "I know this man was bigger than me, I wasn't going to be able to fight him."[69] In an interview with the Saint Louis County Police Department the day after the shooting, Wilson further elaborated:

> Brown had already manipulated I was not in control of the gun. I was able to tilt myself a little bit and push it down and away towards the side of my hip and kinda lock my wrist into my leg to where he couldn't get it back up 'cause I did not have enough strength to come up and force him off of me. He was—he had completely overpowered while I was sittin' in the car.[70]

This was not a Black teenager who was afraid of being shot by a white police officer who has stated that Ferguson "is just not a very well-liked community."[71] This was not a teen who had more leverage because he was standing, and the officer was sitting, as Brown's friend Johnson did argue. This was not a teen of relatively equal size and weight as Wilson. Instead, this was a demon, Hulk Hogan, he, or it, depending on Wilson's requirements. Brown was hypermasculine and hyperstrong, trying to take the gun away from Wilson, for no reason. Wilson argued that he "had to shoot," as doing so may ensure that he "saved" the lives of himself and others.[72] If we follow Bennett's discussion of matter, Wilson had to do what was necessary to restore the it (i.e., to return Brown/matter) to its submissive place to man. It is Wilson who can select Brown, not the other way around. The violent policing of Black communities, then, speaks back to the long sociotechnological Darwinian assumption: the Negro must be re-rendered as a mediator of man's Western, self-determined, anthropocentric, human power.

The capacity to digitally animate Brown via Wilson's words reflects both a commodification of Brown as information (content) and Wilson's access to Brown's body—or Wilson's capacity to ungender Brown, to make, remake, and unmake Brown as a hyperviolent, hypermasculine demon (form), depending on the context. Brown's presumably demonic qualities weighed the same as Wilson's gun (they may outweigh his gun). The most disturbing point is this: pussy/demon/it/he allows Wilson to claim victimhood by giving Brown a hypermasculine, racial Blackness that Brown *never actually had*, but Wilson always had the power to give him. Wilson's presumably nonracist description of Brown—nonracist as defined by those who had no intentions of convicting Wilson for murder—never foreclosed the highly racist and gendered implications of Wilson's ability to gender, ungender, and regender Brown as a he, an it, or a demon whenever Wilson saw fit. This is because Brown was more so matter for Wilson in that fatal moment, as well as the state, than a teenaged, high school graduate, with family and friends.

Brown could not engage in self-determination, as per Wilson, without fully threatening the entirety of Wilson's and the state's anthropocentric position in the world. Indeed, for Black people to fight back too much is to also suggest the fabricated nature of the white world—a fear at the surface of Black radical thought and action. Spillers might argue Brown was ungendered. Likewise, for me, Brown was acted on by and for Wilson and the digital animators, in ways that mirror what the Negro has signified throughout Western discourses: *matter*, or elements that have no self-determination outside (McLuhanesque, social Darwinian) man's will.

## THE LIMITS OF NEWTONIAN (BLACK) BODIES AND THE LIMITS OF WESTERN MEDIA PHILOSOPHY

Like the commodities that Marx theorized, the Negro was inseparable from the natural, and the project of capitalism was to use nature to its excess.[73] Early on in volume 1 of *Capital*, one of Marx's examples of a commodity pulled from nature was the linen coat. Obtained from flax fibers, linen emerged via processing, transformed via labor, into the coat that could be taken to market.[74] Marx's coat holds within it a Western construct of nature, which is to say, the coat's raw materials (fibers) were the underexamined *content* of the coat (medium).

If we take seriously Marshall McLuhan's argument that media can be clothing, then we cannot ignore the natural materials and labor necessary to make such media possible.[75] Similar Western constructs of nature and matter remain in the Western, white supremacist concept of the Negro today. Like the golds, coppers, and mercuries that go into our contemporary digital media, the invention of Africa as a dark continent, as closer in proximity to nature than to Western man, has never left the bodies that we as Black people are often reduced to within a white supremacist society. In fact, what the West has called natural materials, elements, matter, and the *its* are not neutral descriptors of what is transformed into commodities via labor, but they lay the foundation for Western man's produced and imaginary social evolutionary standing above Black and brown people.[76]

Black media philosophy illustrates what Western media philosophy cannot: that matter was a central foundation of the Negro, particularly if we take into consideration what matter has meant throughout Western discourses of knowledge. For the West, matter has largely been seen as a substance that has mass and takes up space, a substance that can be physically touched. Such substances can become the raw materials that go into the commodity. As such, matter is defined in relation to human capacity to physically engage with it. In the eighteenth century, philosopher Immanuel Kant brought a description of matter into philosophy, heavily influenced by the work Isaac Newton, that sounds like our above description. According to Kant, matter and form were in relation with one another, and central to his concepts of space and time, respectively. Form was of a higher order than matter, and that which required further examination:

> That in the appearance which corresponds to sensation I term its matter; but that which so determines the manifold of appearance that it allows of being ordered in certain relations, I term the form of appearance. That in which alone the sensations can be posited and ordered in a certain form, cannot itself be sensation; and therefore, while the matter of all appearance is given to us a posteriori only, its form must lie ready for the sensations a priori in the mind, and so must allow of being considered apart from all sensation.[77]

In this quote from *Critique of Pure Reason*, one of Kant's central treatises on moral philosophy, he argued that form was a priori, or that which existed prior to human experience; matter was a posteriori, or that which we come to know through experience. Of course, Kant privileged form over matter and sought to engage in what he called a "transcendental aesthetic" to better understand form. However, we should also pay attention to matter. Matter was passive, and it lacked any self-determination, coming into existence via man's experience of it. As I have argued elsewhere, such characterizations of matter have made it an important topic of study for Black feminist new materialist scholarship.[78] Indeed, conceptions of Black enslaved people, as passive, lacking self-determination outside of enslavers, undoubtedly mirror Kant's matter.

Via Black media philosophy, then, we can now reread the Negro within a Western discourse of epistemology, influential on Kant and Darwin: Newton's three laws of motion. Indeed, due to dominant Western media philosophy's acceptance of the colonial construct of nature (meaning media philosophy rarely engages in the raced, sexed, and gendered assumptions of nature), I argue that Newton's laws are the *only* place that Blackness makes sense for much of Western media philosophy, again, speaking to the need for something new. Newton's first law of motion, inertia, contends that if there were no gravity, and the net force acting upon an object is balanced, the object will not accelerate or slow down but continue forward. Yet if the net force acting on an object is unbalanced—say, if one were to push matter hard enough—the second law states that this would cause an acceleration that would transform what that matter is without ever making it fully disappear.

What does this have to do with Michael Brown, one may ask? The mattering of the Negro, its mass never fully disappears but is transformed based on the net force of the new, digital media economy exerted against it. One could picture that different media/forces change conceptions of commodification under white supremacist, heterosexist, capitalist, patriarchal, ableist society, which remakes the Negro from racial slavery (physical commodification) to our present digital media context (or information and everybody's commodification). Here Brown remains in far closer proximity to matter than to man, or Wilson and the state. The argument is not that Brown was a perpetual slave. Instead, he is interconnected with commodification, via the carryover of the Negro into new forms of racial violence; and today the net force of the larger digital media economy (along with other forces, of course) transforms what such an interconnected relationship to commodification even means. It is here that we can understand Du Bois's conversation with his white friend about 1920s racism as not slavery but inseparable from slavery's commodification; new forces were under way, and such new forces are not distinct from the media economy one lives in.

This leaves only Newton's third law of motion. The white supremacist, capitalist, patriarchal, heterosexual society is not unaffected by the laws of motion. It does not stand above the fray, untouched. It, too, transforms to fit its twisted image of the Negro. In I. Bernard Cohen's retelling of Newton's third law of motion, he states:

> If a body A exerts a force F on a second body B, then that body B will exert on body A an oppositely directed force of magnitude equal to F. The common error is to assume that these two forces, equal in magnitude and opposite in

direction, can produce a condition of equilibrium. Thus, in arguing for a bicameral legislature at the end of the eighteenth century, John Adams drew on his faulty recollections of college physics to declare that his opponent, Benjamin Franklin, had forgotten "one of Sir Isaac Newton's laws of motion, namely,—'that reaction must always be equal or contrary to action,' or there can never be any *rest*." Adams believed that for the American Congress to attain the kind of equilibrium needed for stability, there must be a balance between an elected House of Representatives and an appointed Senate, and he quite wrongly supposed that his position was supported by an analogy with Newton's third law. He had forgotten that the forces in the third law act on different bodies and so cannot produce a balance or equilibrium.[79]

Cohen notes that the transformation happens not only on the bodies in motion but the force as well. Although far from equal, both force and bodies transform. I bring in the argument between Adams and Franklin on purpose. Adams and Franklin were debating which form of government was necessary in a newly formed United States. These were debates central to the maintenance of slavery and the new colonialism, which was no longer British but would now be carried out through U.S. imperialism in North America and beyond. Thus such discussions were central to the continuance of the Negro as only one commodity/medium/matter in the Americas, with no self-determination, far from the only. As matter formed via labor processes of Western, U.S. colonial rule, Black enslaved people presumably required white males to determine their worlds. In the process, whiteness and maleness in the United States, too, transformed, from colonial subjects to sovereign overseers of the colony, from British maintainers of commodities to the establishment of the post-Enlightenment, U.S. bourgeoisie. The Negro was inseparable from the transformation of Western property relationships here. And these property relations, I argue, are also media histories.

The Negro, as one medium of this book, does not contradict the discourses of matter in new materialism but contributes more theoretical weight to them. You could say that the Negro (not Black people) comes into existence through white/human sensation, itself productive. The dynamism and life of multiple Black people has been cut short in recent, highly publicized police killings because of a white society's need to reduce us to Negroes; similar forms of racial violence have taken out brown and Indigenous people across North America in ways that reduce all of us to mere bodies. Whether implicitly or explicitly, Western media philosophy often does similar work. Based on the Negro's proximity to matter (which, of course, assumes nature), the Negro exists not in and of itself, as per humanist readings, but by and for another.

#BLM is one digitally discursive reminder that we must articulate media and matter not as wholly distinct, but as assemblages, always already overlapping. Yet #BLM also reminds us that the media economy ensures that we cannot view the Negro in the same light today as during the nineteenth century, at a time when the commodification of the Negro was taken for granted by all. The rise of digital media, the central vehicle for organizing #BLM, not only changes conceptions of Blackness, but changes conceptions of commodification under capitalism as well. And even as these commodity relations continually transform, we must continually find new ways to state out loud the title of one Sylvia Wynter's many important works: "Do not call us Negroes."[80] By pointing out those racial implications of Western media philosophy and the mediated lives of Black people far beyond Western conceptual limits, Black media philosophy is one way to illustrate the limits of the Negro for media studies.

## ALTERNATIVE BLACK LIVES

What we have above is a shift in concepts of commodification: on the one hand, the Negro, as a white supremacist imagination, is a commodity; on the other hand, our information that we willfully place online is sold by social media platforms to corporations that seek to do everything from surveil us, to sell us products, to influence our political elections. The Negro as commodity appears in both digital concepts of commodities and the longer history of U.S. commodification. Without accounting for the racialized implications of the commodity, we may read Brown in a limited fashion as a sovereign subject who made a self-determined decision to lunge at an armed white police officer. However, if we incorporate the racialized history of the Negro as a medium, that which includes and exceeds information economies, it is more likely that Brown was killed by a police officer who has learned that commodities (the Negroes) were inferior to him. The fact that this killing, along with the steadily increasing list of Black women and men killed by the police and white citizens, led to no conviction furthers Wilson's belief.

However, the Negro's commodification unfortunately does not stop here in a digital media economy. Brown (not as a human but as a digital discourse) is online, as we speak. Or rather, Brown—like several other digitally animated Black victims of police and white violence—is digitally reanimated via the information he placed online about himself prior to the killing, as well as the information that others continue to circulate about him. Coupled with his relationship to matter, information about Brown online is recirculating on social media platforms, speaking to a new relationship of commodification that enslaved Black people would have never seen coming. Of course, the multiple commodity relations are not all that Blackness is, even if we decided to accept the Western epistemological concerns. Commodification and matter do not foreclose radical potentiality. Quite the opposite.

If we follow the Black-body-as-matter/media trope to its conclusion, this situates Blackness as what Jane Bennet refers to as "vibrant" and Karen Barad calls "agential matter," or a rupturing of the anthropocentric logics of Western man as distinct from that nonhuman matter that he fabricated.[81] In other words, matter does not even follow man's own rules. If the Negro is matter, it is so within a world where its existence reveals the holes within the entire structure of matter that man fabricated from the start. Because it begins on the premise that the Black body cannot self-determine, or is a "dead object," the West's own construct of matter, and the human, ring hollow.[82] As such, the West cannot fully understand what Blackness is, even as it is central to the transmission of whiteness, capitalism, and maleness. Whether they are situated in questions of recognition or not, #BLM discourses and other critiques of Brown's killing ensure that matter always strikes back, that matter holds a vibrancy, one now potentially mobilized via online media platforms.

Spillers's work can be applied to the information economy to show how matter strikes back, particularly via her reading of the Western articulation of Black enslaved people as captive bodies. There is much left behind, ignored by white people in the racial violence that produces captive Black bodies as the functioning media toward man's continuance.[83] The Black body as a commodity, among other commodities, animates radicalism, as white requirements of the Black body give way to an unclassifiable *flight of the flesh*, which breaks apart "violently the laws of American behavior that make such syntax [as the Black body] possible," while initiating a "new *semantic* field/fold more appropriate to his/her own historic movement."[84] Put differently, the production of the Negro as a medium necessitates a flight from such reductions, an impossible classification that has animated everything from the Underground Railroad to the Black Panther Party (as discussed in chapters 2 and 3, respectively). Blackness animates a life that does not look like Western man (or even his conception of the Negro) but a world and a human life that such genres of man lack the imagination and capacity to think of.

We can think about the organizations inspired by #BLM as attempts to use the media of the categorizer to undo the racialized categorization. Indeed, antiracist organizations today are disproportionately utilizing online media to organize, so much so that there are now legitimate concerns that they are being surveilled by the FBI (and others) both offline and online.[85] We can debate if such a use of the categorizer's online tools does the work that Spillers points to; we can ask if the violent syntax is being challenged via hashtags. However, we cannot debate that Black people have tried, in highly creative ways, to produce new forms of living, existing, resisting, and surviving, oftentimes using multiple media technologies to do so.

I want to conclude by way of pointing our attention toward one continuous debate on what the new, future-oriented forms of living, existing, resistance, and surviving could look like, a long debate that has been raging in the United States for more than a century, although it is currently being examined in increasingly troubling ways in our digital context: reparations for slavery. It is here that I want to point in a different direction from some current discussions of reparations in the United States. I want to consider reparations alongside Black studies, cultural studies, environmental studies, and media philosophy: reparation cannot be reduced to the descendants of Black people in the United States but must also consider the media philosophical implications of destroying the natural environment in order to make up Western media economies. In short, reparations are also about the interrelationship between race and the earth.

# Conclusion

## The Reparations of the Earth

Although arguments concerning death-of-media may be useful as a tactic to oppose dialog that only focuses on the newness of media, we believe that media never dies [*sic*]: it decays, rots, reforms, remixes, and gets historicized, reinterpreted and collected. It either stays as residue and in the air as concrete dead media, or is reappropriated through artistic, tinkering methodologies.

—Garnet Hertz and Jussi Parikka

This book illustrates the interconnected relationships between media, gender, sexuality, race, Blackness, and alternative forms of humanness. Thus far, I have examined two elements of these interconnected relations. The first shows how the Negro (as materialized via the social Darwinian articulation of artificial selection, or McLuhan's media philosophy) not only has a connection to Western constructs of nature but also acts as a *middle point* between Western concepts of tribalism and civilization. The second, related element shows that Black people have always pushed back against the terms of our bodies as media functions by and for others, often in ways that poke holes in the solidity of Western man himself. The second part is of most importance; we would be remiss to assume that Black people have never fought back against Western classifications of ourselves as media. Just as important, that fight-back has never been reducible to Black people in the United States, but it is a transnational project, one that positions the "Black" in Black studies as a mode of exploring new forms of humanness and knowledge.

This conclusion turns our attention to what is next, to what Kara Keeling calls Black futures—futures that are not predictable, but open. In short, Blackness points to new modes of thinking, being, and becoming, what Alexander Weheliye calls "sonic Afro-modernity."[1] These Black/Afro futures can be, and must be, for all of us, not just Black people in the United States. In fact, if we seek to survive a forthcoming global climate crisis, one inseparable from the social Darwinian conception of nature that violently put what Frantz Fanon called the *livery* of racialized Negro-ness onto our bodies, we must imagine differently.

As scholars like Harold Innis have taught, our media relations point toward new worldmaking capability. For Innis, that worldmaking involved the articulation of time and space, meaning some media showed a bias toward time, or cultural longevity due to their heavy weight and durability, while other media were reflective of a space bias, meaning that they often showed a bias toward space because such media were easily transportable over vast distances.[2] For Innis, a healthy balance between both time and space was a sign of an effective empire, but most often cultures would lean heavily toward one bias over another. Although Innis's nostalgic plea for time over space has been critiqued, the biases that he introduces have been important for helping media philosophers to see the material implications of media on conceptions of time and space. As Jody Berland argues, Innis pointed toward a media philosophy that assists us with a far better understanding of the relation between media theory and colonialism, one that shined light on the ways that space-biased cultures (colonizer) so often violently and technologically fabricated their superiority over time-biased cultures (colonized).[3]

Today we can extend an Innisian (colonial) media theory even further. For example, as Jussi Parikka has argued, the majority of people walking around in Western societies today are likely carrying "small pieces of Africa in our pockets, referring to the role, for instance, of coltan in digital media technologies."[4] The continual overextraction of natural materials from Africa remains central to our contemporary, spatially biased media environments, carrying over former colonial relations into present Western lives. The Western capacity to conceive of space as easily navigatable via our media is inseparable from natural resource extraction from the same people and places that the West has historically deemed as proximate to nature and, as such, backward, temporally biased, or tribal. Our digital media economy is simply the latest in a long trend of the overuse of natural materials toward the creation of new media technologies but also the recreation of a world inseparable from colonial, racial, hierarchal relations.[5]

But according to Parikka, it has also been the goal of media archaeology to point attention to the new life and activity that raw materials take on in media technologies. In our iPhones lie a complex mix of earth elements used for everything from "the phone's battery, as well as to help give the display screen color and make the phone vibrate when you get a text, among other uses."[6] Nature lies inside our media; no, nature *is* our media, and vice versa. Rather than making enough media technologies to suit a societal need, capitalism creates the excess of "standing-reserves" that pull from nature to its extreme, just so technologies can lie in factories, awaiting use.[7] This necessarily creates what Jonathan Sterne calls a "giant trash heap waiting to happen."[8] According to Sterne and Parikka, these media relations also ensure that there is no such thing as "dead media," where a medium goes out of function and then quietly disappears often into the earth, never to be seen or heard from again. Specifically, Parikka contends, every medium has a new "zombified" life, where toxic chemicals seep into the earth, air, and water, poisioning the natural environment. Even the media presumed to be dead are not, as they will continue to impact and threaten our lives well into the future. The need for new digital media, which do not die but become zombies, is a significant contributor to the contemporary climate crisis. The zombies, which are alive not just because they have been reanimated but as their decomposing bodies participate in ecologies of energy transfer, wreak havoc on all those who arrogantly presume they are more alive, or more human than the zombies.[9] Likewise, zombie media are living deads with an afterlife in new contexts, new hands, new screens, and new landfills.[10] They fundamentally transform our world.

Similar to much of media philosophy, the media of zombie media are presented as raceless. Yet as media philosophers, going forward we would do well to remember the history of the zombie, a history that Tavia Nyong'o argues is always situated in Black people's relationship to Africa, the Caribbean, chattel slavery, and capitalism.[11] As per Nyong'o, despite the continued fascination with the zombie within popular culture and white imaginations, the zombie begins as Black, connected to Western fantasies/fears of Black revolution in Saint-Domingue/Haiti. The Saint-Domingue Revolution lasted from 1791 to 1804, and in it the enslaved people fought for their freedom from French colonial rule and reenslavement. C.L.R. James would write that "on no portion of the globe did" racial slavery yield so much wealth as the colony of Saint-Domingue did for France.[12] It would be such wealth that would motivate major colonial powers to try, and fail, to take Saint-Domingue back from the the Black revolutionaries. Indeed, the French were not the only ones to be defeated by the Black revolutionaries of Saint-Domingue; they would also fight off the British and the Spanish before the revolution's end.[13]

Nyong'o argues during the battle against their reenslavement, it is said that some of the Black people of Saint-Domingue believed one of two things: first, that dying would release them back to Africa, to live a peaceful afterlife; second, some who died would be unfortunately judged to "skulk the Hispaniola plantations for eternity, an undead slave at once denied their own bodies and yet trapped inside them," what can be called "a soulless zombie."[14] The first death mirrors what James said the Black revolutionaries believed in; they each hoped that "if they were killed they would wake again in Africa."[15] Nyong'o argues the second death is what the Black people fighting for their freedom hoped against. Today's iteration of the zombie has routes in the second death, the fear that Black revolutionaries felt at dying, yet never leaving the plantations, of living on undead at the whims of their white enslavers.

This fear, lined in Black radicalism, also lined the pockets of Hollywood executives, organizing the raceless, radicaless reinterpretation of the zombie that persists to this day. Black radicalism is of infrastructural importance to contemporary zombie media. Like the zombie in general, Black radicalism organizes the *zombie* of zombie media. It is the West's fear of Black radicalism that lingers in the background, always misunderstood, awaiting the perfect time to strike, whether in Hollywood's zombie trope or in zombie media. This is not the zombie trope as discussed by Eric Watts, as a metaphor for postracial fantasy, necessary for the continuance of the United States.[16] This is the zombie as the material instantiation of a Black/environmental struggle, inseparable from a challenge to the Western world. But such struggle is not guaranteed to lead to an apocalyptic end of the world, which Achille Mbembe argues is a largely Western, white concern; it is more concerned with the welcoming of the unknown.[17]

Fights against the Anthropocene and Black revolutionary fervor have a commonality: both threaten the solidity on which Western man sits. The Anthropocene and Black radicalism force new futures, whether Western man is ready for them or not. What our zombie media and the Anthropocene speak to is what Black radicalism had long illustrated:

that the Western world is not all that exists, and such a realization at this time is of deadly necessity. Furthermore, Black radicalism speaks to another concern of this book: alternative epistemologies. In terms of media philosophy, I have argued that McLuhan has been one central theorist who pushed a disciplinary approach to knowledge, which remains important for contemporary media philosophers. What C.L.R. James reminds us is that the epistemological concerns of scholars such as McLuhan are far from universal but often leave out (or overlook) alternative concepts of knowledge.

One of those most left out conceptions has been Blackness itself, which is so often reduced to "race" in popular and academic study. But as Walter Rodney argued, Blackness is "not simply what the white world says, but also how individuals percieve each other."[18] Under these terms Blackness is not easily reduced to Western racial catergorization but to the worldmaking terms of global Black radicals over centuries. What I have concerned myself with is, what does epistemology look like when media philosophy takes seriously the thoughts and philosophies of Black people? The response is the cry of Black studies and cultural studies. I contend that, when doing so, it is no longer media philosophy that we are talking about per se, but Black media philosophy—an alternative approach to media, knowledge, and philosophy, largely ignored in media philosophy's acceptance of the Western world as the only world.

As communication and media philosophers, if we are increasingly interested in materialist readings of communication, readings that situate our modes of communicating in questions of the environment, Western concepts of nature, and how to stop harming the natural environment, then we would do well to remember how alternative epistemologies provide us with new tools to think about that natural environment. Doing so forces us to think about the fight against white supremacy as always already the fight against the climate crisis. A Black studies approach to Parikka's zombie media may do some of this work. Parikka argues zombie media must be theorized as twofold: first, they must be theorized as "discarded outside normal use in everyday life," or that which is typically thought about as dead even as it has the potential to take life; and second, and what most concerns me, zombie media deserve theorization in order to consider their *futurity*, artistic and otherwise, rarely thought by those who have tossed these media to the side.[19]

I want to center zombie media in the discussion of an alternative future, of Black epistemologies, where, as Keeling argues, "one conception of the world might emerge as the result of planning, visioning, risk-taking, and radical love rooted in another conception of the world."[20] Indeed, this is a future that, like the climate crisis, is not waiting for man but is already here whether he likes it or not. Part of this new futurity is not really new at all. Instead, it is based on a far older cry, one that should not be allowed to let die. It is a call for a future that just might end up saving us all. We can call this "reparations," a central theme of Black studies work that remains future-oriented, untouched by media philosophy until now.[21] But to call it "reparations" may not do it full justice because the discourse of reparations has a long and politically charged history. Alternatively, I want to call this "reparations of the earth," that which must deal with the zombie, in all its forms. Another way to say this is we are concerned with a reparations that does not dwell in death, or white definitions of Black people (Black bodies, the Negro, media) but Black radical life, a reparations that starts with the premise that a people for which the zombie was even a possibility deserve some level restitution. This is a reparations that could end up saving us all, a reparations not routed in the well-being of one population in the United States but a new worldmaking project. And as Innis reminds us, new worldmaking assumes media.

## REPARATIONS FOR ALL

Most Hollywood productions of zombies suggest an apocalytpic end to the world: the (Western) world can no longer return to its previous imaginary glory, as death and destruction finds its way to our doors. But, as Haiti reminds us, the zombie does not reside solely under the terms of the West or of its apocalytpic, world-ending thought. In other words, the binarization of the end versus the beginning centers the West as the location of all politics. Stephano Harney and Fred Moten reject similar positions. As they wrote in *The Undercommons*: "What is, so to speak, the object of abolition? Not so much the abolition of prisons but the abolition of a society that could have prisons, that could have slavery, that could have the wage, and therefore not abolition as the elimination of anything but abolition as the founding of a new society."[22] Here they argue for a "right of refusal." Such a right might be used for our purposes not as an acceptance of the traditional binarized structure that one is either *for* something or *against* something (for example, reparations); instead, a right-of-refusal is a call for an end to the idea in which the necessity of something like reparations exists in the first place. In other words, a right-of-refusal lies against the legitimization of financial compensation as a fair repair for the materiality of racial violence, something for which fair repair will remain elusive.

Both of these positions, for and against reparations, are negligent because they cannot imagine an outside; they are in denial of a third position toward the end of Western conceptions as the norm. The undercommons—or the "we," for Moten and Harney, who "refuse to ask for recognition and instead we want to take apart, dismantle, tear down the structure that, right now, limits our ability to find each other, to see beyond it and to access the places that we know lie outside its walls"— do not seek recognition as per Western conceptual terms.[23] Instead, Moten's and Harney's *we* speaks to a need for the creation of new forms of consciousness under the twenty-first century context of Western capitalist crises. This would necessarily be a different consciousness than what Huey Newton had in mind in the 1970s (see chapter 3). The conjuncture has changed too drastically for the required consciousness to remain the same.

Although they are not fully discussing reparations throughout their book, Harney and Moten can be pushed into thinking about reparations, as they suggest such calls for and against reparations may be too simplistic.[24] For example, delivered to the House of Representatives on January 3, 2019, one of the most recent political discourses that takes up racial reparations in the United States is the H.R. 40 bill. Congresswoman Sheila Jackson Lee of Texas delivered H.R. 40 to the House to consider reparations for "African-Americans" due to the "fundamental injustice, cruelty, brutality, and inhumanity of slavery" in the former British colonies and in the United States, "between *1619* and *1865*," along with the "subsequent de jure and de facto racial and economic discrimination against African-Americans, and the impact of these forces on living African-Americans."[25] Via H.R. 40, Jackson Lee seeks to establish the "Commission to Study and Develop Reparation Proposals for African-Americans," a commission designed to build documentation on the institution of slavery and to recommend "remedies" to be reported to Congress no later than one year after the date of the first meeting of the commision.[26]

As it stands, the passage of H.R. 40 has been viewed as highly unlikely. Mitch McConnell, who was Senate Majority Leader at the time, argued that racial "reparations for slavery was not 'a good idea,'" as "it would 'be pretty hard to figure out who to compensate,'" especially as the people "responsible" for slavery and the enslaved people were all dead.[27] Partly in response to McConnell's statement, Ta-Nehisi Coates argued at a House hearing on the topic that "well into this century, the United States was still paying out pensions to the heirs of Civil War soldiers," and the U.S. honors "treaties that date back some 200 years, despite no one being alive who signed those treaties."[28] Coates's statement on the payments sent to some over others, despite the deals being made outside of our lifetimes, has much academic backing.[29]

Despite not being a popular position in the U.S. government, Jackson Lee is not alone in her push for reparations. Some of the debate online and offline for reparations is being taken up by a group called the American Descendants of Slaves (ADOS). Under the leadership of Los Angeles defense attorney Antonio Moore and Yvettte Carnell, a former aide to Democratic lawmakers in Washington, ADOS has positioned itself as a group largely against Black (and other forms of) immigration to the United States, specifically calling for a nationalistic form of "reparations for the brutal system of slavery upon which the United States was built."[30] In short, rather than the globalized framing of Blackness articulated by the Black studies movement (see chapter 3), the definition of Black for ADOS is specifically linked to those of us who are the descendents of transatlantic enslaved people in what is now geographically the United States.

ADOS is a highly Black nationalist-capitalist approach to reparations, often striking similar conservative immigration tones as former president Donald Trump. For both, Black and brown immigrants hurt the political and economic mobility of Black people born in the United States. It is for this reason that 1619 is so important to ADOS and Jackson Lee. Despite the longer trajectory of Western colonial rule, it is the British and English-speaking colonial project in North America that is positioned as where reparations should begin, as this English-speaking population would be deemed as necessary for the foundation of the United States. Here we can presumably dismiss the violence and colonial relations that precedes 1619; the sole need for remedy lies in the nationalistic terms of Black English-speaking people in the United States.

As one side of the current political debate goes, racial reparations will benefit Black people in the United States due to the long history of systematic violence we have faced in this country and, as such, reparations should be fought for (Jackson Lee's and ADOS's argument). As for the other side of the debate, reparations only benefits Black people in the United States, unfairly harming the overall political and economic system of the country, particularly for those who had no role in slavery

(McConnell's argument), and therefore reparations should be fought against. But what if we were to refuse the binary terms of racial reparations as they currently sit in front of conservatives and liberals alike? What if the concept of racial reparations was to be recreated, in which the argument is not that reparation will only benefit U.S. Black people, but reparations will create new potentialities beyond the West's limited racial categories? This would require refusing the entire conception of reparations as it currently sits in a logic of 1619. And such a refusal may start with understanding the fabricated articulation of the Negro (in the United States, but not only in the United States, and not only the Negro) to nature, which is to say media—a Black studies, Black Anthropocene–informed rethinking of politics in order to see the saving of Black people as the saving of us all. The assessment of the Combahee River Collective in the 1970s still holds true: "If Black women were free, it would mean that everyone else would have to be free since our freedom would necessitate the destruction of all the systems of oppression."[31] Reparations should benefit a world of people.

In Black studies fashion, then, I contend that rethinking reparations would need to go back to 1492, not 1619—to what Sylvia Wynter calls the Western, Columbian construction of a New World view.[32] This would necessarily exceed the nationalistic borders of the United States. This rethinking would also require thinking about the zombie as always connected to media, and vice versa—a concern with how the Western concept of nature (both associated with the bodies of people of color and foundational to the media technologies we continue to use) has led toward the brink of climate crisis. The more radical reparations discourses have never reduced reparations to Black people in the United States only, but point to rethinking racial reparations via land redistribution, free college tuition, the abolition of policing, prisons, and war, and the end of tax-exempt statuses, to name a few options.[33]

Indeed, much of these arguments come out of an undertaking also gaining popular traction as of late, despite it being a stronghold of Black radical organizing for decades: the prison abolition movement. This is the project of scholars and activists such as Angela Davis, Ruth Wilson Gilmore, and Mariame Kaba in their critique of what they call the prison industrial complex, where prisons, Davis argues "are identified for their potential as consumers and for their potential cheap labor."[34] The focus on the mobilization of prison labor pushes Gilmore to argue that the problem of prison lies not in the prisoners, but in the state's weddedness to capitalism, meaning that prisons are "a consequence of state failure," not innate criminality, they are "geographical solutions to social and economic crises, politically organized by a racial state that is itself in crisis."[35] One of those crises, Gilmore argues, can be in part addressed via ending the death penalty.

Likewise, as Davis argues in *Abolition Democracy*, prison could be one way of rethinking what constitutes reparations, a way of seeing how prisons injure all people: "One of the major priorities of the reparations movement should be the abolition of the death penalty."[36] As the death penalty has killed prisoners of *all* races, reparations/abolishing the death penalty would be not solely for Black people in the United States but for a world of people impacted by the prison industrial complex. I want to focus on an important distinction that scholars like Davis and Gilmore make in the reparations debate, a distinction missing in the framing by Jackson Lee, ADOS, and McConnell: a "struggle for reparations shouldn't be seen as mutually exclusive from the struggle for universal programs," as reparations is "not just the financial redress" but equally necessary for the United States to question "how do we deal with the long-term political aftermath of racism in our society?"[37] Reparations do not save Black, English-speaking people in the United States only; to fight for reparations is to fight for a new future for all, a new future that does not exist yet and is also far from guaranteed.

For Gilmore and Davis, to think about reparations going forward, we may need to ask new questions: How do we create a world toward refusal, one that would require different groups of people to view reparations as for the betterment of all? Building on Gilmore's argument that everyone from farmworkers, to prisoners's families, to immigrant activists, to environmentalists, to prison abolitionists can find common ground, I argue that to do so would require connecting the discussions of racial reparations to the Black Anthropocene (which always means connecting this discussion to the zombie media, which poison the earth).[38]

To create a world toward refusal would mean that we would need to reposition the always already racialized zombie media—that which is not currently deemed as racial in media philosophy—as consistent with the current threat to the climate and to the world. Zombie media are not solely our old laptops oozing in trash heaps; they are also those of us who have fought our reduction to media. To toss us aside is to toss everyone and everything to the side as well. But to save us all would require new forms of planning, it would require pointing ourselves to and beyond a world organized by what Leilani Nishime and Kim Hester Williams call "racial ecologies," where planetary destruction and racial violence are entwined.[39] It would even require us considering the role of planetary destruction on the "wealth of chances for viruses to evolve," like the planetary spread of the novel coronavirus in late 2019 and early 2020—an ongoing crisis that we have yet to get out of.[40] A new reparations project might just be a direct attack on racial ecologies in total, one that refuses the postracial discourse of environmentalism, while steeped in the futures that Nishime and Williams argue we need to think about for planetary survival. And the beginnings of a such a refusal owe much of their legacy to the thought, politics, and (eco)socialist fights of the Global South, those who I argue must be a part of the racial reparations debate in the United States.[41]

## TOWARD THE END OF OWING; OR ON BLACK AND BROWN FUTURITIES

The problem of Western economic thinking runs deep in contemporary progressive discussions of justice. Harney and Moten wrote *Undercommons* with such a contradiction in mind: "It is not credit we seek nor even debt but bad debt which is to say real debt, the debt that cannot be repaid, the debt at a distance, the debt without creditor, the black debt, the queer debt, the criminal debt. Excessive debt, incalculable debt, debt for no reason, debt broken from credit, debt as its own principle."[42] Likewise, the problem of racial reparations is a problem of economic thought, meaning it speaks to an inability to unthink the Western economic world as it currently sits. And the climate crisis ensures that such a need to unthink Western capitalism is coming, whether we are prepared for it or not.

Many non-Western thinkers have long considered what new forms of reparations might look like. For example, in his classic book, *The Wretched of the Earth*, Frantz Fanon argued that Europe could only save itself via some form of reparations to the colonies. Arguably, it is in this text that we see Fanon's strongest Marxist influence. In fact, Fanon argued that such reparations were not only logical, as European wealth rested on colonial occupation; but without reparations, Europe would ultimately end itself, in ways that seem to speak to the contemporary climate crisis we are in: "If through lack of intelligence—not to mention ingratitude—the capitalist countries refused to pay up, then the unrelenting dialectic of their own system would see to it that they are asphyxiated."[43] Colonialism and capitalism, and its goals of limitless expansionism without end, would *suffocate* the West itself, not just the colonies. Fanon's discussion of such an asphyxiation appears to be more metaphorical than literal, but it can be read today in the context of the climate crisis, particularly as vast swaths of California are regularly on fire, hurting the lungs of people throughout the state, but especially the majority Black and brown inmates fighting the fires.[44]

Colonialism/capitalism, Fanon suggests, would literally create a world in which the West's air would toxify, killing the West itself. That which is presumably dead (the colonized and, for me, the zombie media) would haunt the West into its own self-destruction. This is not an apocalytic end to the *world* but an end to the West (which may be phyisical, social, economical, etc.)—or rather, this is the unseating of the West as representative of the entirety of the world. Of course, Fanon was not naive enough to think that Europe would pay up easily but he did believe that such payments would be necessary for the reintroduction of "man into the world, man in his totality," which could only come not by the leadership of Europe's bourgeoisie, but only with the "crucial help of the European masses," the proletariat who have often backed the bourgeoisie's wishes in terms of colonialism.[45] The Western proletariat must join the global Black, brown, and Indigenous revolution, for Fanon. Rather than lead it, the Western proletariat must come to understand that global Black revolution is welcoming and awaiting them.

Since the early 2000s, such countries as Bhutan, Bolivia, Malaysia, Micronesia, Paraguay, Sri Lanka, and Venezuela have all argued to the United Nations that they are owed a "climate debt" in ways that somewhat to align with Fanon's suggestion of the impending climate crisis's threat to the West. Within these reports to the United Nation, a fundamental, unarguable point has emerged: Western nations are the leading cause of the climate crisis, disproportionately effecting non-Western people. The recent Bolivian UN report on the state of the climate crisis illustrates that glacier "retreat has accelerated compromising water supplies, food security and potentially hydropower generation," increasing flood risks "during extreme precipitation events"; during dry seasons more intense and longer droughts have been "observed in around 40% of Bolivian territory, home of 70% of the population and the poorest"; and lastly, such shifts in the climate have endangered the survival of Indigenous people, like the Uru Chipaya, a twenty-five-hundred-year-old Bolivian culture, "making them among the first internal climate change refugees."[46] It is for these reasons of dispossession and overextraction that Western nations, like the United States and European nations, *owe* non-Western nations facing the brunt of the climate crisis.

The road to repaying climate debt consists of two parts: adaptation debt and emissions debt. Adaptation debt is the failure to "provide compensation to developing countries" based on the excesses of wealthy Western countries. In other words, there is a debt owed to poorer nations from wealthier nations to protect people where they currently live; to protect those climate exiles who can no longer live in their previous homes; to cope with the warming that is going to happen in the future and to acknowledge the harms that such warming will create for all; and to prevent a continued, uninterrupted path toward more climate harm. We can think about an adaptation debt as that which Western nations need to "pay" to help people adapt to the troubles that are already here and that are on the way. Unlike adaptation debt, emissions debt is a call for "climate credit," one that contends that the fault of the climate crisis cannot be equally put on Western people and non-Western people, as if both emit carbon dioxide at the same rate. As the non-Western nations have not emitted at the same level as Western nations, emissions debt states that all non-Western nations should be allotted higher emissions rates than Western nations in order to help with their development.

To fully understand emissions debt, one must understand emissions budgets—the upper limit of total carbon dioxide that can be emitted worldwide so that the world can stay under a specific global average temperature.[47] Emissions budgets are divided into national budgets, specifically so individual nations can mitigate their harm. Ideally (maybe idealistically), if all nations throughout the world meet or come under their budgeted emissions rates, we could begin mitigating the harms already done to the environment. According to the Climate Debt website, Western nations like the United States always try to set their emission budgets high, which requires that places like Bolivia must have lower emissions levels, even though they do not emit as much carbon dioxide as the United States.[48] An emission debt involves what we might call a back payment, a credit given to the poorer nations of the world that would allow for them to have higher emissions going forward so that they can "develop," while also calling for the United States to have massive restrictions on its own emissions budget going forward.

In countries like the United States, such discussions of "Western debt" have been deemed highly threatening. In part, due to Bolivia's socialist, environmentalist critique of capitalist policies, the United States helped to support a coup in Bolivia in 2019, which has been largely viewed as an attempt to suppress the democratically elected Movement Toward

Socialism Party, Bolivia's Indigenous, leftist political party. Largely underreported in Western nations, right-wing factions of Bolivia, supported by the United States, participated in subversion against socialist and pro-democratic protesters, in what is now known as the 2019 massacres, leading to the ousting of the Movement Toward Socialism from power and the full establishment of a right-wing provisional leadership. In the United States, the discourse on the massacre at both the political level and the news media level often "evolved in support of the coup, with supposed 'foreign policy experts' across the political spectrum... spouting outright falsehoods to depict the destruction of Bolivian democracy as the salvation of it."[49]

Of course, Bolivia is far from the first country where the United States has supported right-wing factions. Even as Bolivia recently voted to reestablish the Movement Toward Socialism as the governing power for the country, we can see that, at least from the United States's view, Cold War policies against socialism have yet to die.[50] To presume that the United States owes anything is tantamount to antidemocracy, even if the United States must undermine your democracy to save its name. My argument is not that the coup in Bolivia was started because of climate debt; rather, the push to discuss climate debt is a part of a broader socialist-friendly development that we can see throughout the world, one that pushes toward a world far more concerned with the well-being of the majority than the minority. And, importantly, this concern with the climate crisis has been deemed a threat to the United States—a country that deemed Bolivia (like other places) as being *selected* for intervention. Under such terms the United States "owes" more than just U.S. Black people.

Recently, Bolivia's former president Evo Morales Ayama argued that the United States's colonial mindset is not solely a challenge to socialism but is inseparable from Bolivia's attempt to challenge climate crisis. Thus:

> [A U.S.-based] colonialism—which puts our planet in a state of crisis today, devours natural resources, and concentrates wealth that is generated from devastation—says that our laws of *vivir bien* ["living well"] are utopian. But if our dreams of equilibrium with *Pachamama* ["Mother Earth"], of freedom, and social justice are not yet a reality, or if they have been cut short, it is primarily because imperialism has set out to interfere in our political, cultural, and economic revolutions, which promote sovereignty, dignity, peace, and fraternity among all people.[51]

Pulling from Davis, Gilmore, and Fanon, climate debt may point toward another way to think about reparations in the United States. Even still, I lay out some problems with climate debt as a discourse not to critique the heroic efforts of Bolivia's socialist push, but to note what I hope to keep in mind for futures of Black and brown and socialist organizing, thought, and life. The way that many are proposing to fight the climate crisis is highly structured by a grammar of capitalism: debt, credit, budgets, payment, development, and more. As it currently stands, such a grammar assumes that capitalism (inseparable from Western media) will save us. However, as I have shown throughout this book, Western capitalism, media, and grammars are inseparable from the destruction that got us into the climate crisis in the first place.

The Western construct of nature (and its relationship to media, racism, and capitalism) lay a foundation for the current climate crisis. Like the contemporary mining of African lands for natural materials that will eventually go into our cellphones and laptops, for centuries Africans were violently ripped from Africa in the service of producing the Negro, which also extended Western concepts of humanness.[52] We have now put McLuhan in a place he could not imagine: the Negro serves the media function. If media are any extension of Western man, the Negro's connection to the natural also extends man into what he now takes for granted as his whiteness and maleness, as his superiority, progress, and development. Herein lies the problem unthought in many theories of environmental racism in communication and media studies: environmental destruction occurs not only in locations disproportionately inhabited by Black and brown people but also in the harming of Black and brown people, of which coups outside the United States are a part.[53]

In other words, to destroy the environment is to destroy those items related with the environment as well, which have been Black and brown bodies for the West. The complicity of the United States in the Bolivian coup is just one example of this, just as slavery and Indigenous genocide are others. If this is the foundation on which we were to think about environmental racism, then to theorize survival must consider not only our media representations of environmental racism, not only our melting icecaps, not only rising emissions levels, but also the materiality of some people's bodies in a world of Western arrogance. To be owed a back year of overextraction of resources for development may be a limited way to get us out of the problem of the West. Indeed, we must think beyond capitalistic grammars and, even more importantly, we must think beyond Black nationalist terms, if we hope to reimagine what reparations for the earth could look like.

I want to build off Bolivia's discussion of climate debt and credit to reconsider it in relation to the Negro and Harney's and Moten's work:

"Only debt makes credit possible, only debt lets credit rule."[54] Two sides of the same coin, the grammar of debt and credit used in the climate debt discourses may always already be wedded to the same politics of development that the United States presented as neutral. Much of the contemporary climate debt discourse is steeped in the idea that non-Western places like Bolivia are owed a boom. But I want to say that we may need to, at some point in the future, say something different: there is a debt that cannot be repaid, there is an unforgiveable debt that a boom will never fill. Like Jackson Lee's and McConnell's debate, there is something that is never acknowledged in climate debt discourses: the West has created a world in which there is no amount of financial repayment that can ever equalize everything and everyone, especially as repayment and development are structured under Western terms.[55] As such, it may be time to think about ending all forms of overextraction, rather than distributing overextraction more equitably. Indeed, raise Bolivia's limit, and massiviely cut the United States's, but toward the end of all forms of overextraction.

How do we imagine a way forward for a population deemed little more than media technologies by the larger institutions of Western societies? It will not come in the same politics and grammars that got us here. It may come via the refusal of such grammars. The climate crisis cannot be fixed with debt and credit logics as they currently sit, but it could be addressed via the Black radical tradition.[56] It is in such a tradition that alternative thought is possible, as we can see that the Negro serves a function for Western societies, and that function has everything and nothing to do with the Darwinian construct of nature. Furthermore, it is from here that we can see an isomorphism between the Negro and Western media: both are pulled from natural, raw materials, regardless of the potentiality for environmental destruction. Because we live in a world that has fabricated nature as a thing to be overly utilized and we live in a world that has fabricated some people's proximity to nature, distinct from civilization, nature is Black.

In order for us to save the planet, to save us all, we must save Black people. This is not tantamount to saying we must save Black people *first* or even we must *only* save Black people, which seem closer to the U.S.-focused, racial reparations debates. Instead, it is to say, much like Rodney, that Black people are a global people, inseparable from the tenacles of Western colonial rule.[57] It is also to say, much like Davis, that to consider how Black people are affected in the United States and to solve such problems extends out to solving other problems as well. For example, both Davis and Atiya Husain contend that to end the militarization of policing in Black ghettoes could impact U.S. militarized approaches to the war on terror, which also has inspired other country's approaches to the war on terror.[58] In a similar vein, to take seriously the raced, gendered, and sexual assumptions of nature in our climate crisis discussions would not only point toward Black people, but toward the role of the Western-led climate crisis on the lives and futures of non-Western locales that have been deemed unworthy of saving by the West. In such a context, racial reparations are not solely about U.S. Black people, even as they are about us; reparations become inseparable from considerations of saving our environment—the time-space where we all live.

One potential mode for thinking about surviving environmental racism lies in the collective, planned, organized demand for racial reparations. I say "collective, planned, and organized" because reparations cannot go to one race of people only, but they must go to many, they must be articulated by a collective, new consciousness. As noted earlier, for decades reparations thinking has approached questions of monetary payment as only one way to think about reparations. If we begin with the premise that the Negro is a medium, then the zombified apocalypse can be reimagined, particularly by refocusing our discussion of reparations toward the environment as well. The discourse of reparations opens a space to think about new ways to survive under our crisis if a payment was ever made. Much of this rethinking of reparations could look like the free relocation of Black and brown people to locations that will in the future receive far less flooding and wildfires, or (for the love of God!) fixing the water filtration systems in Flint, Michigan, or other forms of transformation that we have not even imagined yet.

The point being, however, that reparations is future-oriented, and it will take not the conclusion of a book, but a world of people, in and outside the United States, to point us toward new ways of thinking. It is for this reason that racial reparations exceed the limited imaginations of a United States–focused approach of Jackson Lee, ADOS, and McConnell, and may point far closer to Bolivia, even as we may eventually need to push past climate debt as an organizing principle. Reparations is a transnational project, one where Western nations must consider what they have wrought on the people and the earth, before both rise up, undead, to strike back.

# Notes

INTRODUCTION

*Epigraph*: C.L.R. James, "*The Black Scholar* Interviews: C.L.R. James," *The Black Scholar* 2, no. 1 (1970): 43.

1. For examples of Black media studies, see Nancy Wang Yuen, "Playing 'Ghetto': Black Actors, Stereotypes, and Authenticity," in *Black Los Angeles: American Dreams and Racial Realities*, ed. Darnell Hunt and Ana-Christina Ramon (New York: New York University Press, 2010), 232–242; Michael Eric Dyson, *The Michael Eric Dyson Reader* (New York: Basic Civitas Books, 2004); bell hooks, *Yearning: Race, Gender, and Cultural Politics* (Cambridge, MA: South End Press, 1990); George Lipsitz, "The Hip-Hop Hearings: The Hidden History of Deindustrialization," in *The Race and Media Reader*, ed. Gilbert Rodman (New York: Routledge, 2014), 294–312; Mark Orbe, "Representations of Race and Reality TV: Watch and Discuss," *Critical Studies in Media Communication* 25, no. 4 (2008): 345–352; Tricia Rose, *Black Noise: Rap Music and Black Culture in Contemporary America* (Indianapolis: Wesleyan Publishing House, 1994), and "Fear of a Black Planet: Rap Music and Black Cultural Politics in the 1990s," in *The Race and Media Reader*, ed. Gilbert Rodman (New York: Routledge, 2014), 120–131; and Eric King Watts, "Border Patrolling and 'Passing' in Eminem's *8 Mile*," *Critical Studies in Media Communication* 22, no. 3 (2005): 187–206. There are, of course, notable exceptions to this list. An influential contingent of media scholars are pushing far more materialist readings of media and Blackness. See Ruha Benjamin, *Race after Technology: Abolitionist Tools for the New Jim Code* (New York: Polity Press, 2019); Simone Browne, *Dark Matters: On the Surveillance of Blackness* (Durham, NC: Duke University Press, 2015); Andre Brock, *Distributed Blackness: African American Cybercultures* (New York: New York University Press, 2020); Timothy Havens, *Black*

*Television Travels: African American Media around the Globe* (New York: New York University Press, 2013); Kara Keeling, *The Witch's Flight: The Cinematic, the Black Femme, and the Image of Common Sense* (Durham, NC: Duke University Press, 2007); and Alexander Weheliye, *Phonographies: Grooves in Sonic Afro-Modernity* (Durham, NC: Duke University Press, 2005).

2. Marshall McLuhan Collection, Thomas Fisher Rare Book Library, University of Toronto Libraries, accessed October 2, 2020, https://fisher.library.uto ronto.ca/sites/fisher.library.utoronto.ca/files/mcluhanFA-june2014.pdf.

3. Jade Davis argues that McLuhan's work operates in similar ways as Frantz Fanon's, particularly pointing to the implication that the Black body has a media relation. See Davis, "Second Iteration: A Letter to Fanon & McLuhan," *Jadedid* (blog), 2013, http://jadedid.com/blog/2013/02/13/second-iteration-a-let ter-to-fanon-mcluhan. For McLuhan's own words on race, see McLuhan, "Playboy Interview: 'Marshall McLuhan—A Candid Conversation with the High Priest of Popcult and Metaphysician of Media," in *Essential McLuhan*, ed. Eric McLuhan and Frank Zingrone (New York: Basic Books, 1995), 233–269.

4. See Ginger Nolan, *The Neocolonialism of the Global Village* (Minneapolis: University of Minnesota Press, 2018); and Armond Towns, "Toward a Black Media Philosophy," *Cultural Studies* 43, no. 6 (2020): 851–873.

5. Richard Cavell, introduction to *McLuhan on the Nature of Media: Essays, 1952–1978)*, ed. Cavell (Berkeley, CA: Gingko Press, 2016), 10–11, emphasis added.

6. Towns, "Toward a Black Media Philosophy."

7. Indeed, as C.L.R. James was central to Black studies and in contact with cultural studies scholars like E. P. Thompson and Stuart Hall, the distinctions between the two are not that important for me. See C.L.R. James, *You Don't Play with Revolution: The Montreal Lectures of C.L.R. James* (Chico, CA: AK Press, 2009), 260.

8. In his letter to Eric Havelock, to express excitement for Havelock's book, *Preface to Plato*, McLuhan argues: "I have tried to avoid making personal value judgements about these processes [of technology's role on societal changes] since they seem far too important and too large in scope to deserve a merely private opinion." See McLuhan, "Letter to Eric Havelock," May 22, 1970, Library and Archives of Canada, http://data2.archives.ca/e/e447/e011165482-v8.jpg.

9. Alexander Ross, "The High Priest of Pop Culture," *Maclean's*, July 3, 1965, https://archive.macleans.ca/article/1965/7/3/the-high-priest-of-pop-cultu re.

10. James Carey, *Communication as Culture* (New York: Routledge, 2009); and Raymond Williams, *Television: Technology and Cultural Form* (New York: Routledge, 2003).

11. "Annie Hall: Full Cast & Crew," *IMDb*, accessed October 2, 2020, www.imdb.com/title/tt0075686/fullcredits?ref_=ttfc_ql_1.

12. In addition to Carey and Williams, see another critique of McLuhan: Eric Jenkins and Peter Zhang, "Deleuze the Media Ecologist? Extensions of and Advance on McLuhan," *Explorations in Media Ecology* 15, no. 1 (2016): 55–72.

13. Alison Nastasi, "10 of the Most Fascinating 'Playboy' Interviews," *Fla-*

*vorwire*, August 31, 2013, www.flavorwire.com/412697/10-of-the-most-fascina ting-playboy-interviews.

14. McLuhan, "Playboy Interview," 249.

15. Aniko Bodroghkozy, *Groove Tube: Sixties Television and the Youth Rebellion* (Durham, NC: Duke University Press, 2001).

16. Bodroghkozy, *Groove Tube*, 25.

17. Grant Havers, "The Right-Wing Postmodernism of Marshall McLuhan," *Media, Culture & Society* 25, no. 4 (2003): 511–525.

18. Marshall McLuhan Collection, 1963–1965, MG31.D56.89.58, Library and Archives of Canada, Ottawa, Ontario, Canada.

19. Daniel Geary, "The Moynihan Report: An Annotated Edition," *The Atlantic*, September 14, 2015, www.theatlantic.com/politics/archive/2015/09/the -moynihan-report-an-annotated-edition/404632/#Chapter%20I.

20. Cavell, introduction to *McLuhan on the Nature of Media*; and Achille Mbembe, *Necropolitics* (Durham, NC: Duke University Press, 2019), 138.

21. For example, in his discussion of radio as a "tribal drum," McLuhan held that there was always an African laying *within* Western man, potentially reawakening via the proliferation of radio's presumed potential to return man to some precivilized, tribal mind-set (though never fully reawakening man from detribalism, as man was "too civilized"—i.e., too literate). Putting aside his inability to fathom the complexity and diversity of the African continent, the "African within" for McLuhan was not a product of Africans having the radio first and the West copying them. The "African within" was the product of the Western, Guglielmo Marconi–inspired invention of the radio toward the end of the nineteenth century as well as that radio's presumed ability to return the West back to a *tribal* time period of communality that he argued existed well before electronic media. See McLuhan, "Radio: The Tribal Drum," *AV Communication Review* 12, no. 2 (1964): 133–145.

22. The concept of "man" is used throughout this book to signal not the human in general but the Western conception of the human, which I argue people like McLuhan pulled from Charles Darwin, or at least Darwin-inspired thought. This is a human who is in relation with nature but can utilize nature toward highly sophisticated technological ends. Thus for Darwin, and McLuhan, that use of nature has hierarchal assumptions, depending on the human.

23. See Sylvia Wynter, "The Ceremony Found: Towards the Autopoetic Turn/Overturn, Its Autonomy of Human Agency and Extraterritoriality of (Self-)Cognition," in *Black Knowledges/Black Struggles: Essays in Critical Epistemology*, ed. Jason Ambroise and Sabine Broeck (Liverpool, UK: Liverpool University Press, 2015), 186–252. Towns, "Toward a Black Media Philosophy."

24. Mark Smith, *How Race Is Made: Slavery, Segregation, and the Senses* (Chapel Hill: University of North Carolina Press, 2006).

25. Ronald Judy, *DisForming the American Canon: African-Arabic Slave Narratives and the Vernacular* (Minneapolis: University of Minnesota Press, 1993), 128.

26. Although Judy's latest, important book seems to say this explicitly: that the Negro can be thought about as "mimetic media." See Judy, *Sentient Flesh:*

*Thinking in Disorder, Poiesis in Black* (Durham, NC: Duke University Press, 2020), 13.

27. See Brock, *Distributed Blackness*.

28. See Austin, "Introduction: In Search of a National Identity: C.L.R. James and the Promise of the Caribbean," in *You Don't Play with Revolution*, 9–13.

29. National Defense Education Act of 1958, H.R. 13247, September 2, 1958, www.govinfo.gov/content/pkg/STATUTE-72/pdf/STATUTE-72-Pg1580 .pdf, 1584, emphasis added.

30. National Defense Education Act of 1958, 1584.

31. Central Intelligence Agency, "The Break-up of the Colonial Empires and Its Implications of US Security," September 3, 1948, www.cia.gov/readingroom /docs/DOC_0000258342.pdf.

32. Roderick Ferguson, *The Reorder of Things: The University and Its Pedagogies of Minority Difference* (Minneapolis: University of Minnesota Press, 2012).

33. Jeff Pooley, "Wilbur Schramm and the 'Four Founders' History of U.S. Communication Research," *Tom* 2, no. 4 (2017): 7.

34. Pooley, "Wilbur Schramm," 8.

35. Indeed, at the turn of the twentieth century, we see the development of terms like "media" and "communication" as scientific concepts designed to be distinguished from art forms like "rhetoric" and "propaganda." It would not be long before they entered into the U.S. state as legitimate areas of study. See John Guillory, "Genesis of the Media Concept," *Critical Inquiry* 36 (2010): 321–362.

36. Alexis Madrigal, "Gil Scott-Heron's Poem, 'Whitey on the Moon,'" *The Atlantic*, September 14, 2015, www.theatlantic.com/technology/archive/2011 /05/gil-scott-herons-poem-whitey-on-the-moon/239622/.

37. Rey Chow, "The Age of the World Target: Atomic Bombs, Alterity, Area Studies," in *The Rey Chow Reader*, ed. Paul Bowman (New York: Columbia University Press, 2010), 2–19.

38. Ferguson, *Reorder of Things*.

39. National Defense Education Act of 1958, 1594.

40. Chow, "Age of the World Target," 2–19.

41. Vincent Harding, "The Vocation of the Black Scholar and the Struggles of the Black Community," in *Education and Black Struggle: Notes for the Colonized World*, ed. The Institute of the Black World (Cambridge, MA: Harvard Educational Review, 1974), 4.

42. Robin Kelley, "Western Civilization Is Neither: Black Studies' Epistemic Revolution," *The Black Scholar: Journal of Black Studies and Research* 50, no. 3 (2020): 7.

43. National Defense Education Act of 1958, 1596.

44. Pooley, "Wilbur Schramm."

45. Bodroghkozy, *Groove Tube*, 41.

46. A major influence on McLuhan, J. C. Carothers made racist arguments about the African mind. See Carothers, *The African Mind in Health and Disease: A Study of Ethnopsychiatry* (Geneva: World Health Organization, 1953).

47. Ferguson, *Reorder of Things*, 27.

48. Greg Carr, "What Black Studies Is Not: Moving Crisis to Liberation in Africana Intellectual Work," *Socialism and Democracy* 25, no. 1 (2011): 178.

49. Frantz Fanon, *The Wretched of the Earth* (New York: Grove Press, 2004), 181.

50. Kwame Ture and Charles Hamilton, *Black Power: The Politics of Liberation* (New York: Vintage Books, 1992), 6.

51. Harding, "Vocation of the Black Scholar," 6.

52. Martha Biondi, *The Black Revolution on Campus* (Berkeley: University of California Press, 2012), 34.

53. Lerone Bennett, *The Challenge of Blackness* (Chicago: Johnson, 1972).

54. Derrick White, *The Challenge of Blackness: The Institute of the Black World and Political Activism in the 1970s* (Gainesville: University Press of Florida, 2012), 20.

55. White, *Challenge of Blackness*.

56. Nathaniel Norment Jr., introduction to *The African American Studies Reader*, second edition, ed. Norment (Durham, NC: Carolina Academic Press), xxxi.

57. As a faculty member at the University of Virginia, Robinson founded the Carter G. Woodson Institute for African-American and African Studies in 1981. For his work at Yale, see Armstead Robinson, "A Concluding Statement," in *Black Studies in the University*, ed. Robinson, Craig Foster, and Donald Ogilvie (New Haven, CT: Yale University Press, 1969), 207–214.

58. Biondi, *Black Revolution*, 125–126; June Jordan, *Moving Towards Home: Political Essays* (London: Virago, 1989); and Ferguson, *Reorder of Things*, 78.

59. Carole Boyce Davies, *Left of Marx: The Political Life of Black Communist Claudia Jones* (Durham, NC: Duke University Press, 2008).

60. Kelley, "Western Civilization."

61. Walter Rodney, *The Groundings with my Brothers* (London: Bogle-L'Ouverture Publications, 1996).

62. Jesse Benjamin and Robin Kelley, "Introduction: An 'African' Perspective," in *The Russian Revolution: A View from the Third World*, ed. Benjamin and Kelley (Brooklyn, NY: Verso Books, 2018), xix–lxxiii.

63. Walter Rodney, *How Europe Underdeveloped Africa* (Brooklyn, NY: Verso, 2018).

64. Kelley, "Western Civilization," 7.

65. Interdisciplinarity during the mid-twentieth-century cultural studies push was *not* the interdisciplinarity that often shows up today. For example, Kara Keeling argues that the term *interdisciplinary* has been appropriated by corporations recently for profit building. See Keeling, *Queer Times, Black Futures* (New York: New York University Press, 2019).

66. Antonio Gramsci, *Selections from the Prison Notebooks* (New York: International Publishers, 2008), x.

67. Raymond Williams, *Culture and Materialism* (New York: Verso, 2005), 31.

68. David Scott, *Conscripts of Modernity* (Durham, NC: Duke University Press, 2004), 26–27.

69. Stuart Hall, "Gramsci and Us," *Verso*, February 10, 2017, www.versobo oks.com/blogs/2448-stuart-hall-gramsci-and-us, para 6.

70. Hardt's work would crucially call for a critical communication studies, inspired by cultural studies, that would turn communication studies into a political project. Indeed, we can see much influence from Hall's discussion of the necessity for intervention into the conjuncture here. See Carey, *Communication*; Hanno Hardt, "Beyond Cultural Studies—Recovering the 'Political' in Critical Communication Studies," *Journal of Communication Inquiry* 21, no. 2 (1997): 70–78; and Hardt, *Critical Communication Studies: Essays in Communication, History and Theory in America* (New York: Routledge, 1992).

71. Stuart Hall, "Marxist Structuralism," in *Cultural Studies: 1983*, ed. Jennifer Daryl Slack and Lawrence Grossberg (Durham, NC: Duke University Press, 2016), 123.

72. Stuart Hall, "Encoding/Decoding," in *The Cultural Studies Reader*, ed. Simon During (New York: Routledge, 1993), 100.

73. Neil Postman, *Technopoly: The Surrender of Culture in Technology* (New York: Vintage Books, 1993), 21.

74. Karl Marx, *Capital: A Critique of Political Economy*, volume 1 (London: Lawrence & Wishart, LTD, 2003), 60.

75. See Deborah Cook, *Adorno on Nature* (New York: Routledge, 2011); and Max Horkheimer and Theodor Adorno, *Dialectic of Enlightenment* (Stanford, CA: Stanford University Press, 2002).

76. Marshall McLuhan, *Understanding Media: The Extensions of Man* (Berkeley, CA: Gingko Press, 2003).

77. Elizabeth Dickinson, "The Misdiagnosis: Rethinking 'Nature-Deficit Disorder,'" *Environmental Communication* 7, no. 3 (2013): 315–335; Darrel Enck-Wanzer, "Race, Coloniality, and Geo-Body Politics: *The Garden* as Latin@ Vernacular Discourse," *Environmental Communication* 5, no. 3 (2011): 363–371; Cheryl Lousley, "Charismatic Life: Spectacular Biodiversity and Biophilic Life Writing," *Environmental Communication* 10, no. 6 (2016): 704–718; and Phaedra Pezzullo, *Toxic Tourism: Rhetorics of Pollution, Travel, and Environmental Justice* (Tuscaloosa: University of Alabama Press, 2009).

78. Jody Berland, *Virtual Menageries: Animals as Mediators in Network Cultures* (Cambridge, MA: MIT Press, 2019); Mél Hogan, "Big Data Ecologies: Landscapes of Political Action," *Ephemera: Theory & Politics in Organization* 18, no. 3 (2018): 631–657; Friedrich Kittler, *Gramophone, Film, Typewriter* (Stanford, CA: Stanford University Press, 1999); Shannon Mattern, *Code and Clay, Data and Dirt: Five Thousand Years of Urban Media* (Minneapolis: University of Minnesota Press, 2017); Jussi Parikka, *A Geology of Media* (Minneapolis: University of Minnesota Press, 2015); Lisa Parks, *Cultures in Orbit: Satellites and the Televisual* (Durham, NC: Duke University Press, 2005); and John Durham Peters, *The Marvelous Clouds: Toward a Philosophy of Elemental Media* (Chicago: University of Chicago Press, 2015).

79. Parikka, *Geology of Media*, 46.

80.  Maybe the closest examples of the relation between media and nature that exists, comparable to my work, is the work of Jody Berland, Melody Jue, and Nicole Starosielski. Each discusses nature as having colonial implications that media theory must address. For more information on this, see Berland, *Virtual Menageries*; Jue, *Wild Blue Media: Thinking through Seawater* (Durham, NC: Duke University Press, 2020); and Starosielski, *The Undersea Network* (Durham, NC: Duke University Press, 2015).

81.  Hazel Carby, *Race Men* (Cambridge, MA: Harvard University Press, 1998); Paul Gilroy, *Against Race: Imagining Political Culture beyond the Color Line* (Cambridge, MA: Harvard University Press, 2000); and Kobena Mercer, *Welcome to the Jungle: New Positions in Black Cultural Studies* (New York: Routledge, 1994).

82.  Gilroy, *Against Race*, 33.

83.  Mbembe, *Necropolitics*, 134.

84.  Sybille Krämer, *Medium, Messenger, Transmission: An Approach to Media Philosophy* (Amsterdam: Amsterdam University Press, 2015).

85.  Peters, *Marvelous Clouds*; and Lance Strate, "The Medium and McLuhan's Message," *Razon Y Palabra*, accessed October 2, 2020, www.razonypalabra.org.mx/N/N80/V80/00A_Strate_V80.pdf.

86.  Raymond Williams, "The Analysis of Culture," in *Cultural Theory and Popular Culture*, ed. John Storey (Athens: University of Georgia Press, 1998), 48–56. Hall, "Marxist Structuralism."

87.  Stuart Hall, "Gramsci's Relevance for the Study of Race and Ethnicity," *Journal of Communication Inquiry* 10, no. 2 (1986): 15.

88.  Lawrence Grossberg, *Cultural Studies in the Future Tense* (Durham, NC: Duke University Press, 2010), 191.

89.  Wendy Hoi Kyong Chun, "Introduction: Race and/as Technology, or How to Do Things to Race," *Camera Obscura* 70, 24, no. 1 (2009): 7–35.

90.  Krämer, *Medium, Messenger, Transmission*, 35.

## CHAPTER 1. TECHNOLOGICAL DARWINISM

*Epigraph*: Charles Darwin, *The Descent of Man, and Selection in Relation to Sex* (Princeton, NJ: Princeton University Press, 1981), 232, emphasis added.

1.  J.S. Henslow, "From J.S.: 24 August 1831," *Darwin Correspondence Project*, accessed October 22, 2020, www.darwinproject.ac.uk/letter/DCP-LETT-105.xml.

2.  Also, due to his father not wanting him to go, Darwin initially rejected Henson's recommendation. But Darwin's father changed his mind after receiving correspondence from Darwin's grandfather, Josiah Wedgewood. See Henslow, "From J.S.: 24 August 1831"; and Charles Darwin, "To J.S. Henslow: 30 [August 1831]," *Darwin Correspondence Project*, accessed October 22, 2020, www.darwinproject.ac.uk/letter/DCP-LETT-107.xml.

3.  Charles Darwin, *On the Origin of Species by Means of Natural Selection* (1859; Mineola, NY: Dover Publications, 2006).

4.  In addition to Darwin's intimacy, much has been written on FitzRoy's

attempt to return three captives that he had captured from Tierra del Fuego on the first mission of the H.M.S. Beagle between 1826 and 1830. The Fuegians were "neither enslaved laborers nor free colonial subjects but" were "objects of scientific and cultural curiosity." Thus scientific inquiry exceeded Darwin's notebook and FitzRoy's surveying to include the captive Fuegians as *objects* of Western scientific fascination. Even though Darwin disapproved of the kidnapping, by the time he wrote *On the Origin of Species*, he still described "those of Tierra del Fuegian" as "savages," which is to say they were *undomesticated*, unlike those *civilized* people who had kidnapped them. The Fuegians were close to a "state of nature," or what Western social contract theorists once argued was the "condition of *all* men" at one time or another. The state of nature was deemed a state in which humans were once closer in thought and action to animals than to what the West today calls "civilization." Unlike the Fuegians, their Western European kidnappers were presumably able to emerge out of nature long ago and into civilization. This effectively meant that the Fuegians were stuck in the past, in the state of nature, while white Western Europeans and North Americans progressed forward. For a description of the ways that the Fuegians were objects of scientific inquiry, see Nihad Farooq, *Undisciplined: Science, Ethnography, and Personhood in the Americas, 1830–1940* (New York: New York University Press, 2016); for more on Darwin's descriptions of the Fuegians, see Darwin, *On the Origin of Species*, 12; for more on the state of nature, see Charles Mills, *The Racial Contract* (Ithaca, NY: Cornell University Press, 1997), 12.

5. Farooq, *Undisciplined*, 166–173.

6. Farooq, *Undisciplined*.

7. Charles Darwin, *Journal of Researches into the Natural History and Geology of the Countries Visited during the Voyage of H.M.S. Beagle Round the World, under the Command of Capt. Fitz Roy, R.N.* (New York: D. Appleton and Company, 1871), 500.

8. Cedric Robinson, "The Inventions of the Negro," *Social Identities* 7, no. 3 (2001): 343.

9. Darwin, *Voyage of H.M.S. Beagle*, 499.

10. Darwin, *On the Origin of Species*, 3, emphasis added.

11. Darwin, *Descent of Man*, 381–382, 388, emphasis added.

12. See Carothers, *The African Mind in Health and Disease*; and Herbert Spencer, *The Principles of Psychology* (London: Longman, Brown, Green, Longmans, 1855), 461.

13. Banu Subramaniam, *Ghost Stories for Darwin: The Science of Variation and the Politics of Diversity* (Champaign: University of Illinois Press, 2014), 47.

14. Saidiya Hartman, *Scenes of Subjection: Terror, Slavery, and Self-Making in Nineteenth-Century America* (New York: Oxford University Press, 1997), 38.

15. Candice Jenkins, *Private Lives, Proper Relations: Regulating Black Intimacy* (Minneapolis: University of Minnesota Press, 2007), 18–19.

16. Jenkins, *Private Lives, Proper Relations*, for licentious, see p. 8; for republican family ideals, see p. 5.

17. For more on this relationship between racial violence, intimacy, and

eroticism, see the work of Sharon Patricia Holland, *The Erotic Life of Racism* (Durham, NC: Duke University Press, 2012).

18. Brian Hochman, *Savage Preservation: The Ethnographic Origins of Modern Media Technology* (Minneapolis: University of Minnesota Press, 2014), 19–29.

19. Sylvia Wynter, "Unsettling the Coloniality of Being/Power/Truth/Freedom: Towards the Human, after Man, Its Overrepresentation—An Argument," *The New Centennial Review* 3, no. 3 (2003): 257–337.

20. Sylvia Wynter, "On How We Mistook the Map for the Territory, and Re-imprisoned Ourselves in Our Unbearable Wrongness of Being, of Désêrtre: Black Studies Toward the Human Project," in *Not Only the Master's Tools: African-American Studies in Theory and Practice*, ed. Lewis Gordan and Jane Gordan (Boulder, CO: Paradigm Publishers, 2006), 126.

21. Lisa Lowe, *The Intimacy of Four Continents* (Durham, NC: Duke University Press, 2015), 36.

22. Scott, *Conscripts of Modernity*, 27.

23. James, *You Don't Play with Revolution*, 218. And C.L.R. James, *The Black Jacobins: Toussaint L'Ouverture and the San Domingo Revolution* (1938, New York: Vintage, 1989).

24. Central Intelligence Agency, "Break-up of the Colonial Empires."

25. James, *You Don't Play with Revolution*, 64.

26. Carothers, *The Psychology of Mau Mau* (Nairobi: Colony and Protectorate of Kenya, 1955), https://ufdc.ufl.edu/UF00023305/00001/1j, 6.

27. Carothers, *Psychology of Mau Mau*, 6.

28. Carothers, *Psychology of Mau Mau*, 23.

29. Carothers, *African Mind in Health and Disease*, 7.

30. Johannes Fabian, *Time and the Other: How Anthropology Makes Its Object* (1983; New York: Columbia University Press, 2014).

31. Bernard Stiegler, *Technics and Time, 2: Disorientation* (Stanford, CA: Stanford University Press, 2008).

32. Walter Rodney, *How Europe Underdeveloped Africa*, 8.

33. Carothers, *African Mind in Health and Disease*, 8

34. For more information, see the Marshall McLuhan Collection at Library and Archives of Canada.

35. Smith, *How Race Is Made*.

36. Neda Atanasoski and Kalindi Vora, *Surrogate Humanity: Race, Robots, and the Politics of Technological Futures* (Durham, NC: Duke University Press, 2019), 121–123.

37. Atanasoski and Vora, *Surrogate Humanity: Race*, 123.

38. McLuhan, *Understanding Media*, 19.

39. I put biological sex in quotes to speak to the long line of research that notes less distinctions between gender and sex than Darwin. But biological sex is more accurate of a terminology for Darwin's own time period. To see the complexity, see the work of Judith Butler, *Gender Trouble* (New York: Routledge, 2007).

40. John Tyler Bonner and Robert May, introduction to *The Descent of*

*Man, and Selection in Relation to Sex*, ed. Bonner and May (Princeton, NJ: Princeton University Press, 1981), ix.

41. Darwin, *Descent of Man*, 56. Elizabeth Grosz, *The Nick of Time: Politics, Evolution, and the Untimely* (Durham, NC: Duke University Press, 2004).

42. Darwin, *Descent of Man*, 249–250, emphasis added.

43. Grosz, *Nick of Time*, 91.

44. Though influenced by Grosz, this book takes an alternative position: I see sexual and artificial selection as inseparable, but, unlike Grosz, I ask the question of racial difference along the line of artificiality (*man's* selection, or man's toolmaking capacity). Maybe a better way to say this is that we must make even less of a distinction between artificial and sexual selection.

45. Robinson, "Inventions of the Negro."

46. Cedric Robinson, *Black Marxism: The Making of the Black Radical Tradition* (Chapel Hill: University of North Carolina Press, 2000).

47. Nahum Chandler, *X—The Problem of the Negro as a Problem for Thought* (New York: Fordham Press, 2013).

48. Natural selection was the process by which individual and inherited variations in different species allowed for some to survive based on changes in nature, while others died out. In other words, natural selection is a theory designed to "determine how far the new characters thus arising shall be preserved" in later generations. Natural selection was efficient, particularly when conditions of one species had reached saturation. Survival of a species was often at random, made up of missteps and luck that might end up preserving the fittest, or those whose variation assisted them with the changing conditions. Still, survival was no guarantee, just somewhat likely. Via natural selection, biological entities like plants and animals could die off or survive based on nature's assortment of factors introduced into the larger ecosystem. Some of the factors could be an abundance of food or an increase in predators; threats and/or benefits could likewise fluctuate based on everything from rising shore tides, to expanding deserts, and extended winters. For more on this, see Darwin, *On the Origin of Species*, 10.

49. Spencer, *Principles of Psychology*.

50. T. J. Demos, *Decolonizing Nature: Contemporary Art and the Politics of Ecology* (Cambridge, MA: MIT Press, 2016); and Doreen Massey, *Space, Place, and Gender* (Minneapolis: University of Minnesota Press, 1994).

51. In important works like Michael Stamm's *Dead Tree Media*, for example, the tree (nature) is selected by man and then artificially turned into media for one of his largest institutions—the newspaper publishing industry. See Stamm, *Dead Tree Media: Manufacturing the Newspaper in Twentieth Century North America* (Baltimore, MD: John Hopkins University Press, 2018).

52. Peters, *Marvelous Clouds*, 6–7.

53. Massey, *Space, Place, and Gender*.

54. Similarly, Tiffany King argues that there are "other kinds of (and often forgotten) relationships" that must be remembered that captive "Black bodies have to plants, objects, and non-human life forms." Likewise, as I have argued, those *other relationships* call for us to theorize the Negro not solely as a subject

or occupier of space but as consistent with the Western discourses of space, nature, raw materials, *and*, I argue, media. For more on this, see Tiffany King, "The Labor of (Re)reading Plantation Landscapes Fungible(ly)," *Antipode* 48, no. 4 (2016): 1023; and Towns, "Black 'Matter' Lives," *Women's Studies in Communication* 41, no. 4 (2018): 351.

55. See Tiffany King, *The Black Shoals: Offshore Formations of Black and Native Studies* (Durham, NC: Duke University Press, 2019).

56. Martin Heidegger, *The Question Concerning Technology and Other Essays* (New York: Garland Publishing, 1977).

57. Frantz Fanon, *Black Skin, White Mask* (New York: Grove Press, 2008), 93, emphasis in the original.

58. Fanon, *Wretched of the Earth*.

59. Fanon, *Black Skin*, 93.

60. Fanon, *Black Skin*, 119.

61. Ronald Judy, "Fanon's Body of Black Experience," in *Fanon: A Critical Reader*, ed. Lewis Gordon, T. Sharpley-Whiting, and Renee White (Hoboken, NJ: Wiley-Blackwell, 1996), 53–73.

62. Cleve Wootson Jr., "A Black Yale Student Fell Asleep in Her Dorm's Common Room. A White Student Called the Police," *Washington Post*, May 11, 2018, www.washingtonpost.com/news/grade-point/wp/2018/05/10/a-bla ck-yale-student-fell-asleep-in-her-dorms-common-room-a-white-student-called -police/?utm_term=.d91d97c17c90.

63. Hortense Spillers, *Black, White, and in Color: Essays on American Literature and Culture* (Chicago: University of Chicago Press, 2003).

64. Some argue that Darwin allows for an antiracist position that is later misused in racist ways. I do not try to refute these positions as much as show that the presumed "antiracism" of Darwin is structured on the racialization of his conceptions of time and space as objective modes of reading the world. For those who try to point to Darwin's antiracist potential, or at least the misuse of Darwin for racist ends, see Grosz, *Nick of Time*; and Arun Saldanha, "Reontologising Race: The Machinic Geography of Phenotype," *Environment and Planning D: Society and Space* 24 (2006): 17.

65. Sylvia Wynter, "The Ceremony Found: Towards the Autopoetic Turn/ Overturn, Its Autonomy of Human Agency and Extraterritoriality of (Self-) Cognition," in *Black Knowledges/Black Struggles*, ed. Jason Ambroise and Sabine Broeck (Liverpool, UK: Liverpool University Press, 2015), 241.

66. William Wells Brown, *Clotel; or, The President's Daughter; a Narrative of Slave Life in the United States* (1853; New York: Collier Books, 1970).

67. Krämer argues that all media assume a morbidity, which dates back to the myth of Pheidippides, the Greek messenger who died while delivering a message of victory over the Persians in the Battle of Marathon. I am pulling this argument into a discussion of the Negro. See Krämer, *Medium, Messenger, Transmission*.

68. Brown, *Clotel*, 43.

69. Katherine McKittrick, *Demonic Grounds: Black Women and the Car-*

*tographies of Struggle* (Minneapolis: University of Minnesota Press, 2006), 65–66.

70. Krämer, *Medium, Messenger, Transmission*, 43.

71. Darwin, *On the Origin of Species*, 19–20, emphasis added.

72. Darwin, *On the Origin of Species*, 19.

73. Zakiyyah Iman Jackson, "Losing Manhood: Animality and Plasticity in the (Neo)Slave Narrative, *Qui Parle: Critical Humanities and Social Sciences* 25, nos. 1–2 (2016): 95–136.

74. W.E.B. Du Bois, *Black Reconstruction in America, 1860–1880* (New York: The Free Press, 1992), 35.

75. Darwin, *Descent of Man*, 296, emphasis added.

76. Nick Fagge, "Picks, Pans and Bare Hands: How Miners in the Heart of Africa Toil in Terrible Conditions to Extract the Rare Minerals That Power Your iPhone," *Daily Mail*, October 22, 2015, www.dailymail.co.uk/news/article-3280872/iPhone-mineral-miners-Africa-use-bare-hands-coltan.html; and Parikka, *Geology of Media*, 46.

77. G.W.F. Hegel, *The Philosophy of History* (Kitchener, ON: Batoche Books, 2001), 111, emphasis added.

78. Hegel, *Philosophy of History*, 113.

79. Robinson, "Inventions of the Negro"; and Wynter, "On How We Mistook the Map for the Territory."

80. Christian Fuchs, "Karl Marx & Communication @ 200: Towards a Marxian Theory of Communication," *tripleC* 16, no. 2 (2018): 518–534; and Vincent Mosco, *The Political Economy of Communication* (New York: Sage Publications, 2009).

81. Krämer, *Medium*, 43.

82. Darwin, *Descent of Man*, 34.

83. Armond Towns, "The (Black) Elephant in the Room: McLuhan and the Racial," *Canadian Journal of Communication*, 44, no. 4 (2019): 553.

84. Darwin, *Descent of Man*, 296.

85. Grosz, *Nick of Time*, 65, emphasis added.

86. Kittler, *Gramophone, Film, Typewriter*, 16.

87. Jonathan Amos, "America Colonisation 'Cooled Earth's Climate,'" BBC News, January 31, 2019, www.bbc.com/news/science-environment-47063973; Oliver Milman, "European Colonization of the Americas Killed So Many It Cooled Earth's Climate," *The Guardian*, January 31, 2019, www.theguardian.com/environment/2019/jan/31/european-colonization-of-americas-helped-cause-climate-change; and "European Colonization of Americas 'Cooled Earth's Climate,' *MSN*, February 1, 2019, www.msn.com/en-us/travel/news/european-colonization-of-americas-cooled-earths-climate/vp-BBT1dPo.

88. Milman, "European Colonization."

89. Milman, "European Colonization."

90. Milman, "European Colonization."

91. Parikka, *Geology of Media*.

92. Kathryn Yusoff, *A Billion Black Anthropocenes or None* (Minneapolis: University of Minnesota Press, 2018).

93.  Harold Innis, *Empire and Communications* (New York: Rowman & Littlefield, 2007).

94.  King, "Labor of (Re)reading Plantation Landscapes."

## CHAPTER 2. BLACK ESCAPISM ON THE UNDERGROUND (BLACK) ANTHROPOCENE

An earlier version of this chapter appeared in the journal *Communication and Critical/Cultural Studies*. I would like to thank the journal and the former editor, Greg Dickinson, for permission to reprint certain parts of the article for this chapter. See Armond R. Towns, "Rebels of the underground: Media, Orality, and the Routes of Black Emancipation," *Communication and Critical/Cultural Studies* 13, no. 2 (2016): 184–197.

*Epigraph*: Walter Ong, *Orality and Literacy* (New York: Routledge, 2012), 2.

1.  Michelle Oliver, "A Look at the Roots of the Underground Railroad in Detroit," *Click on Detroit*, February 21, 2019, www.clickondetroit.com/black -history-month/a-look-at-the-roots-of-the-underground-railroad-in-detroit.

2.  David Blight, *Passages to Freedom: The Underground in History and Memory* (New York: Harper Paperbacks, 2006).

3.  Katherine McKittrick critiques this tendency in "Freedom Is a Secret," in *Black Geographies and the Politics of Place*, ed. McKittrick and Clyde Woods (New York: South End Press, 2007), 97–114.

4.  McKittrick, *Demonic Grounds*.

5.  See the first chapter of Fred Moten, *In the Break: The Aesthetics of the Black Radical Tradition* (Minneapolis: University of Minnesota Press, 2003).

6.  Simone Browne "Digital Epidermalization: Race, Identity and Biometrics," *Critical Sociology* 36, no. 1 (2010): 131–150.

7.  Ong, *Orality and Literacy*, 8.

8.  Walter Ong, *An Ong Reader: Challenges for Further Inquiry*, ed. Thomas Farrell and Paul Soukup (New York: Hampton Press, 2002).

9.  Paul Levinson, *Digital McLuhan: A Guide to the Information Millennium* (New York: Routledge, 1999).

10.  Hochman, *Savage Preservation*, 4.

11.  Darwin, *Descent of Man*, 296, emphasis added.

12.  Hochman, *Savage Preservation*, 11.

13.  Carmen Kynard, *Vernacular Insurrections: Race, Black Protest, and the New Century in Composition-Literacies Studies* (Albany, NY: SUNY Press, 2013), 4.

14.  Armond Towns, "Rebels of the Underground: Media, Orality, and the Routes of Black Emancipation," *Communication and Critical/Cultural Studies* 13, no. 2 (2016): 184–197.

15.  Judy, *DisForming the American Canon*, 161.

16.  Innis, *Empire and Communications*.

17.  Keeling, *Queer Times, Black Futures*.

18.  Paul Gilroy, *The Black Atlantic: Modernity and Double-Consciousness* (Cambridge, MA: Harvard University Press, 1993).

19. In Lisa Gitelman's important work she talks about "scriptural economies" as a way of pushing back against McLuhan's print culture. Print culture
assumes, for Gitelman, that the printing press is the central medium of transformation. Alternatively, Gitelman argues that scriptural economies assume a complex mixture of media, which always blur what constitutes "print" in the first
place. In the process, both Gutenberg's press and the Xerox are a part of a larger
economy of recording. I am, likewise, using media economy to point to the in-
terrelation between multiple media and how they always interact depending on
context. Furthermore, Gitelman points to how such economies have epistemological implications. It is here that I see alternative epistemologies as important,
those that we focus on in Black studies have a media studies association as well.
For more information on this, see Lisa Gitelman, *Paper Knowledge: Toward a
Media History of Documents* (Durham, NC: Duke University Press, 2014).

20. Lewis Morgan, "Ancient Society" (The Project Gutenberg), accessed
April 4, 2020, www.gutenberg.org/files/45950/45950-h/45950-h.htm, p. 41.

21. Carey, *Communication as Culture*; Jeremy Packer, "Rethinking Dependency: New Relations of Transportation and Communication," in *Thinking with James Carey: Essays on Communications, Transportation, History*, ed.
Packer and Craig Robertson (Bern, Switzerland: Peter Lang, 2016), 79–100;
and Jonathan Sterne, "Transportation and Communication: Together as You've
Always Wanted Them," in *Thinking with James Carey*, 117–136.

22. E. Delorus Preston Jr., "The Genesis of the Underground Railroad,"
*Journal of Negro History* 18, no. 2 (1933): 166.

23. "Voices Remembering Slavery: Freed People Tell Their Stories," Library
of Congress, accessed April 4, 2020, www.loc.gov/collections/voices-remem
bering-slavery/about-this-collection/.

24. "Dr. D.B. Gaines, Little Rock, Arkansas," Library of Congress, accessed
April 4, 2020, www.loc.gov/resource/mesn.023/?sp=7.

25. W.E.B. Du Bois, "The Talented Tenth: Memorial Address," in *W.E.B.
Du Bois: A Reader*, ed. David Levering Lewis (New York: Henry Holt and
Company, 1995), 353; and Du Bois, *Black Reconstruction in America*.

26. During the early nineteenth century, for example, some would contest
the slave narratives and their arguments of harsh treatment, suggesting that
Black people who ran away did so only because they were suffering from a
severe mental illness. At the Underground Railroad's height, for example, the
physician Samuel Cartwright coined the term "drapetomania," an illness that
he fabricated to describe the actions of Black people who ran from their enslavement. For Cartwright, drapetomania was what caused Black people to flee
in the first place, potentially placing themselves into life-threatening situations
in the process, away from the presumable safe haven of enslavement, which
included mostly benevolent white masters. See Samuel Cartwright, "Diseases
and Peculiarities of the Negro Race," in *The Case of the South*, ed. Paul Paskoff
and Daniel Wilson (Baton Rouge: Louisiana State University Press, 1982), 35.

27. Gitelman, *Paper Knowledge*.

28. Judy, *DisForming the American Canon*, 246.

29. Harold Innis, *The Biases of Communication* (Toronto: University of To-

ronto Press, 2008), 33; and Karl Marx, *Grundrisse* (New York: Random House, 1973), 539.

30. Judy, *DisForming the American Canon*, 2.

31. Preston, "Genesis of the Underground Railroad," 148–149, 170.

32. Preston, "Genesis of the Underground Railroad," 155, 169.

33. Preston, "Genesis of the Underground Railroad," 167, emphasis added.

34. McKittrick, *Demonic Grounds*; and McKittrick, "Freedom Is a Secret."

35. Media philosophers have long made links between geography and communication. For example, see Carey, *Communication as Culture*. However, I am adding race to these discussions.

36. McLuhan, *Understanding Media*.

37. Sean Cubitt, *Finite Media: Environmental Implications of Digital Technologies* (Durham, NC: Duke University Press, 2017), 20.

38. Donna Haraway, "Anthropocene, Capitalocene, Plantationocene, Chthulucene: Making Kin," *Environmental Humanities* 6 (2015): 159.

39. Parikka, *Geology of Media*.

40. Yusoff, *Billion Black Anthropocenes*, 61.

41. Haraway, "Anthropocene, Capitalocene, Plantationocene, Chthulucene," 159.

42. Janae Davis, Alex Moulton, Levi Van Sant, and Brian Williams, "Anthropocene, Capitalocene,… Plantationocene?: A Manifesto for Ecological Justice in an Age of Global Crisis," *Geography Compass* 13, no. 5 (2019): 5.

43. Katherine McKittrick, "Plantation Futures," *Small Axe: A Caribbean Journal of Criticism* 13, no. 3, 42 (2013): 10.

44. McKittrick, "Plantation Futures," 2.

45. McKittrick, "Plantation Futures," 3.

46. Robin Kelley, *Freedom Dreams: The Black Radical Imagination* (New York: Beacon Press, 2003).

47. Of course, this is not an entirely new argument, as there have been multiple calls to rethink the different genres of human as in line with Western conceptions of nature and how the Black Anthropocene opens up this space. Yet I am pointing to the use of such conceptions *for* media philosophy, an area silent on the Black Anthropocene. Indeed, plantations can be argued to function as what Lisa Parks and Nicole Starosielski classify as "media infrastructures": they are materialist/discursive constructs; only for me, such constructs are concerned with the production and distribution of the Negro as a medium. For more on media infrastructures, see Lisa Parks and Nicole Starosielski, introduction to *Signal Traffic: Critical Studies of Media Infrastructures*, ed. Parks and Starosielski (Champaign: University of Illinois Press, 2015), 5.

48. See "Journey to Freedom: Underground Railroad," *National Geographic*, accessed November 4, 2019, www.nationalgeographic.org/interactive /journey-freedom-underground-railroad/. Recently there have been reports that many white visitors do not want to hear about slavery on plantation tours, even as they continue to sign up for them. See Gillian Brockell, "Some White People Don't Want to Hear about Slavery at Plantations Built by Slaves," *Washington*

*Post*, August 8, 2019, www.washingtonpost.com/history/2019/08/08/some-whi
te-people-dont-want-hear-about-slavery-plantations-built-by-slaves/.

49. For more information, see Gilroy, *Black Atlantic*; and McKittrick, "Freedom Is a Secret."

50. Hochman, *Savage Preservation*, 4.

51. Davis et al., "Anthropocene, Capitalocene,... Plantationocene?"

52. William Wells Brown, "Narrative of William Wells Brown, a Fugitive Slave (Excerpts)," in *Slave Narratives of the Underground*, ed. Christine Rusdisel and Bob Blaisdell (Mineola, NY: Dover Publications, 2014), 11, emphasis added.

53. Josiah Henson, "An Autobiography of the Reverend Josiah Henson," in *Four Fugitive Slave Narratives*, ed. Robin Winks (Reading, MA: Addison-Wesley Publishing Company, 1969), 59.

54. Frederick Douglass, *Narrative of the Life of Frederick Douglass, an American Slave* (New York: Barnes & Noble Classics, 2003), 78.

55. Eber Pettit, "Margaret: Born on a Slave Ship," in *Slave Narratives of the Underground*, ed. Christine Rusdisel and Bob Blaisdell (Mineola, NY: Dover Publications, 2014), 167.

56. Benjamin Drew, "The Refugee: A North-Side View of Slavery," in *Four Fugitive Slave Narratives*, ed. Robin Winks (Reading, MA: Addison-Wesley Publishing Company, 1969), 182–183.

57. Drew, "The Refugee," 15.

58. Henson, "Autobiography of the Reverend Josiah Henson," 81.

59. Peters, *Marvelous Clouds*.

60. This draws from Sarah Sharma's important concept "power chronography," which argues that temporality is experienced at the intersections of power. People can exist in what may seem like the same space, but the time in which they experience that space suggests differential power relations. For more on this, see Sharma, *In the Meantime: Temporality and Cultural Politics* (Durham, NC: Duke University Press, 2014).

61. Douglass, *Narrative of the Life of Frederick Douglass*, 78.

62. Sharma, *In the Meantime*.

63. For more on this, see Browne, *Dark Matters*.

64. Toni Morrison, *Beloved* (New York: Penguin Books, 2004); and William Still, "Abolitionist in the Underground," in *Slave Narratives of the Underground*, ed. Christine Rusdisel and Bob Blaisdell (Mineola, NY: Dover Publications, 2014), 21–38.

65. Indeed, as Sylviane Diouf reminds us, 15–20 percent of enslaved Black people brought to the Americas were Muslim, Arabic-speaking (and likely Arabic-writing) people. See Sylviane Diouf, *Servants of Allah: African Muslims Enslaved in the Americas* (New York: New York University Press, 2013).

66. My thinking on this builds off of Talal Asad's work, which holds that the Western liberal idea of dying and killing largely misunderstands all dying and killing within its only secularized framework. For more on this, see Talal Asad, *On Suicide Bombing* (New York: Columbia University Press, 2007).

67. Sarah Bradford, "'Harriet Tubman': *Harriet Tubman: The Moses of*

*Her People* (Excerpts)," in *Slave Narratives of the Underground*, ed. Christine Rusdisel and Bob Blaisdell (Mineola, NY: Dover Publications, 2014), 183–190.

68. Bradford, "'Harriet Tubman.'"

69. Austin Steward, "Austin Steward: Twenty-Two Years a Slave and Forty Years a Freeman," in *Four Fugitive Slave Narratives*, ed. Robin Winks (Reading, MA: Addison-Wesley Publishing Company, 1969), 68.

70. Drew, "The Refugee," 29.

71. C. Riley Snorton, *Black on Both Sides: A Racial History of Trans Identity* (Minneapolis: University of Minnesota, 2017), 57–59.

72. Still, "Abolitionist in the Underground," 39.

73. Browne, *Dark Matters*, 55.

74. Audre Lorde, *Sister Outsider: Essays and Speeches by Audre Lorde* (New York: Random House Press, 2007), 112.

75. McKittrick, "Freedom Is a Secret," 100.

76. Hartman, *Scenes of Subjection*.

77. McLuhan, *Understanding*; Marshall McLuhan and Bruce Powers, *The Global Village: Transformations in World Life and Media in the 21st Century* (New York: Oxford University Press, 1992), 9; and Ong, *Orality and Literacy*.

78. Judy, *DisForming the American Canon*, 147.

79. James Cone, *A Black Theology of Liberation* (New York: Orbis Books, 2010).

80. Du Bois, *Black Reconstruction in America*, 124, emphasis added.

81. Andre Carrington, *Speculative Blackness: The Future of Race in Science Fiction* (Minneapolis: University of Minnesota Press, 2016), 2.

82. Carey, *Communication as Culture*.

83. Guillory, "Genesis of the Media Concept."

## CHAPTER 3. TOWARD A THEORY OF INTERCOMMUNAL MEDIA

*Epigraph*: Lynn Spigel and Michael Curtin, introduction to *The Revolution Wasn't Televised: Sixties Television and Social Conflict*, ed. Spigel and Curtin (New York: Routledge, 1997), 5.

1. There were a number of reasons that Newton sought to illustrate the Party's intellectual plan, but maybe the most pressing was that he sought to end the bloodshed. In the five years since the Party started in 1966, the FBI, local police, and government officials throughout the country perpetrated the harshest forms of racial violence against the organization, including everything from policy changes, to wiretaps, to COINTELPRO, to political incarceration, to actual assassinations. See Joshua Bloom and Waldo Martin Jr., *Black against Empire: The History and Politics of the Black Panther Party* (Berkeley: University of California Press, 2013).

2. Jane Rhodes, *Framing the Black Panthers: The Spectacular Rise of a Black Power Icon* (Champaign: University of Illinois Press, 2017).

3. Zayd-Malik Shakur, "Fascist Pigs Murder Man Frame Connecticut Panthers," *The Black Panther: Black Community News Service* (San Francisco), June 7, 1969, 11.

4. Bloom and Martin, *Black against Empire*; and John Narayan, "The Wages of Whiteness in the Absence of Wages: Racial Capitalism, Reactionary Intercommunalism and the Rise of Trumpism," *Third World Quarterly* (2017): 1–19, DOI: 10.1080/01436597.2017.1368012.

5. Michael Fischbach, *Black Power and Palestine: Transnational Countries of Color* (Redwood City, CA: Stanford University Press, 2019), 27.

6. Bodroghkozy, *Groove Tube*.

7. Bloom and Martin, *Black against Empire*; and Sohail Daulatzai, *Fifty Years of "The Battle of Algiers": Past as Prologue* (Minneapolis: University of Minnesota Press, 2016).

8. Huey Newton, "The Technology Question: 1972," in *The Huey P. Newton Reader*, ed. David Hilliard and Donald Weise (New York: Seven Stories Press, 2002), 256–266.

9. This is not to say no forms of U.S. Black solidarity with the Third World existed prior to electronic media. As Susan Buck-Morss argues, for example, many white people throughout the Americas sought to keep Black enslaved people from reading about the Haitian revolution, so as to prevent a larger Black solidarity with those revolutionaries. Thus the more important point was that electronic media, like other media beforehand, were mobilized by the Black Panther Party to solidify what was already there. For more on the Haitian revolution and media, particularly newspapers, see Susan Buck-Morss, "Hegel and Haiti," *Critical Inquiry* 26, no. 4 (2000): 821–865.

10. C.L.R. James, *The Black Jacobins: Toussaint L'Ouverture and the San Domingo Revolution* (New York: Vintage, 1989).

11. Gitelman, *Paper Knowledge*.

12. Newton, "Intercommunalism," in *The Huey P. Newton Reader*, ed. David Hilliard and Donald Weise (New York: Seven Stories Press, 2002), 184.

13. Newton, "Intercommunalism," 185.

14. Newton, "Intercommunalism," 185.

15. Newton, "Intercommunalism," 185.

16. Ture and Hamilton, *Black Power*.

17. Newton, "Intercommunalism," 185.

18. Newton, "Intercommunalism," 185, emphasis added.

19. Newton, "Intercommunalism," 186.

20. Charlton McIlwain, *Black Software: The Internet and Racial Justice, from the AfroNet to Black Lives Matter* (New York: Oxford University Press, 2020), 8.

21. While these tensions are not the explicit focus of this chapter, some Party members did not agree with Newton's intercommunalism, and publicly stated as much. But often, the confusion over the term was not as publicly stated. Donna Murch rightly notes that for "much of the rank and file, the concept of 'intercommunalism' remained elusive." Likewise, with the majority of the funding for the Party's political prisoners going to trials like Newton's, while less funds went to other high-profile cases such as Party members in New York City, a major break in the Party had already been brewing by the time Newton began to theorize intercommunalism. Some of the tensions between the Oakland-based Party

and other chapters throughout the United States would be a disagreement on the usage of militant, guerilla war style tactics. These important tensions can be better seen in some of the histories and personal stories and biographies of the Party, which are not my focus. Still, intercommunalism would be the position of the Party until its end. See Donna Murch, *Living for the City: Migration, Education, and the Rise of the Black Panther Party in Oakland, California* (Chapel Hill: University of North Carolina Press, 2010), 193–196.

22. Newton, "Intercommunalism," 188, emphasis added.

23. Marshall McLuhan, *Understanding Me: Lectures and Interviews* (Cambridge, MA: MIT Press, 2005), 62.

24. McLuhan, *Understanding Media*, 6–7, emphasis added.

25. While the Party made somewhat progressive public statements on patriarchy, gender, and sexuality, privately some of its Black male leaders engaged in sexist and homophobic behaviors. As Elaine Brown noted, "We didn't get these brothers from revolutionary heaven." Newton was often one of the worst offenders. Toward the end of Newton's life, he became increasingly violent and erratic, particularly with some of his closest male friends and multiple female lovers. See Elaine Brown, *A Taste of Power: A Black Woman's Story* (New York: Random House, 1994); Safiya Bukhari, *The War Before: The True Life Story of Becoming a Black Panther, Keeping the Faith in Prison and Fighting for Those Left Behind* (New York: The Feminist Press, 2010); Bloom and Martin, *Black against Empire*; and Stanley Nelson, dir., *The Black Panthers: Vanguard of the Revolution* (motion picture) (New York: Public Broadcasting Service, 2015).

26. Katherine McKittrick, "Mathematics Black Life," *The Black Scholar* 44, no. 2 (2014): 23.

27. White, *Challenge of Blackness*.

28. This positions Newton as in line with later theorists, like Michael Hardt and Antonio Negri, all of which have outlined theoretical foundations of Global South solidarities. See Michael Hardt and Antonio Negri, *Multitude: War and Democracy in the Age of Empire* (New York: Penguin Books, 2005).

29. Ashley Farmer, *Remaking Black Power: How Black Women Transformed an Era* (Chapel Hill: University of North Carolina Press, 2017); and Murch, *Living for the City*.

30. Of course, this is not to argue that global concerns of racism and capitalism were unknown in the United States prior to television. Yet media used by the Party (radio, film, television, newspapers, etc.) are part of a larger, changing media economy that Newton called the global village—not reducible to electronic media alone. For more work that considers media, transnational critiques, and their relationship to the Black Power movements, see Sohail Daulatzai, *Black Star, Crescent Moon: The Muslim International and Black Freedom beyond America* (Minneapolis: University of Minnesota Press, 2012).

31. Murch, *Living for the City*, 4.

32. Clyde Woods, "'Sittin' on Top of the World': The Challenges of Blues and Hip Hop Geography," in *Black Geographies and the Politics of Place*, ed. Katherine McKittrick and Clyde Woods (Toronto, ON: Between the Lines Press, 2007), 56.

33.  Keeanga-Yamahtta Taylor, *From #BlackLivesMatter to Black Liberation* (Chicago: Haymarket Books, 2016).

34.  See White, *Challenge of Blackness*, 107–108.

35.  Even though technology is a central component of intercommunalism, Newton did not provide a complex definition of technology. Newton delivered nothing more than a few vague references to technology, as airplanes, advertisements, space shuttles, and television. However, Newton's reference to the global village suggests that his theory of technology was influenced by McLuhan's theory of electronic media. With the rapid spread of information and the new relations of involvement and participation, despite physical distances, one can see why Newton might find some interest in McLuhan's metaphor of the global village.

36.  Ture and Hamilton, *Black Power*, 6.

37.  Fanon, *Wretched of the Earth*.

38.  For discussions on media as extensions, see McLuhan, *Understanding Media*. For discussions on man as overrepresented as white and male, see Wynter, "Unsettling the Coloniality of Being/Power/Truth/Freedom."

39.  Heidegger, *Question Concerning Technology*, 14.

40.  Newton, "Technology Question," 256.

41.  See Mehrsa Baradaran, *The Color of Money: Black Banks and the Racial Wealth Gap* (Cambridge, MA: Harvard University Press, 2017).

42.  Baradaran, *Color of Money*.

43.  In his autobiography, *Revolutionary Suicide*, Newton provides one example of such sexism. During the early stages of the Party, Newton's autobiography recalls a sexual relationship that he had with a woman named Dolores. At this time, the Party had just developed "communal living," or "Panther Pads," where members could live with one another and engage in sexual activity, without the traditional familial structures. For Newton, such communal living moved away from bourgeois relations of possession, toward principles of "nonpossessiveness." He argued that the reason that it was necessary to move away from such possession was because possession of a partner, in similar ways as the possession of property, "absorbed all of a man's energies and did not leave him free to develop potential talents, to be creative, or make a contribution in other areas of life." Dolores was one of the many women who Newton was involved with at these Panther Pads. Newton told Dolores that she needed to move away from the idea of possessing him and toward accepting an open sexual relationship with him. On paper, Newton's critique of possession sounds good; in practice, the sexism of some Party members prevented a maturation of politics. According to Newton, (Black) *man's* energies were *sapped* by the traditional familial roles, but not traditional gender and sexuality roles, which allowed men to engage in sex with as many women as possible, with no thought of the role gender and sexuality played in normalizing these behaviors. While Newton critically thought about the bourgeois family as a part of the colonial foundation, he could not link his own gendered and sexual behaviors to the same structure, as it benefited him. Indeed, Dolores tried to kill herself after coming to Newton's parents' home to discover that he was there with another

woman. Though sad about Dolores, who survived the attempt on her own life, the encounter did not teach Newton about sexism; instead it "reinforced, in the end, my conviction that the demands two people make upon each other can be crippling and destructive." This example taught him that communal living was a revolutionary engagement in the world, rather than a continuation of dominant gendered and sexual politics produced in concert with the reactionaries that he so hated. For more information on this, see Newton, *Revolutionary Suicide* (New York: Penguin Books, 2009), 94 and 98.

44. Karl Marx and Friedrich Engels, *The Communist Manifesto* (New York: Penguin Books, 2002), 196.

45. Newton, "Speech Delivered at Boston College: November 18, 1970," in *The Huey P. Newton Reader*, ed. David Hilliard and Donald Weise (New York: Seven Stories Press, 2002), 166; and Mao Zedong, "On Contradiction," *Marxists*, August 1938, accessed December 24, 2017, www.marxists.org/reference/archive/mao/selected-works/volume-1/mswv1_17.htm.

46. Hegel, *Philosophy of History*, 361.

47. Kelley, *Freedom Dreams*; and Robin Kelley, introduction to *A History of Pan-African Revolt*, by C.L.R. James (Oakland, CA: PM Press, 2012), 1–33.

48. C.L.R. James, *Notes on Dialectics: Hegel, Marx, Lenin* (Westport, CT: Lawrence Hill & Co., 1981).

49. Walter Rodney, *The Russian Revolution: A View from the Third World* (Brooklyn, NY: Verso, 2018), 20.

50. Davies, *Left of Karl Marx*, 38.

51. Amilcar Cabral, "Connecting the Struggles: An Informal Talk with Black Americans," in *Return to the Source: Selected Speeches of Amilcar Cabral*, ed. African Information Service (New York: Monthly Review Press, 1973).

52. Even Marx's reading of the lumpen proletariat as a criminal class that is anti-revolutionary should be read within Marx's context. In nineteenth-century Europe, arguments were circulating that the proletariat were the true criminal class and undeserving of any esteem. Marx sought to displace such thinking by turning attention away from the proletariat to the lumpen. Marx sought to politically situate the proletariat as a potentially radical group that could mobilize toward worldwide revolution. To do so, he had to push back against arguments that the proletariat were prone to crime. For more on this, see Gareth Stedman Jones, introduction to *Karl Marx and Friedrich Engels: The Communist Manifesto* (New York: Penguin Books, 1967), 3–185. Also see Fanon, *Wretched of the Earth*.

53. Bloom and Martin, *Black against Empire*, 73.

54. Roderick Ferguson talks about the romanticization of "the people" by groups like the Party. Such romanticization led to sexist, homophobic, and ableist positions in the Party. While important to note, I am more interested in the Party's idea that the people were not only a construct, but supposed to make their own decisions about what constituted revolution. For a critique of the people, however, see Roderick Ferguson, *The Reoder of Things*.

55. Stuart Hall, "The Problem of Ideology – Marxism without Guarantees," *Journal of Communication Inquiry* 10, no. 2 (1986): 28–44.

56. Newton, "Intercommunalism," 187.

57. Lynn Spigel, "Housing Television: Architectures of the Archives," *The Communication Review* 13, no. 1 (2010): 62.

58. Jonathan Sterne, "Out with the Trash: On the Future of New Media," in *Residual Media*, ed. Charles Acland (Minneapolis: University of Minnesota Press, 2007), 16–31.

59. Lynn Spigel, *Welcome to the Dreamhouse: Popular Media and Postwar Suburbs* (Durham, NC: Duke University Press, 2001).

60. Spigel, *Welcome to the Dreamhouse*.

61. McLuhan, "Playboy Interview," 245.

62. Baradaran, *Color of Money*.

63. Huey Newton, "Dialectics of Nature: 1974," in *The Huey P. Newton Reader*, ed. David Hilliard and Donald Weise (New York: Seven Stories Press, 2002), 310.

64. Innis, *Bias of Communication*.

65. Ferguson, *Reorder of Things*.

66. Benjamin, *Race after Technology*; and Browne, *Dark Matters*.

67. Brown, *Taste of Power*, 277–278.

68. Brown, *Taste of Power*, 279–281.

69. Unlike McLuhan, who Aniko Bodroghkozy argues viewed the death of nationalism as a potentially good thing—sparked via television's influence on (white) youth—Newton held no utopian view about the death of the nation. Newton argued this death of the nation could fully benefit the capitalist/intercommunalists and likely would. See Bodroghkozy, *Groove Tube*.

70. Michel Foucault, *The Order of Things* (New York: Vintage Books, 1994), 318.

71. It is important to note that Newton had more than one Boston College speech. The one cited at the beginning of this chapter is from 1971, where he outlines his theory of intercommunalism. The one referenced in this note is from 1970. See Newton, "Speech Delivered at Boston College," 166.

72. Newton, "Technology Question," 256, emphasis added.

73. For more on Stuart Hall's analysis of popular culture and U.S. imperialism, see Hall, *Cultural Studies 1983: A Theoretical History* (Durham, NC: Duke University Press, 2016).

74. Navin Bapat, *Monsters to Destroy: Understanding the War on Terror* (New York: Oxford University Press, 2019), 13.

75. Bapat, *Monsters to Destroy*, 17.

76. Newton, "Dialectics of Nature: 1974," 308–309.

77. Newton, "Dialectics of Nature: 1974," 311–312.

78. Newton, "Speech Delivered at Boston College," 166.

79. McKenzie Wark, *Capital Is Dead: Is This Something Worse?* (Brooklyn, NY: Verso Books, 2019), 3.

80. Newton, "Speech Delivered at Boston College," 168.

81. Fred Nolan, "Black Cultural Nationalism," *The Black Panther: Black Community News Service* (San Francisco), December 21, 1968, p. 15.

82. Newton, "Technology Question," 260.

83. Narayan, "Wages of Whiteness," 4.

84. Daulatzai, *Black Star, Crescent Moon*; and Malcolm X, *Malcolm X Speaks: Selected Speeches and Statements* (New York: Grove Press, 1994).

85. Newton, *Revolutionary Suicide*, 75.

86. Murch, *Living for the City*, 119.

87. Murch, *Living for the City*, 119.

88. Both Huggins and Alprentice "Bunchy" Carter were killed on UCLA's campus in 1969 in a shootout with members of the Black cultural nationalist organization, US. Both groups were infiltrated by the FBI leading up to the shootout. The Party's newspaper did a story two years after the killing, checking up on Ericka Huggins, communications secretary for the Party's Los Angeles chapter and wife of Huggins, and their child, Mai. See "About Ericka & Mai," *The Black Panther: Black Community News Service* (San Francisco), January 30, 1971, p. 10. "Los Angeles Panthers Await Justice for 'US' Organization Pigs," *The Black Panther: Black Community News Service* (San Francisco), February 2, 1969, p. 4.

89. Daulatzai, *Fifty Years*, 6.

90. Daulatzai, *Fifty Years*, 6; and "Eldridge Warmly Recieved [*sic*] by the People of Algiers," *The Black Panther: Black Community News Service* (San Francisco), August 9, 1969, 3.

91. Hutton was both the first person to join the Party at sixteen and the first Party member to be killed.

92. "Eldridge Warmly Recieved [*sic*] by the People of Algiers," 3.

93. Murch, *Living for the City*. Also see Cleaver's own work, *Soul on Ice* (New York: Delta, 1999).

94. Yahia Zoubir, "The United States, the Soviet Union and Decolonization of the Maghreb, 1945–1962," *Middle Eastern Studies* 31, no. 1 (1995): 58–84.

95. McLuhan, *Understanding Media*, 419.

96. McLuhan, *Understanding Media*, 39.

97. McLuhan, *Understanding Media*, 40.

98. Bodroghkozy, *Groove Tube*.

99. For example, Palestinians have provided tips on Twitter for how to deal with tear gas for Black protestors in Ferguson, Missouri, after the killing of Michael Brown by Ferguson police officer Darren Wilson. See Mark Molloy and agencies, "Palestinians Tweet Tear Gas Advice to Protestors in Ferguson," *The Telegraph*, August 15, 2014, www.telegraph.co.uk/news/worldnews/northamerica/usa/11036190/Palestinians-tweet-tear-gas-advice-to-protesters-in-Ferguson.html.

100. Keeling, *Queer Times, Black Futures*, 111.

101. The work of Keeling fits in here as well. Particularly thinking about the ways, beyond solely media content, that film can both play a role in capitalist maintenance and create alternative ways of navigating time and space for Black people. See Keeling, *Witch's Flight*.

102. Daulatzai, *Fifty Years*, 49.

103. Williams, *Television*, 132–133.

104. Brown, *Taste of Power*, 281.

105. Zoubir, "The United States, the Soviet Union and Decolonization of the Maghreb"; and Fanon, *Wretched of the Earth*, 4.

106. Lewis Gordon, *Fanon and the Crisis of European Man: An Essay on Philosophy and the Human Sciences* (New York: Routledge, 1995), 65.

107. Huey Newton, "On the Relevance of the Church," in *The Huey P. Newton Reader*, ed. David Hilliard and Donald Weise (New York: Seven Stories Press, 2002), 225, emphasis added.

108. Subramaniam, *Ghost Stories for Darwin*, 50.

109. Sarah Jane Cervenak and J. Kameron Carter, "Untitled and Outdoors: Thinking with Saidiya Hartman," *Women & Performance: A Journal of Feminist Theory* 27, no. 1 (2017): 46.

110. This is pulled from Fanon's discussion of the Black body as "livery," a creation of white people: "Whether he likes it or not, the black man has to wear the livery the white man has fabricated for him." See Fanon, *Black Skin, White Mask*, 17.

111. Randa Aboubakr, "New Directions of Internet Activism in Egypt," *Communications: European Journal of Communication Research* 38, no. 3 (2013): 251–265; Ben Berkowitz, "To Occupy Wall Street, Occupy the Internet First," *Reuters*, October 4, 2011, www.reuters.com/article/us-wallstreet-pr otests-media/to-occupy-wall-street-occupy-the-internet-first-idUSTRE79377 W20111004; and W. Lance Bennett and Alexandra Segerberg, "The Logic of Connective Action," *Information, Communication & Society* 15, no. 5 (2012): 739–768.

112. Wark, *Capital Is Dead*.

113. "Amazon Best Sellers," Amazon, accessed November 23, 2019, www .amazon.com/Best-Sellers-Books-132780010-Marx-Karl/zgbs/books/917096.

114. Levinson, *Digital McLuhan*.

CHAPTER 4. BLACK "MATTER" LIVES: MICHAEL BROWN AND DIGITAL AFTERLIVES

*Epigraph*: Barbara Ransby, *Making All Black Lives Matter: Reimaging Freedom in the 21st Century* (Berkeley: University of California Press, 2018), 48.

1. Larry Buchanan, Ford Fessenden, K. K. Rebecca Lai, Haeyoun Park, Alicia Parlapiano, Archie Tse, Tim Wallace, Derek Watkins, and Karen Yourish, "What Happened in Ferguson?" *New York Times*, August 10, 2015, www.ny times.com/interactive/2014/08/13/us/ferguson-missouri-town-under-siege-after -police-shooting.html.

2. Jon Swaine and Oliver Laughland, "Darren Wilson Will Not Face Federal Charges in Michael Brown Shooting," *The Guardian*, March 4, 2015, www .theguardian.com/us-news/2015/mar/04/darren-wilson-federal-criminal-char ges-michael-brown-shooting.

3. For clarity's sake, this is a chapter not about the groups organized under the BLM hashtag (#BLM) but the implications of the hashtag itself. In particular, the chapter is concerned with the commodity relations that are implied, in both online and offline context, and how #BLM points our attention to the

inseparability between online and offline life. For a reading of the organizational/organizing histories, see Andrea Boyles, *You Can't Stop the Revolution: Community Disorder and Social Ties in Post-Ferguson* (Berkeley: University of California Press, 2019); and Ransby, *Making All Black Lives Matter.*

4. Ransby, *Making All Black Lives Matter,* 2

5. Boyles, *You Can't Stop the Revolution,* 62.

6. Ransby, *Making All Black Lives Matter,* 6.

7. Interestingly, Keeanga-Yamahtta Taylor, Barbara Ransby, and Christopher J. Lebron outline the context that organizations influenced by the hashtag #BLM emerge within, but they leave out one important thing: the fact that #BLM largely relies on the web for its political articulation. Though less so for Ransby (see *Making All Black Lives Matter,* 100–103), the web is treated as a transparent mode of expressing Black anger by Taylor and Lebron. See Lebron, *The Making of Black Lives Matter: A Brief History of an Idea* (New York: Oxford University Press, 2017); Ransby, *Making All Black Lives Matter;* and Taylor, *From #BlackLivesMatter to Black Liberation.*

8. Deen Freelon, Charlton McIlwain, and Meredith Clark, *Beyond the Hashtags: #Ferguson, #Blacklivesmatter, and the Online Struggle for Offline Justice* (Washington, DC: Center for Media and Social Impact, 2016).

9. Towns, "Black 'Matter' Lives," 350.

10. Denise Ferreira da Silva, "1 (Life) ÷ 0 (Blackness) = ∞ − ∞ or ∞ / ∞: On Matter beyond the Equation of Value," *E-Flux* 79 (2017), www.e-flux.com/journal/79/94686/1-life-o-blackness-or-on-matter-beyond-the-equation-of-value/.

11. Jane Bennett, *Vibrant Matter: A Political Ecology of Things* (Durham, NC: Duke University Press, 2010), 5.

12. Towns, "Black 'Matter' Lives," 350–351.

13. W.E.B. Du Bois, *Darkwater: Voices from within the Veil* (Mineola, NY: Dover, 1999), 131.

14. Ransby, *Making All Black Lives Matter,* 48.

15. Wark, *Capital Is Dead.*

16. I am pulling the invention of the Negro from Cedric Robinson's article. In particular, he argues that "the invention of the Negro, the inferiorised Black, coincides with the construction of English national identity." See Robinson, "Inventions of the Negro," 332.

17. Keeling, *Queer Times, Black Futures,* 122.

18. Meredith Broussard, *Artificial Unintelligence: How Computers Misunderstand the World* (Cambridge, MA: MIT Press, 2019); Virginia Eubanks, *Automating Inequality* (London: Picador, 2019); Cathy O'Neil, *Weapons of Math Destruction: How Big Data Increases Inequality and Threatens Democracy* (New York: Crown, 2017); and Roopika Risam, *New Digital Worlds: Postcolonial Digital Humanities in Theory, Praxis, and Pedagogy* (Evanston, IL: Northwestern University, 2018).

19. Wynter, "Unsettling the Coloniality of Being/Power/Truth/Freedom," 257–337.

20. Eugene McLaughlin and John Muncie, *The Sage Dictionary of Criminology* (Thousand Oaks, CA: Sage Publishing, 2013).

21. Lisa Nakamura, "Afterword: Racism, Sexism, and Gaming's Cruel Optimism," in *Gaming Representation*, ed. Jennifer Malkowski and TreaAndrea Russworm (Bloomington: University of Indiana Press, 2017), 245–250.

22. Guillory, "Genesis of the Media Concept," 321–362.

23. Pooley, "Wilbur Schramm and the 'Four Founders' History," 5–18.

24. Wark, *Capital Is Dead*, 11.

25. Safiya Noble, *Algorithms of Oppression: How Search Engines Reinforce Racism* (New York: New York University Press, 2018).

26. In the AAFS's 2015 conference, the Colorado Justice Project's founder Donald Fymbo applied to be an associate member of the AAFS. See AAFS, "Academy News," accessed October 22, 2017, https://aafs.org/common/Uploa ded%20files/Resources/News%20Library/2014/July14.pdf, 40.

27. Benjamin, *Race after Technology*; Browne, *Dark Matters*; and Shosana Magnet, *When Biometrics Fail: Gender, Race, and the Technology of Identity* (Durham, NC: Duke University Press, 2011).

28. Simone Browne, "Digital Epidermalization," 134.

29. Levinson, *Digital McLuhan*.

30. Starosielski, *Undersea Network*, 10, emphasis added.

31. For example, many still argue for the decentralized argument, contending that increases in digital, informational media should lead to decreases in racist, sexist, homophobic, ableist, and transphobic interactions. In support of the use of cashier-free, facial recognition technology at Amazon stores, journalists Daniel Castro and Michael McLaughlin argue that "many people already face discrimination today and using facial recognition technologies for certain applications, like store surveillance could reduce the impact of human biases." However, as humans create these technologies, there are no guarantees of a removal of human biases from them as promised. The circulation of digital technologies throughout society feeds into perceptions that the world will be improved when humans no longer engage with other humans but with machines. For more information, see Daniel Castro and Michael McLaughlin, "Facial Recognition Technology Can Minimize Racial Discrimination against Shoppers," *Inside Sources*, December 28, 2018, www.insidesources.com/facial-recognition-techn ology-can-minimize-racial-discrimination-against-shoppers/.

32. Denise Ferreira da Silva, *Toward a Global Idea of Race* (Minneapolis: University of Minnesota Press, 2007), 15.

33. Da Silva, *Toward a Global Idea*.

34. Neda Atanasoski and Kalindi Vora, "Surrogate Humanity: Posthuman Networks and the (Racialized) Obsolescence of Labor," *Catalyst: Feminism, Theory, Technoscience* 1, no. 1 (2015): 28.

35. Risam, *New Digital Worlds*.

36. Benjamin, *Race after Technology*, 10.

37. Mbembe, *Necropolitics*, 113.

38. Magnet, *When Biometrics Fail*.

39. Tara McPherson, "U.S. Operating Systems at Mid-Century: The Inter-

twining of Race and UNIX," in *Race after the Internet*, ed. Lisa Nakamura and Peter Chow-White (New York: Routledge, 2011), 24.

40.  Similarly, Sarah Sharma argues the pains of capitalism evoke cultural fantasies of "exit," fantasies that are divided along gendered and racialized lines. Rather than address sociopolitical problems of Western man's own making, "the white patriarchal penchant for exit rears its ugly head at any hint of having to live with one's supremacy in question." See Sarah Sharma, "Exit and the Extensions of Man," *Transmediale/Art and Digital Culture*, August 5, 2017, https://transmediale.de/content/exit-and-the-extensions-of-man, paragraph 6.

41.  Benjamin, *Race after Technology*, 66.

42.  This is not an entirely new argument. Shoshana Magnet, Simone Browne, and Neda Atanasoski and Kalindi Vora all makes similar points. However, I outline a trajectory of the different media relations of man. I combine these readings to note that man resituates his former transparency inside digital technologies, which is to say they function to assist him with his own maintenance. Darren Wilson is no neutral classifier here but connected to a history that assumes his transparency before he starts. Digital animations, and their connection to a longer history of Western commodification, further back Wilson's arguments in a new media environment. For a similar argument, see Browne, *Dark Matters*, 110.

43.  What the works of Nakamura and Starosielski point to is that we must consider the technological context in which #BLM emerges if we want to understand those influenced by #BLM and those in disagreement with #BLM. An increase in research on #BLM, as well as the movements it has sparked, has been circulating since 2016. Much of this work has centered the history of not just the hashtag but the way in which those who employ it speak back to earlier Black critiques of racism, such as racial slavery and Jim Crow. Lebron's *Making of Black Lives Matter* locates different forms of #BLM inside the activism of figures like Frederick Douglass and Ida B. Wells. It is no exaggeration to argue that Wells and Douglass are two of the most important voices to criticize anti-Black violence in U.S. history. However, the problem of Lebron and much of the #BLM research lies in understanding how the contexts of the late-nineteenth and early twentieth century drastically differ from our current context. Wilson, McCulloch, juries, and media outlets remained hesitant to suggest that Brown was killed due to racism; there were no similar questions about whether the violence faced by Douglass or Wells was racist. Therefore, Brown's context differs significantly from Douglass's and Wells's. And I contend that media lie at the center of understanding these different contexts. For more on some of these problems, see Lebron, *Making of Black Lives Matter*, 32.

44.  John Feather, *The Information Society* (London: Facet Publishing, 2000), 38–39; and Ken Hillis, *Online a Lot of the Time: Ritual, Fetish, Sign* (Durham, NC: Duke University Press, 2008), 39.

45.  Wark, *Capital Is Dead*, 15.

46.  Wark, *Capital Is Dead*.

47.  Noble, *Algorithms of Oppression*.

48.  Siva Vaidhyanathan, *Antisocial Media: How Facebook Disconnects Us and Undermines Democracy* (New York: New York University Press, 2018).

49. Robinson, "Inventions of the Negro."

50. This is well fleshed out in Nick Srnicek's *Platform Capitalism* (Hoboken, NJ: Wiley, 2016).

51. See McKittrick, "Mathematics Black Life," 16–28.

52. Brock, *Distributed Blackness*, 21.

53. Christina Sharpe, *In the Wake: On Blackness and Being* (Durham, NC: Duke University Press, 2016), 83.

54. Immanuel Kant, *Critique of Pure Reason* (Boston, MA: Bedford/St. Martin's, 1965); and Marx, *Capital*.

55. McLaughlin and Muncie, *Sage Dictionary*.

56. "State of Missouri v. Darren Wilson" (Saint Louis, MO: Gore Perry Reporting & Video, September 16, 2014), 224–225.

57. "State of Missouri v. Darren Wilson."

58. "State of Missouri v. Darren Wilson," 281.

59. Boyles, *You Can't Stop the Revolution*, 27.

60. Boyles, *You Can't Stop the Revolution*.

61. Jake Halpern, "The Cop," *The New Yorker*, August 10, 2015, www.new yorker.com/magazine/2015/08/10/the-cop.

62. Daniel Bates, "Darren Wilson's '$1 Million' Warchest Revealed by Woman Organizing Support for Officer—and Who Says: 'Michael Brown Made a Bad Choice That Day," *Daily Mail*, November 28, 2014, www.dailymail.co .uk/news/article-2851213/Darren-Wilson-receive-1-million-funding-support ers-woman-organizing-officer-s-friends-group-says-Michael-Brown-bad-choice -day.html.

63. Spillers, *Black, White, and in Color*.

64. "State of Missouri v. Darren Wilson," 224–225.

65. "State of Missouri v. Darren Wilson," 224–225.

66. "Darren Wilson Interview," Saint Louis County Police Department, August 10, 2014, pp. 105–106.

67. "State of Missouri v. Darren Wilson," 207.

68. "State of Missouri v. Darren Wilson," 212.

69. "State of Missouri v. Darren Wilson," 34.

70. "Darren Wilson Interview," 7.

71. "State of Missouri v. Darren Wilson."

72. "State of Missouri v. Darren Wilson."

73. Marx, *Capital*, volume 1, 50.

74. Marx, *Capital*, volume 1, 60.

75. McLuhan, *Understanding Media*, 163.

76. Kathryn Yusoff, *A Billion Black Anthropocenes or None* (Minneapolis: University of Minnesota Press, 2018).

77. Kant, *Critique of Pure Reason*, 65–66.

78. Towns, "Black 'Matter' Lives."

79. I. Bernard Cohen, "A Guide to Newton's *Principia*," in Isaac Newton's *The Principia: Mathematical Principles of Natural Philosophy*, trans. I. Bernard Cohen, Anne Whitman, and Julia Budenz (Berkeley: University of California Press, 1999), 117–118, emphasis in the original.

80. See Sylvia Wynter, *"Do Not Call Us Negros": How Multicultural Textbooks Perpetuate Racism* (San Francisco: Aspire Books and Magazines, 1992).

81. Karen Barad, *Meeting the Universe Halfway: Quantum Physics and the Entanglement of Matter and Meaning* (Durham, NC: Duke University Press, 2007); and Bennett, *Vibrant Matter.*

82. Bennett, *Vibrant Matter.*

83. Spillers, *Black, White, and in Color,* 206

84. Spillers, *Black, White, and in Color,* 226, emphasis in the original.

85. Lee Fang, "Why Was an FBI Joint Terrorism Task Force Tracking a Black Lives Matter Protest?" *The Intercept,* March 12, 2015, https://theintercept.com/2015/03/12/fbi-appeared-use-informant-track-black-lives-matter-protest/.

## CONCLUSION

*Epigraph*: Garnet Hertz and Jussi Parikka, "Zombie Media: Circuit Bending Media Archaeology into an Art Method," *Leonardo* 45, no. 5 (2012): 430.

1. Weheliye, *Phonographies.*

2. Innis, *Bias of Communication.*

3. Jody Berland, *North of Empire: Essays on the Cultural Technologies of Space* (Durham, NC: Duke University Press, 2009).

4. Parikka, *Geology of Media,* 46.

5. See Starosielski, *Undersea Network.*

6. Jeremy Berke, "Here's How Much Metal It Takes to Make Your iPhone," *Business Insider,* July 11, 2018, www.businessinsider.com/how-much-metal-in-an-iphone-2018-6.

7. Heidegger, *Question Concerning Technology,* 14.

8. Sterne, "Out with the Trash," 17.

9. Shaka McGlotten, "Dead and Live Life: Zombies, Queers, and Online Sociality," in *Generation Zombie: Essays on the Living Dead in Modern Culture,* ed. Stephanie Boluk and Wylie Lenz (Jefferson, NC: McFarland Press, 2011), 190.

10. Parikka, *What Is Media Archaeology* (Cambridge, UK: Polity, 2012), 3.

11. Tavia Nyong'o, "The Scene of Occupation," *TDR: The Drama Review* 56, no. 4 (2012): 146.

12. James, *Black Jacobins,* 46.

13. James, *History of Pan-African Revolt.*

14. Mike Mariani, "The Tragic, Forgotten History of Zombies," *The Atlantic,* October 28, 2015, www.theatlantic.com/entertainment/archive/2015/10/how-america-erased-the-tragic-history-of-the-zombie/412264/.

15. James, *Black Jacobins,* 108.

16. Eric King Watts, "Postracial Fantasies, Blackness, and Zombies," *Communication and Critical/Cultural Studies* 14, no. 4 (2017): 318.

17. Mbembe, *Necropolitics,* 29.

18. Rodney, *Groundings with My Brothers,* 28.

19. Parikka, *What Is Media Archaeology,* 147–148.

20. Keeling, *Queer Times, Black Futures,* 23.

21. The Black studies work on reparations is extensive. I do not pretend to offer something new to it. Rather, I seek to simply point media philosophy toward these conversations with the hope of thinking about how these areas may be generative for one another. A short, highly incomplete list of the Black studies work on reparations includes Ana Lucia Araujo, *Reparations for Slavery and the Slave Trade: A Transnational History* (London: Bloomsbury, 2017); Charles Henry, *Long Overdue: The Politics of Racial Reparations* (New York: New York University Press, 2007); Ali Al'Amin Mazrui, *Black Reparations in the Era of Globalization* (Binghamton, NY: Institute of Global Cultural Studies, 2002); and Clarence Munford, *Race and Reparations: A Black Perspective for the Twenty-First Century* (Trenton, NJ: Africa World Press, 1996).

22. Stefano Harney and Fred Moten, *The Undercommons: Fugitive Planning and Black Study* (Brooklyn, NY: Autonomedia, 2013), 42.

23. Jack Halberstam, "The Wild Beyond: With and for the Undercommons," in *Undercommons*, ed. Stefano Harney and Fred Moten (Brooklyn, NY: Autonomedia, 2013), 6.

24. In the final chapter Moten hints at a discussion of reparations but solely through a lens of recognition. The discussion of reparations happening here does not have to rely on a discussion of recognition but a realization that reparations must benefit all. For more on Moten's discussion of reparations, see Harney and Moten, *Undercommons*, 152.

25. H.R. 40, House of Representatives, 116th Congress, 1st session, January 3, 2019, www.congress.gov/116/bills/hr40/BILLS-116hr40ih.pdf, 1, emphasis added.

26. H.R. 40, 9.

27. Alex Samuels, "On Juneteenth, Sheila Jackson Lee Spearheads Congressional Hearing on Reparations, Calling Them 'Long Overdue,'" *Texas Tribune*, June 19, 2019, www.texastribune.org/2019/06/19/sheila-jackson-lee-reparations-juneteenth/.

28. Jasmine Aguilera, "Author Ta-Nehisi Coates Criticized Mitch McConnell for Saying Slavery's Effects Were in the Past," *Time*, June 19, 2019, https://time.com/5610151/ta-nehisi-coates-criticized-mcconnell-reparations/.

29. See Edward Baptist, *The Half Has Never Been Told: Slavery and the Making of American Capitalism* (New York: Basic Books, 2016); and Baradaran, *Color of Money*.

30. Farah Stockman, "'We're Self-Interested': The Growing Identity Debate in Black America," November 8, 2019, www.nytimes.com/2019/11/08/us/slavery-black-immigrants-ados.html.

31. The Combahee River Collective, "The Combahee River Collective Statement," in *How We Get Free: Black Feminism and the Combahee River Collective*, ed. Keeanga-Yamahtta Taylor (Chicago, IL: Haymarket Books, 2017), 22–23.

32. Sylvia Wynter, "1492: A New World View," in *Race, Discourse, and the Origin of the Americas: A New World View*, ed. Vera Lawrence Hyatt and Rex Nettleford (Washington, DC: Smithsonian Institution Press, 1995), 5–57.

33. In addition to public memorialization, there are other debates on what a new form of reparations might look like happening at institutions of higher

education such as Georgetown University, the Princeton Theological Seminary, and the Virginia Theological Seminary, which are creating scholarships for descendants of racial slavery. Likewise, the city of Evanston, Illinois, a suburb of Chicago, is currently dealing with its own unique reparations debate. With a decrease in its Black population due to the inability to afford to live there, Evanston has sought to create a fund that "will be financed by revenue from cannabis" to "encourage minority business startups and help longtime [Black] residents" to continue to afford living in Evanston. For more on the relations between higher educatiton and reparations, see Mark Anthony Neal, "How Universities Are Addressing Slavery and Reparations," *NewBlackMan in (Exile)*, November 17, 2019, www.newblackmaninexile.net/2019/11/how-universi ties-are-addressing-slavery.html?m=1. For more information on Evanston and reparations, see Jermont Terry, "City of Evanston to Use Cannabis Revenue for Reparations Fund for African-American Residents," CBS Chicago, November 27, 2019, https://chicago.cbslocal.com/2019/11/27/evanston-recreational-can nabis-reparations-african-american-residents/.

34. Angela Davis, *Abolition Democracy: Beyond Empire, Prisons, and Torture* (New York: Seven Stories Press, 2005), 36.

35. Ruth Wilson Gilmore, "Fatal Couplings of Power and Difference: Notes on Racism and Geography," *The Professional Geographer* 54, no. 1 (2002): 16.

36. Davis, *Abolition Democracy*, 32.

37. Keeanga-Yamahtta Taylor and Adolph Reed, "The Reparations Debate," *Dissent Magazine*, June 24, 2019, www.dissentmagazine.org/online_articles/the-reparations-debate.

38. Ruth Wilson Gilmore, *Golden Gulag: Prison, Surplus, Crisis, and Opposition in Globalizing California* (Berkeley: University of California Press, 2007), 250.

39. Leilani Nishime and Kim Hester Williams, "Introduction: Why Racial Ecologies?" in *Racial Ecologies*, ed. Nishime and Williams (Seattle: University of Washington Press, 2018), 3–4.

40. Sarah Kaplan, "Climate Change Affects Everything—Even the Coronavirus," *Washington Post*, April 15, 2020, www.washingtonpost.com/climate-so lutions/2020/04/15/climate-change-affects-everything-even-coronavirus/?arc40 4=true.

41. The thinking of Thea Riofrancos fits in here. See Riofrancos, *Resource Radicals: From Petro-Nationalism to Post-Extractivism in Ecuador* (Durham, NC: Duke University Press, 2020).

42. Harney and Moten, *Undercommons*, 61.

43. Fanon, *Wretched of the Earth*, 59.

44. Jared Brock, "As California Wildfires Raged, Incarcerated Exploited for Labor," *USA Today*, November 11, 2020, www.usatoday.com/story/opinion/po licing/2020/11/11/california-wildfires-raged-incarcerated-exploited-labor-colu mn/6249201002/.

45. Fanon, *Wretched of the Earth*, 62.

46. The Plurinational State of Bolivia, "Climate Debt: The Basis of a Fair and Effective Solution to Climate Change," *UNFCCC*, accessed January 24,

2020, https://unfccc.int/files/meetings/ad_hoc_working_groups/lca/application/pdf/4_bolivia.pdf, p. 2.

47. "Emissions Debt," *Climate Debt*, accessed January 24, 2020, http://climate-debt.org/climate-debt/emissions-debt/.

48. "Emissions Debt."

49. Glenn Greenwald, "The U.S.-Supported Coup in Bolivia Continues to Produce Repression and Tyranny, While Revealing How U.S. Media Propaganda Works," *The Intercept*, July 23, 2020, https://theintercept.com/2020/07/23/the-u-s-supported-coup-in-bolivia-continues-to-produce-repression-and-tyranny-while-revealing-how-u-s-media-propaganda-works/.

50. David Adler, "Facts & Fantasies in the Fight Against Fascism: What Can Bolivia Teach Us about the Defence of Democracy?" *Verso*, October 29, 2020, www.versobooks.com/blogs/4895-facts-amp-fantasies-in-the-fight-against-fascism-what-can-bolivia-teach-us-about-the-defence-of-democracy.

51. Evo Morales Ayama, preface to *Washington Bullets: A History of the CIA, Coups, and Assassinations*, by Vijay Prashad (New York: Monthly Review, 2020), 11.

52. Parikka, *Geology of Media*.

53. Elizabeth Dickinson, "The Misdiagnosis: Rethinking 'Nature-Deficit Disorder,'" *Environmental Communication* 7, no. 3 (2013): 315–335; Darrel Enck-Wanzer, "Race, Coloniality, and Geo-Body Politics: *The Garden* as Latin@ Vernacular Discourse," *Environmental Communication* 5, no. 3 (2011): 363–371; and Cheryl Lousley, "Charismatic Life: Spectacular Biodiversity and Biophilic Life Writing," *Environmental Communication* 10, no. 6 (2016): 704–718.

54. Harney and Moten, *Undercommons*, 66.

55. As just one example, a recent report from *Aljazeera* estimates that British colonization netted $45 trillion from India alone. See Jason Hickel, "How Britain Stole $45 Trillion from India," *Aljazeera*, December 19, 2018, www.aljazeera.com/indepth/opinion/britain-stole-45-trillion-india-181206124830851.html.

56. Harney and Moten, *Undercommons*, 68.

57. Rodney, *Groundings*.

58. See Davis, *Abolition Democracy*. Likewise, Atiya Husain makes a similar argument in her important article. See Husain, "Terror and Abolition," *Boston Review*, June 11, 2020, http://bostonreview.net/race/atiya-husain-terror-and-abolition.

# Bibliography

Aboubakr, Randa. "New Directions of Internet Activism in Egypt." *Communications: The European Journal of Communication Research* 38, no. 3 (2013): 251–265.

"About Ericka & Mai." *The Black Panther: Black Community News Service* (San Francisco), January 30, 1971, p. 10.

Adler, David. "Facts & Fantasies in the Fight against Fascism: What Can Bolivia Teach Us about the Defence of Democracy?" *Verso*, October 29, 2020. www .versobooks.com/blogs/4895-facts-amp-fantasies-in-the-fight-against-fasci sm-what-can-bolivia-teach-us-about-the-defence-of-democracy.

Aguilera, Jasmine. "Author Ta-Nehisi Coates Criticized Mitch McConnell for Saying Slavery's Effects Were in the Past." *Time*, June 19, 2019. https://time .com/5610151/ta-nehisi-coates-criticized-mcconnell-reparations/.

"Amazon Best Sellers." *Amazon*. Accessed November 23, 2019. www.amazon .com/Best-Sellers-Books-132780010-Marx-Karl/zgbs/books/917096.

American Academy of Forensic Sciences (AAFS). "Academy News." Accessed October 22, 2017. https://aafs.org/common/Uploaded%20files/Resources /News%20Library/2014/July14.pdf.

Amos, Jonathan. "America Colonisation 'Cooled Earth's Climate.'" *BBC News*, January 31, 2019. www.bbc.com/news/science-environment-47063973.

"Annie Hall: Full Cast & Crew." *IMDb*. Accessed October 2, 2020. www.imdb .com/title/tt0075686/fullcredits?ref_=ttfc_ql_1.

Araujo, Ana Lucia. *Reparations for Slavery and the Slave Trade: A Transnational History*. London: Bloomsbury, 2017.

Asad, Talal. *On Suicide Bombing*. New York: Columbia University Press, 2007.

Atanasoski, Neda, and Kalindi Vora. "Surrogate Humanity: Posthuman Networks and the (Racialized) Obsolescence of Labor." *Catalyst: Feminism, Theory, Technoscience* 1, no. 1 (2015): 1–40.

———. *Surrogate Humanity: Race, Robots, and the Politics of Technological Futures.* Durham, NC: Duke University Press, 2019.

Bapat, Navin. *Monsters to Destroy: Understanding the War on Terror.* New York: Oxford University Press, 2019.

Baptist, Edward. *The Half Has Never Been Told: Slavery and the Making of American Capitalism.* New York: Basic Books, 2016.

Barad, Karen. *Meeting the Universe Halfway: Quantum Physics and the Entanglement of Matter and Meaning.* Durham, NC: Duke University Press, 2007.

Baradaran, Mehrsa. *The Color of Money: Black Banks and the Racial Wealth Gap.* Cambridge, MA: Harvard University Press, 2017.

Bates, Daniel. "Darren Wilson's '$1 Million' Warchest Revealed by Woman Organizing Support for Officer—and Who Says: 'Michael Brown Made a Bad Choice That Day.'" *Daily Mail*, November 28, 2014. www.dailymail.co.uk /news/article-2851213/Darren-Wilson-receive-1-million-funding-supporters -woman-organizing-officer-s-friends-group-says-Michael-Brown-bad-choice -day.html.

Benjamin, Jesse, and Robin Kelley. "Introduction: An 'African' Perspective." In *The Russian Revolution: A View from the Third World*, edited by Jesse Benjamin and Robin Kelley, xix– lxxiii. Brooklyn, NY: Verso Books, 2018.

Benjamin, Ruha. *Race after Technology: Abolitionist Tools for the New Jim Code.* New York: Polity Press, 2019.

Bennett, Jane. *Vibrant Matter: A Political Ecology of Things.* Durham, NC: Duke University Press, 2010.

Bennett, W. Lance, and Alexandra Segerberg. "The Logic of Connective Action." *Information, Communication & Society* 15, no. 5 (2012): 739–768.

Berke, Jeremy. "Here's How Much Metal It Takes to Make Your iPhone." *Business Insider*, July 11, 2018. www.businessinsider.com/how-much-metal-in -an-iphone-2018-6.

Berkowitz, Ben. "To Occupy Wall Street, Occupy the Internet First." *Reuters*, October 4, 2011. www.reuters.com/article/us-wallstreet-protests-media/to -occupy-wall-street-occupy-the-internet-first-idUSTRE79377W20111004.

Berland, Jody. *North of Empire: Essays on the Cultural Technologies of Space.* Durham, NC: Duke University Press, 2009.

———. *Virtual Menageries: Animals as Mediators in Network Cultures.* Cambridge, MA: MIT Press, 2019.

Biondi, Martha. *The Black Revolution on Campus.* Berkeley: University of California Press, 2012.

Blight, David. *Passages to Freedom: The Underground in History and Memory.* New York: Harper Paperbacks, 2006.

Bloom, Joshua, and Waldo Martin Jr. *Black against Empire: The History and Politics of the Black Panther Party.* Berkeley: University of California Press, 2013.

Bodroghkozy, Aniko. *Groove Tube: Sixties Television and the Youth Rebellion.* Durham, NC: Duke University Press, 2001.

Bolivia, the Plurinational State of. "Climate Debt: The Basis of a Fair and Effective Solution to Climate Change." *UNFCCC*. Accessed January 24, 2020. https://unfccc.int/files/meetings/ad_hoc_working_groups/lca/application/pdf /4_bolivia.pdf.

Boyles, Andrea. *You Can't Stop the Revolution: Community Disorder and Social Ties in Post-Ferguson America*. Berkeley: University of California Press, 2019 (e-book).

Bradford, Sarah. "'Harriet Tubman': *Harriet Tubman: The Moses of Her People* (Excerpts)." In *Slave Narratives of the Underground*, edited by Christine Rusdisel and Bob Blaisdell, 183–190. Mineola, NY: Dover Publications, 2014.

Brock, Andre. *Distributed Blackness: Africana American Cybercultures*. New York: New York University Press, 2020.

Brock, Jared. "As California Wildfires Raged, Incarcerated Exploited for Labor." *USA Today*, November 11, 2020. www.usatoday.com/story/opinion/policing /2020/11/11/california-wildfires-raged-incarcerated-exploited-labor-column /6249201002/.

Brockell, Gillian. "Some White People Don't Want to Hear about Slavery at Plantations Built by Slaves." *Washington Post*, August 8, 2019. www.was hingtonpost.com/history/2019/08/08/some-white-people-dont-want-hear -about-slavery-plantations-built-by-slaves/.

Broussard, Meredith. *Artificial Unintelligence: How Computers Misunderstand the World*. Cambridge, MA: MIT Press, 2019.

Brown, Elaine. *A Taste of Power: A Black Woman's Story*. New York: Random House, 1994.

Brown, William Wells. *Clotel; or, The President's Daughter; a Narrative of Slave Life in the United States*. New York: Collier Books, 1970.

———. "Narrative of William Wells Brown, a Fugitive Slave (Excerpts)." In *Slave Narratives of the Underground,* edited by Christine Rusdisel and Bob Blaisdell, 8–16. Mineola, NY: Dover Publications, 2014.

Browne, Simone. *Dark Matters: On the Surveillance of Blackness*. Durham, NC: Duke University Press, 2015.

———. "Digital Epidermalization: Race, Identity and Biometrics." *Critical Sociology* 36, no. 1 (2010): 131–150.

Buchanan, Larry, Ford Fessenden, K. K. Rebecca Lai, Haeyoun Park, Alicia Parlapiano, Archie Tse, Tim Wallace, Derek Watkins, and Karen Yourish. "What Happened in Ferguson?" *New York Times*, August 10, 2015. www.nytimes .com/interactive/2014/08/13/us/ferguson-missouri-town-under-siege-after -police-shooting.html.

Buck-Morss, Susan. "Hegel and Haiti." *Critical Inquiry* 26, no. 4 (2000): 821–865.

Bukhari, Safiya. *The War Before: The True Life Story of Becoming a Black Panther, Keeping the Faith in Prison and Fighting for Those Left Behind*. New York: Feminist Press, 2010.

Butler, Judith. *Gender Trouble*. New York: Routledge, 2007.

Cabral, Amilcar. *Return to the Source: Selected Speeches of Amilcar Cabral*. Edited by Africa Information Service. New York: Monthly Review, 1973.

Carby, Hazel. *Race Men*. Cambridge, MA: Harvard University Press, 1998.

Carey, James. *Communication as Culture*. New York: Routledge, 2009.

Carothers, J. C. *The African Mind in Health and Disease: A Study of Ethnopsychiatry.* Geneva: World Health Organization, 1953.

———. *The Psychology of Mau Mau.* Nairobi: Colony and Protectorate of Kenya, 1955.

Carr, Greg. "What Black Studies Is Not: Moving Crisis to Liberation in Africana Intellectual Work." *Socialism and Democracy* 25, no. 1 (2011): 178–191.

Carrington, Andre. *Speculative Blackness: The Future of Race in Science Fiction.* Minneapolis, MN: University of Minnesota Press, 2016.

Cartwright, Samuel. "Diseases and Peculiarities of the Negro Race." In *The Case of the South*, edited by Paul Paskoff and Daniel Wilson, 27–43. Baton Rouge: Louisiana State University Press, 1982.

Castro, Daniel, and Michael McLaughlin. "Facial Recognition Technology Can Minimize Racial Discrimination against Shoppers." *Inside Sources*, December 28, 2018. www.insidesources.com/facial-recognition-technology-can-mi nimize-racial-discrimination-against-shoppers/.

Cavell, Richard. Introduction to *McLuhan on the Nature of Media: Essays, 1952–1978*, edited by Richard Cavell, 9–11. Berkeley, CA: Gingko Press, 2016.

Central Intelligence Agency. "The Break-up of the Colonial Empires and Its Implications of US Security." September 3, 1948. www.cia.gov/readingroom/do cs/DOC_0000258342.pdf.

Cervenak, Sarah Jane, and J. Kameron Carter. "Untitled and Outdoors: Thinking with Saidiya Hartman." *Women & Performance: A Journal of Feminist Theory* 27, no. 1 (2017): 45–55.

Chandler, Nahum. *X—The Problem of the Negro as a Problem for Thought.* New York: Fordham Press, 2013.

Chow, Rey. "The Age of the World Target: Atomic Bombs, Alterity, Area Studies." In *The Rey Chow Reader*, edited by Paul Bowman, 2–19. New York: Columbia University Press, 2010.

Chun, Wendy Hoi Kyong. "Introduction: Race and/as Technology, or How to Do Things to Race." *Camera Obscura* 70, 24, no. 1 (2009): 7–35.

Cleaver, Eldridge. *Soul on Ice.* New York: Delta, 1999.

Cohen, I. Bernard. "A Guide to Newton's *Principia*." In Isaac Newton's *The Principia: Mathematical Principles of Natural Philosophy*, translated by I. Bernard Cohen, Anne Whitman, and Julia Budenz, 11–271. Berkeley: University of California Press, 1999.

The Combahee River Collective. "The Combahee River Collective Statement." In *How We Get Free: Black Feminism and the Combahee River Collective*, edited by Keeanga-Yamahtta Taylor, 15–28. Chicago, IL: Haymarket Books, 2017.

Cone, James. *A Black Theology of Liberation.* New York: Orbis Books, 2010.

Cook, Deborah. *Adorno on Nature.* New York: Routledge, 2011.

Coupland, Douglas. *Marshall McLuhan: You Know Nothing of My Work!* London: Atlas Books, 2010.

Cubitt, Sean. *Finite Media: Environmental Implications of Digital Technologies.* Durham, NC: Duke University Press, 2017.

"Darren Wilson Interview." Saint Louis County Police Department, Saint Louis, MO, August 10, 2014.

Darwin, Charles. *The Descent of Man, and Selection in Relation to Sex*. Princeton, NJ: Princeton University Press, 1981.

———. *Journal of Researches into the Natural History and Geology of the Countries Visited during the Voyage of H.M.S. Beagle Round the World, under the Command of Capt. Fitz Roy, R.N*. New York: D. Appleton and Company, 1871.

———. "To J.S. Henslow: 30 [August 1831]." *Darwin Correspondence Project*. Accessed November 4, 2019.

———. *On the Origin of Species, by Means of Natural Selection*. Mineola, NY: Dover Publications, 2006.

Daulatzai, Sohail. *Black Star, Crescent Moon: The Muslim International and Black Freedom beyond America*. Minneapolis: University of Minnesota Press, 2012.

———. *Fifty Years of "The Battle of Algiers": Past as Prologue*. Minneapolis: University of Minnesota Press.

Davies, Carole Boyce. *Left of Marx: The Political Life of Black Communist Claudia Jones*. Durham, NC: Duke University Press, 2008.

Davis, Angela. *Abolition Democracy: Beyond Empire, Prisons, and Torture*. New York: Seven Stories Press, 2005.

Davis, Jade. "Second Iteration: A Letter to Fanon & McLuhan." *Jadedid* (blog). 2013. http://jadedid.com/blog/2013/02/13/second-iteration-a-letter-to-fanon-mcluhan.

Davis, Janae, Alex Moulton, Levi Van Sant, and Brian Williams. "Anthropocene, Capitalocene,...Plantationocene?: A Manifesto for Ecological Justice in an Age of Global Crisis." *Geography Compass* 13, no. 5 (2019): 1–15.

Demos, T. J. *Decolonizing Nature: Contemporary Art and the Politics of Ecology*. Cambridge, MA: MIT Press, 2016.

Dickinson, Elizabeth. "The Misdiagnosis: Rethinking 'Nature-Deficit Disorder.'" *Environmental Communication* 7, no. 3 (2013): 315–335.

Diouf, Sylviane. *Servants of Allah: African Muslims Enslaved in the Americas*. New York: New York University Press, 2013.

Douglass, Frederick. *Narrative of the Life of Frederick Douglass, an American Slave*. New York: Barnes & Noble Classics, 2003.

"Dr. D.B. Gaines, Little Rock, Arkansas." Library of Congress. Accessed April 4, 2020. www.loc.gov/resource/mesn.023/?sp=7.

Drew, Benjamin. "The Refugee: A North-Side View of Slavery." In *Four Fugitive Slave Narratives*, edited by Robin Winks, xxviii–272. Reading MA: Addison-Wesley Publishing Company, 1969.

Du Bois, W.E.B. *Black Reconstruction in America, 1860–1880*. New York: The Free Press, 1992.

———. *Darkwater: Voices from within the Veil*. Mineola, NY: Dover, 1999.

———. "The Talented Tenth: Memorial Address." In *W.E.B. Du Bois: A Reader*, edited by David Levering Lewis, 347–353. New York: Henry Holt and Company, 1995.

Dyson, Michael Eric. *The Michael Eric Dyson Reader*. New York: Basic Civitas Books, 2004.

"Eldridge Warmly Recieved [*sic*] by the People of Algiers." *The Black Panther: Black Community News Service* (San Francisco), August 9, 1969.

"Emissions Debt." *Climate Debt*. Accessed January 24, 2020. http://climate-de bt.org/climate-debt/emissions-debt/.

Enck-Wanzer, Darrel. "Race, Coloniality, and Geo-Body Politics: *The Garden* as Latin@ Vernacular Discourse." *Environmental Communication* 5, no. 3 (2011): 363–371.

Eubanks, Virginia. *Automating Inequality*. London: Picador, 2019.

"European Colonization of Americas 'Cooled Earth's Climate.'" *MSN*, February 1, 2019. www.msn.com/en-us/travel/news/european-colonization-of -americas-cooled-earths-climate/vp-BBT1dP0.

Fabian, Johannes. *Time and the Other: How Anthropology Makes Its Object*. New York: Columbia University Press, 2014.

Fagge, Nick. "Picks, Pans and Bare Hands: How Miners in the Heart of Africa Toil in Terrible Conditions to Extract the Rare Minerals That Power Your iPhone." *Daily Mail*, October 22, 2015. www.dailymail.co.uk/news/article -3280872/iPhone-mineral-miners-Africa-use-bare-hands-coltan.html.

Fang, Lee. "Why Was an FBI Joint Terrorism Task Force Tracking a Black Lives Matter Protest?" *The Intercept*, March 12, 2015. https://theintercept.com/20 15/03/12/fbi-appeared-use-informant-track-black-lives-matter-protest/.

Fanon, Frantz. *Black Skin, White Mask*. New York: Grove Press, 2008.

———. *The Wretched of the Earth*. New York: Grove Press, 2004.

Farmer, Ashley. *Remaking Black Power: How Black Women Transformed an Era*. Chapel Hill: University of North Carolina Press, 2017.

Farooq, Nihad. *Undisciplined: Science, Ethnography, and Personhood in the Americas, 1830–1940*. New York: New York University Press, 2016.

Feather, John. *The Information Society*. London: Facet Publishing, 2000.

Ferguson, Roderick. *The Reorder of Things: The University and Its Pedagogies of Minority Difference*. Minneapolis: University of Minnesota Press, 2012.

Fischbach, Michael. *Black Power and Palestine: Transnational Countries of Color*. Redwood City, CA: Stanford University Press, 2019.

Foucault, Michel. *The Order of Things*. New York: Vintage Books, 1994.

Freelon, Deen, Charlton McIlwain, and Meredith Clark. *Beyond the Hashtags: #Ferguson, #Blacklivesmatter, and the Online Struggle for Offline Justice*. Washington, DC: Center for Media and Social Impact, 2016.

Fuchs, Christian. "Karl Marx & Communication @ 200: Towards a Marxian Theory of Communication." *tripleC* 16, no. 2 (2018): 518–534.

Geary, Daniel. "The Moynihan Report: An Annotated Edition." *The Atlantic*, September 14, 2015. www.theatlantic.com/politics/archive/2015/09/the -moynihan-report-an-annotated-edition/404632/#Chapter%20I.

Gilmore, Ruth Wilson. "Fatal Couplings of Power and Difference: Notes on Racism and Geography." *The Professional Geographer* 54, no. 1 (2002): 15–24.

———. *Golden Gulag: Prison, Surplus, Crisis, and Opposition in Globalizing California*. Berkeley: University of California Press, 2007.

Gilroy, Paul. *Against Race: Imagining Political Culture beyond the Color Line.* Cambridge, MA: Harvard University Press, 2000.

———. *The Black Atlantic: Modernity and Double-Consciousness.* Cambridge, MA: Harvard University Press, 1993.

Gitelman, Lisa. *Paper Knowledge: Toward a Media History of Documents.* Durham, NC: Duke University Press, 2014.

Gordon, Lewis. *Fanon and the Crisis of European Man: An Essay on Philosophy and the Human Sciences.* New York: Routledge, 1995.

Gramsci, Antonio. *Selections from the Prison Notebooks.* New York: International Publishers, 2008.

Greenwald, Glenn. "The U.S.-Supported Coup in Bolivia Continues to Produce Repression and Tyranny, While Revealing How U.S. Media Propaganda Works." *The Intercept,* July 23, 2020. https://theintercept.com/2020/07/23/the-u-s-supported-coup-in-bolivia-continues-to-produce-repression-and-tyranny-while-revealing-how-u-s-media-propaganda-works/.

Grossberg, Lawrence. *Cultural Studies in the Future Tense.* Durham, NC: Duke University Press, 2010.

Grosz, Elizabeth. *The Nick of Time: Politics, Evolution, and the Untimely.* Durham, NC: Duke University Press, 2004.

Guillory, John. "Genesis of the Media Concept." *Critical Inquiry* 36 (2010): 321–362.

Halberstam, Jack. "The Wild Beyond: With and for the Undercommons." In *The Undercommons: Fugitive Planning & Black Study,* by Stephano Harney and Fred Moten, 2–13. Brooklyn, NY: Autonomedia, 2013.

Hall, Stuart. "Encoding/Decoding." In *The Cultural Studies Reader,* edited by Simon During, 477–487. New York: Routledge, 1993.

———. "Gramsci's Relevance for the Study of Race and Ethnicity." *Journal of Communication Inquiry* 10, no. 2 (1986): 5–27.

———. "Gramsci and Us." *Verso,* February 10, 2017. www.versobooks.com/blogs/2448-stuart-hall-gramsci-and-us.

———. "Marxist Structuralism." In *Cultural Studies: 1983,* edited by Jennifer Daryl Slack and Lawrence Grossberg, 97–126. Durham, NC: Duke University Press, 2016.

———. "The Problem of Ideology—Marxism without Guarantees." *Journal of Communication Inquiry* 10, no. 2 (1986): 28–44.

Halpern, Jake. "The Cop." *The New Yorker,* August 10, 2015. www.newyorker.com/magazine/2015/08/10/the-cop.

Haraway, Donna. "Anthropocene, Capitalocene, Plantationocene, Chthulucene: Making Kin." *Environmental Humanities* 6 (2015): 159–165.

Harding, Vincent. "The Vocation of the Black Scholar and the Struggles of the Black Community." In *Education and Black Struggle: Notes for the Colonized World,* edited by The Institute of the Black World, 3–29. Cambridge, MA: Harvard Educational Review, 1974.

Hardt, Hanno. "Beyond Cultural Studies—Recovering the 'Political' in Critical Communication Studies." *Journal of Communication Inquiry* 21, no. 2 (1997): 70–78.

———. *Critical Communication Studies: Essays in Communication, History and Theory in America*. New York: Routledge, 1992.

Hardt, Michael, and Antonio Negri. *Multitude: War and Democracy in the Age of Empire*. New York: Penguin Books, 2005.

Harney, Stefano, and Fred Moten. *The Undercommons: Fugitive Planning and Black Study*. Brooklyn, NY: Autonomedia, 2013.

Hartman, Saidiya. *Scenes of Subjection: Terror, Slavery, and Self-Making in Nineteenth-Century America*. New York: Oxford University Press, 1997.

Havens, Timothy. *Black Television Travels: African American Media around the Globe*. New York: New York University Press, 2013.

Havers, Grant. "The Right-Wing Postmodernism of Marshall McLuhan." *Media, Culture & Society* 25, no. 4 (2003): 511–525.

Hegel, G.W.F. *The Philosophy of History*. Kitchener, ON: Batoche Books, 2001.

Heidegger, Martin. *The Question Concerning Technology and Other Essays*. New York: Garland Publishing, INC, 1977.

Henry, Charles. *Long Overdue: The Politics of Racial Reparations*. New York: New York University Press, 2007.

Henslow, J. S. "From J.S.: 24 August 1831." *Darwin Correspondence Project*. Accessed, November 4, 2019. www.darwinproject.ac.uk/letter/DCP-LETT -105.xml.

Henson, Josiah. "An Autobiography of the Reverend Josiah Henson." In *Four Fugitive Slave Narratives*, edited by Robin Winks. Reading, MA: Addison-Wesley Publishing Company, 1969.

Hertz, Garnet, and Jussi Parikka. "Zombie Media: Circuit Bending Media Archaeology into an Art Method." *Leonardo* 45, no. 5 (2012): 424–430.

Hickel, Jason. "How Britain Stole $45 Trillion from India." *Aljazeera*, December 19, 2018. www.aljazeera.com/indepth/opinion/britain-stole-45-trillion -india-181206124830851.html.

Hillis, Ken. *Online a Lot of the Time: Ritual, Fetish, Sign*. Durham, NC: Duke University Press, 2008.

Hochman, Brian. *Savage Preservation: The Ethnographic Origins of Modern Media Technology*. Minneapolis: University of Minnesota Press, 2014.

Hogan, Mél. "Big Data Ecologies: Landscapes of Political Action." *Ephemera: Theory & Politics in Organization* 18, no. 3 (2018): 631–657.

Holland, Sharon Patricia. *The Erotic Life of Racism*. Durham, NC: Duke University Press, 2012.

hooks, bell. *Yearning: Race, Gender, and Cultural Politics*. Cambridge, MA: South End Press, 1990.

Horkheimer, Max, and Theodor Adorno. *Dialectic of Enlightenment*. Stanford, CA: Stanford University Press, 2002.

H.R. 40. House of Representatives, 116th Congress, 1st session. January 3, 2019. www.congress.gov/116/bills/hr40/BILLS-116hr40ih.pdf.

Husain, Atiya. "Terror and Abolition." *Boston Review*, June 11, 2020. http:// bostonreview.net/race/atiya-husain-terror-and-abolition.

Innis, Harold. *The Biases of Communication*. Toronto: University of Toronto Press, 2008.

———. *Empire and Communications*. New York: Rowman & Littlefield, 2007.

Jackson, Zakiyyah Iman. "Losing Manhood: Animality and Plasticity in the (Neo)Slave Narrative." *Qui Parle: Critical Humanities and Social Sciences* 25, nos. 1–2 (2016): 95–136.

James, C.L.R. *The Black Jacobins: Toussaint L'Ouverture and the San Domingo Revolution*. 1938, New York: Vintage, 1989.

———. "*The Black Scholar* Interviews: C.L.R. James." *The Black Scholar* 2, no. 1 (1970): 35–43.

———. *A History of Pan-African Revolt*. Oakland, CA: PM Press, 2012.

———. *Notes on Dialectics: Hegel, Marx, Lenin*. Westport, CT: Lawrence Hill & Co., 1981.

———. *You Don't Play with Revolution: The Montreal Lectures of C.L.R. James*. Oakland, CA: AK Press, 2009.

Jenkins, Candice. *Private Lives, Proper Relations: Regulating Black Intimacy*. Minneapolis: University of Minnesota Press, 2007.

Jenkins, Eric, and Peter Zhang, "Deleuze the Media Ecologist? Extensions of and Advance on McLuhan." *Explorations in Media Ecology* 15, no. 1 (2016): 55–72.

Jones, Gareth Stedman. Introduction to *Karl Marx and Friedrich Engels: The Communist Manifesto*, 3–185. New York: Penguin Books, 1967.

Jordan, June. *Moving Towards Home: Political Essays*. London: Virago, 1989.

"Journey to Freedom: Underground Railroad." *National Geographic*. Accessed November 4, 2019. www.nationalgeographic.org/interactive/journey-fre edom-underground-railroad/.

Judy, Ronald. *DisForming the American Canon: African-Arabic Slave Narratives and the Vernacular*. Minneapolis: University of Minnesota Press, 1993.

———. "Fanon's Body of Black Experience." In *Fanon: A Critical Reader*, edited by Lewis Gordon, T. Sharpley-Whiting, and Renee White, 53–73. Hoboken, NJ: Wiley-Blackwell, 1996.

———. *Sentient Flesh: Thinking in Disorder, Poiesis in Black*. Durham, NC: Duke University Press, 2020.

Jue, Melody. *Wild Blue Media: Thinking through Seawater*. Durham, NC: Duke University Press, 2020.

Kaplan, Sarah. "Climate Change Affects Everything—Even the Coronavirus." *Washington Post*, April 15, 2020. www.washingtonpost.com/climate-solu tions/2020/04/15/climate-change-affects-everything-even-coronavirus/?arc4 04=true.

Kant, Immanuel. *Critique of Pure Reason*. Boston, MA: Bedford/St. Martin's, 1965.

Keeling, Kara. *Queer Times, Black Futures*. New York: New York University Press, 2019.

———. *The Witch's Flight: The Cinematic, the Black Femme, and the Image of Common Sense*. Durham, NC: Duke University Press, 2007.

Kelley, Robin. *Freedom Dreams: The Black Radical Imagination*. New York: Beacon Press, 2003.

———. Introduction to *A History of Pan-African Revolt*, by C.L.R. James, 1–33. Oakland, CA: PM Press, 2012.

———. "Western Civilization Is Neither: Black Studies' Epistemic Revolution."

*The Black Scholar: Journal of Black Studies and Research* 50, no. 3 (2020): 4–10.

King, Tiffany. *The Black Shoals: Offshore Formations of Black and Native Studies*. Durham, NC: Duke University Press, 2019.

———. "The Labor of (Re)reading Plantation Landscapes Fungible(ly)." *Antipode* 48, no. 4 (2016): 1022–1039.

Kittler, Fredrich. *Gramophone, Film, Typewriter*. Stanford, CA: Stanford University Press, 1999.

Krämer, Sybille. *Medium, Messenger, Transmission: An Approach to Media Philosophy*. Amsterdam: Amsterdam University Press, 2015.

Kynard, Carmen. *Vernacular Insurrections: Race, Black Protest, and the New Century in Composition-Literacies Studies*. Albany, NY: SUNY Press, 2013.

Lebron, Christopher J. *The Making of Black Lives Matter: A Brief History of an Idea*. New York: Oxford University Press, 2017.

Levinson, Paul. *Digital McLuhan: A Guide to the Information Millennium*. New York: Routledge, 1999.

Lipsitz, George. "The Hip-Hop Hearings: The Hidden History of Deindustrialization." In *The Race and Media Reader*, edited by Gilbert Rodman, 294–312. New York: Routledge, 2014.

Lorde, Audre. *Sister Outsider: Essays and Speeches by Audre Lorde*. New York: Random House Press, 2007.

"Los Angeles Panthers Await Justice for 'US' Organization Pigs." *The Black Panther: Black Community News Service* (San Francisco), February 2, 1969.

Lousley, Cheryl. "Charismatic Life: Spectacular Biodiversity and Biophilic Life Writing," *Environmental Communication* 10, no. 6 (2016): 704–718.

Lowe, Lisa. *The Intimacy of Four Continents*. Durham, NC: Duke University Press, 2015.

Lowy, Michael. *Ecosocialism: A Radical Alternative to Capitalist Catastrophe*. Chicago: Haymarket Books, 2015.

Magnet, Shosana. *When Biometrics Fail: Gender, Race, and the Technology of Identity*. Durham, NC: Duke University Press, 2011.

Madrigal, Alexis. "Gil Scott-Heron's Poem, 'Whitey on the Moon.'" *The Atlantic*, September 14, 2015. www.theatlantic.com/technology/archive/2011/05/gil-scott-herons-poem-whitey-on-the-moon/239622/.

Malcolm X. *Malcolm X Speaks: Selected Speeches and Statements*. New York: Grove Press, 1994.

Mao Zedong. "On Contradiction." *Marxists*, August 1938. www.marxists.org/reference/archive/mao/selected-works/volume-1/mswv1_17.htm.

Mariani, Mike. "The Tragic, Forgotten History of Zombies." *The Atlantic*, October 28, 2015. www.theatlantic.com/entertainment/archive/2015/10/how-america-erased-the-tragic-history-of-the-zombie/412264/.

Marshall McLuhan Collection. Library and Archives of Canada. Ottawa, Ontario, Canada. www.bac-lac.gc.ca/eng/discover/biography-people/mcluhan/Pages/mcluhan.aspx.

Marshall McLuhan Collection. Thomas Fisher Rare Book Library. University of Toronto Libraries. Accessed October 2, 2020. https://fisher.library.utoronto.ca/sites/fisher.library.utoronto.ca/files/mcluhanFA-june2014.pdf.

Marx, Karl. *Capital: A Critique of Political Economy.* Volume 1. London: Lawrence & Wishart, LTD, 2003.

———. *Grundrisse.* New York: Random House, 1973.

Massey, Doreen. *Space, Place, and Gender.* Minneapolis: University of Minnesota Press, 1994.

Mattern, Shannon. *Code and Clay, Data and Dirt: Five Thousand Years of Urban Media.* Minneapolis: University of Minnesota Press, 2017.

Mazrui, Ali Al'Amin. *Black Reparations in the Era of Globalization.* Binghamton, NY: Institute of Global Cultural Studies, 2002.

Mbembe, Achille. *Necropolitics.* Durham, NC: Duke University Press, 2019.

McGlotten, Shaka. "Dead and Live Life: Zombies, Queers, and Online Sociality." In *Generation Zombie: Essays on the Living Dead in Modern Culture,* edited by Stephanie Boluk and Wylie Lenz, 182–193. Jefferson, NC: McFarland Press, 2011.

McIlwain, Charlton. *Black Software: The Internet and Racial Justice, from the AfroNet to Black Lives Matter.* New York: Oxford University Press, 2020.

McKittrick, Katherine. *Demonic Grounds: Black Women and the Cartographies of Struggle.* Minneapolis: University of Minnesota Press. 2006.

———. "Freedom Is a Secret." In *Black Geographies and the Politics of Place,* edited by Katherine McKittrick and Clyde Woods, 97–114. New York: South End Press, 2007.

———. "Mathematics Black Life." *The Black Scholar* 44, no. 2 (2014): 16–28.

———. "Plantation Futures." *Small Axe: A Caribbean Journal of Criticism* 17, no. 13, 42 (2013): 1–15.

McLaughlin, Eugene, and John Muncie. *The Sage Dictionary of Criminology.* Thousand Oaks, CA: Sage Publishing, 2013.

McLuhan, Marshall. "Letter to Eric Havelock." May 22, 1970. Library and Archives of Canada. http://data2.archives.ca/e/e447/e011165482-v8.jpg.

———. "Playboy Interview: 'Marshall McLuhan—A Candid Conversation with the High Priest of Popcult and Metaphysician of Media." In *Essential McLuhan,* edited by Eric McLuhan and Frank Zingrone, 233–269. New York: Basic Books, 1995.

———. "Radio: The Tribal Drum." *AV Communication Review* 12, no. 2 (1964): 133–145.

———. *Understanding Me: Lectures and Interviews.* Cambridge, MA: MIT Press, 2005.

———. *Understanding Media: The Extensions of Man.* Berkeley, CA: Gingko Press, 2003.

McLuhan, Marshall, and Bruce Powers. *The Global Village: Transformations in World Life and Media in the 21st Century.* New York: Oxford University Press, 1992.

McPherson, Tara. "U.S. Operating Systems at Mid-Century: The Intertwining of Race and UNIX." In *Race after the Internet,* edited by Lisa Nakamura and Peter Chow-White, 21–37. New York, Routledge, 2011.

Mercer, Kobena. *Welcome to the Jungle: New Positions in Black Cultural Studies.* New York: Routledge, 1994.

"Michael Brown Shooting (Ferguson)." Colorado Justice Project. Accessed October 22, 2017. http://coloradojusticeproject.com/node/3.

Mills, Charles. *The Racial Contract*. Ithaca, NY: Cornell University Press, 1997.

Milman, Oliver. "European Colonization of the Americas Killed So Many It Cooled Earth's Climate." *The Guardian*, January 31, 2019. www.theguardian.com/environment/2019/jan/31/european-colonization-of-americas-helped-cause-climate-change.

Molloy, Mark, and agencies. "Palestinians Tweet Tear Gas Advice to Protestors in Ferguson." *The Telegraph*, August 15, 2014. www.telegraph.co.uk/news/worldnews/northamerica/usa/11036190/Palestinians-tweet-tear-gas-advice-to-protesters-in-Ferguson.html.

Morales Ayama, Evo. Preface to *Washington Bullets: A History of the CIA, Coups, and Assassinations*, by Vijay Prashad, 9–11. New York: Monthly Review, 2020.

Morgan, Lewis. "Ancient Society." The Project Gutenberg. Accessed April 4, 2020. www.gutenberg.org/files/45950/45950-h/45950-h.htm.

Morrison, Toni. *Beloved*. New York: Penguin Books, 2004.

Mosco, Vincent. *The Political Economy of Communication*. New York: Sage Publications, 2009.

Moten, Fred. *In the Break: The Aesthetics of the Black Radical Tradition*. Minneapolis: University of Minnesota Press, 2003.

Munford, Clarence. *Race and Reparations: A Black Perspective for the Twenty-First Century*. Trenton, NJ: Africa World Press, 1996.

Murch, Donna. *Living for the City: Migration, Education, and the Rise of the Black Panther Party in Oakland, California*. Chapel Hill: University of North Carolina Press, 2010.

Nakamura, Lisa. "Afterword: Racism, Sexism, and Gaming's Cruel Optimism." In *Gaming Representation*, edited by Jennifer Malkowski and TreaAndrea Russworm, 245–250. Bloomington: University of Indiana Press, 2017.

Narayan, John. "The Wages of Whiteness in the Absence of Wages: Racial Capitalism, Reactionary Intercommunalism and the Rise of Trumpism." *Third World Quarterly* (2017): 1–19. DOI: 10.1080/01436597.2017.1368012.

Nastasi, Alison. "10 of the Most Fascinating 'Playboy' Interviews." *Flavorwire*, August 31, 2013. www.flavorwire.com/412697/10-of-the-most-fascinating-playboy-interviews.

National Defense Education Act of 1958. H.R. 13247. September 2, 1958. www.govinfo.gov/content/pkg/STATUTE-72/pdf/STATUTE-72-Pg1580.pdf.

Neal, Mark Anthony. "How Universities Are Addressing Slavery and Reparations." *NewBlackMan in (Exile)* (blog). November 17, 2019. www.newblackmaninexile.net/2019/11/how-universities-are-addressing-slavery.html?m=1.

Nelson, Stanley, dir. *The Black Panthers: Vanguard of the Revolution* (motion picture). New York: Public Broadcasting Service, 2015.

Newton, Huey. "Dialectics of Nature: 1974." In *The Huey P. Newton Reader*, edited by David Hilliard and Donald Weise, 304–312. New York: Seven Stories Press, 2002.

———. "Intercommunalism." In *The Huey P. Newton Reader*, edited by David Hilliard and Donald Weise, 181–199. New York: Seven Stories Press, 2002.

———. "On the Relevance of the Church." In *The Huey P. Newton Reader*, edited by David Hilliard and Donald Weise, 214–226. New York: Seven Stories Press, 2002.

———. "Speech Delivered at Boston College: November 18, 1970." In *The Huey P. Newton Reader*, edited by David Hilliard and Donald Weise, 160–180. New York: Seven Stories Press, 2002.

———. "The Technology Question: 1972." In *The Huey P. Newton Reader*, edited by David Hilliard and Donald Weise, 256–266. New York: Seven Stories Press, 2002.

Nishime, Leilani, and Kim Hester Williams. "Introduction: Why Racial Ecologies?" In *Racial Ecologies*, edited by Leilani Nishime and Kim Hester Williams, 3–15. Seattle: University of Washington Press, 2018.

Noble, Safiya. *Algorithms of Oppression: How Search Engines Reinforce Racism*. New York: New York University Press, 2018.

Nolan, Fred. "Black Cultural Nationalism." *The Black Panther: Black Community News Service* (San Francisco), December 21, 1968.

Nolan, Ginger. *The Neocolonialism of the Global Village*. Minneapolis: University of Minnesota Press, 2018.

Norment Jr., Nathaniel. Introduction to *The African American Studies Reader*, second edition, edited by Nathaniel Norment Jr., xxvii–xlix. Durham, NC: Carolina Academic Press.

Nyong'o, Tavia. "The Scene of Occupation." *TDR: The Drama Review* 56, no. 4 (2012): 136–149.

Oliver, Michelle. "A Look at the Roots of the Underground Railroad in Detroit." *Click on Detroit*, February 21, 2019. www.clickondetroit.com/black-history-month/a-look-at-the-roots-of-the-underground-railroad-in-detroit.

O'Neil, Cathy. *Weapons of Math Destruction: How Big Data Increases Inequality and Threatens Democracy*. New York: Crown, 2017.

Ong, Walter. *An Ong Reader: Challenges for Further Inquiry*, edited by Thomas Farrell and Paul Soukup. New York: Hampton Press, 2002.

———. *Orality and Literacy*. New York: Routledge, 2012.

Orbe, Mark. "Representations of Race and Reality TV: Watch and Discuss." *Critical Studies in Media Communication* 25, no. 4 (2008): 345–352.

Packer, Jeremy. "Rethinking Dependency: New Relations of Transportation and Communication." In *Thinking with James Carey: Essays on Communications, Transportation, History*, edited by Jeremy Packer and Craig Robertson, 79–100. Bern, Switzerland: Peter Lang, 2016.

Parikka, Jussi. *A Geology of Media*. Minneapolis: University of Minnesota Press, 2015.

———. "To Media Study: Media Studies and Beyond." *MAST: Journal of Media Art, Study and Theory* 1, no. 1 (2020): 59–63.

———. *What Is Media Archaeology*. Cambridge, UK: Polity, 2012.

Parks, Lisa. *Cultures in Orbit: Satellites and the Televisual*. Durham, NC: Duke University Press, 2005.

Parks, Lisa, and Nicole Starosielski. Introduction to *Signal Traffic: Critical Studies of Media Infrastructures*, edited by Lisa Parks and Nicole Starosielski, 1–27. Champaign: University of Illinois Press, 2015.

Peters, John Durham. *The Marvelous Clouds: Toward a Philosophy of Elemental Media*. Chicago: University of Chicago Press, 2015.

Pettit, Eber. "Margaret: Born on a Slave Ship." In *Slave Narratives of the Underground*, edited by Christine Rusdisel and Bob Blaisdell, 166–168. Mineola, NY: Dover Publications, 2014.

Pezzullo, Phaedra. *Toxic Tourism: Rhetorics of Pollution, Travel, and Environmental Justice*. Tuscaloosa: University of Alabama Press, 2009.

Pooley, Jeff. "Wilbur Schramm and the 'Four Founders' History of U.S. Communication Research." *Tom* 2, no. 4 (2017): 5–18.

Postman, Neil. *Technopoly: The Surrender of Culture in Technology*. New York: Vintage Books, 1993.

Preston Jr., E. Delorus. "The Genesis of the Underground Railroad." *Journal of Negro History* 18, no. 2 (1933): 144–170.

Ransby, Barbara. *Making All Black Lives Matter: Reimaging Freedom in the 21st Century*. Berkeley: University of California Press, 2018.

Rhodes, Jane. *Framing the Black Panthers: The Spectacular Rise of a Black Power Icon*. Champaign: University of Illinois Press, 2017.

Riofrancos, Thea. *Resource Radicals: From Petro-Nationalism to Post-Extractivism in Ecuador*. Durham, NC: Duke University Press, 2020.

Risam, Roopika. *New Digital Worlds: Postcolonial Digital Humanities in Theory, Praxis, and Pedagogy*. Evanston, IL: Northwestern University Press, 2018.

Robinson, Armstead. "A Concluding Statement." In *Black Studies in the University*, edited by Armstead Robinson, Craig Foster, and Donald Ogilvie, 207–214. New Haven, CT: Yale University Press, 1969.

Robinson, Cedric. *Black Marxism: The Making of the Black Radical Tradition*. Chapel Hill, NC: University of North Carolina Press, 2000.

———. "The Inventions of the Negro." *Social Identities* 7, no. 3 (2001): 329–361.

Rodney, Walter. *The Groundings with My Brothers*. London: Bogle-L'Ouverture Publications, 1996.

———. *How Europe Underdeveloped Africa*. Brooklyn, NY: Verso, 2018.

———. *The Russian Revolution: A View from the Third World*. Brooklyn, NY: Verso, 2018.

Rose, Tricia. *Black Noise: Rap Music and Black Culture in Contemporary America*. Indianapolis, IN: Wesleyan Publishing House, 1994.

———. "Fear of a Black Planet: Rap Music and Black Cultural Politics in the 1990s." In *The Race and Media Reader*, edited by Gilbert Rodman, 120–131. New York: Routledge, 2014.

Ross, Alexander. "The High Priest of Pop Culture." *Maclean's*, July 3, 1965. https://archive.macleans.ca/article/1965/7/3/the-high-priest-of-pop-culture.

Saldanha, Arun. "Reontologising Race: The Machinic Geography of Phenotype." *Environment and Planning D: Society and Space* 24 (2006): 9–24.

Samuels, Alex. "On Juneteenth, Sheila Jackson Lee Spearheads Congressional Hearing on Reparations, Calling Them 'Long Overdue.'" *Texas Tribune*, June 19, 2019. www.texastribune.org/2019/06/19/sheila-jackson-lee-reparations-juneteenth/.

Scott, David. *Conscripts of Modernity*. Durham, NC: Duke University Press, 2004.

Shakur, Zayd-Malik. "Fascist Pigs Murder Man Frame Connecticut Panthers." *The Black Panther: Black Community News Service* (San Francisco), June 7, 1969.

Sharma, Sarah. "Exit and the Extensions of Man." *Transmediale/Art and Digital Culture*, August 5, 2017. https://transmediale.de/content/exit-and-the-extensions-of-man.

———. *In the Meantime: Temporality and Cultural Politics*. Durham, NC: Duke University Press, 2014.

Sharpe, Christina. *In the Wake: On Blackness and Being*. Durham, NC: Duke University Press, 2016.

da Silva, Denise Ferreira. "1 (Life) ÷ 0 (Blackness) = ∞ – ∞ or ∞ / ∞: On Matter beyond the Equation of Value." *E-Flux* 79 (2017). www.e-flux.com/journal/79/94686/1-life-o-blackness-or-on-matter-beyond-the-equation-of-value/.

———. *Toward a Global Idea of Race*. Minneapolis: University of Minnesota Press, 2007.

Smith, Mark. *How Race Is Made: Slavery, Segregation, and the Senses*. Chapel Hill: University of North Carolina Press, 2006.

Snorton, C. Riley. *Black on Both Sides: A Racial History of Trans Identity*. Minneapolis: University of Minnesota, 2017.

Spencer, Herbert. *The Principles of Psychology*. London: Longman, Brown, Green, Longmans, 1855.

Spigel, Lynn. "Housing Television: Architectures of the Archives." *The Communication Review* 13, no. 1 (2010): 52–74.

———. *Welcome to the Dreamhouse: Popular Media and Postwar Suburbs*. Durham, NC: Duke University Press, 2001.

Spigel, Lynn, and Michael Curtin. Introduction to *The Revolution Wasn't Televised: Sixties Television and Social Conflict*, edited by Lynn Spigel and Michael Curtin, 1–20. New York: Routledge, 1997.

Spillers, Hortense. *Black, White, and in Color: Essays on American Literature and Culture*. Chicago: University of Chicago Press, 2003.

Srnicek, Nick. *Platform Capitalism*. Hoboken, NJ: Wiley, 2016.

Stamm, Michael. *Dead Tree Media: Manufacturing the Newspaper in Twentieth Century North America*. Baltimore, MD: Johns Hopkins University Press, 2018.

Starosielski, Nicole. *The Undersea Network*. Durham, NC: Duke University Press, 2015.

"State of Missouri v. Darren Wilson." Saint Louis, MO: Gore Perry Reporting & Video, September 16, 2014.

Sterne, Jonathan. "Out with the Trash: On the Future of New Media." In *Residual Media*, edited by Charles Acland, 16–31. Minneapolis: University of Minnesota Press, 2007.

———. "Transportation and Communication: Together as You've Always Wanted Them." In *Thinking with James Carey: Essays on Communications, Transportation, History*, edited by Jeremy Packer and Craig Robertson, 117–136. Bern, Switzerland: Peter Lang, 2016.

Steward, Austin. "Austin Steward: Twenty-Two Years a Slave and Forty Years a Freeman." In *Four Fugitive Slave Narratives*, edited by Robin Winks, xvi–221. Reading, MA: Addison-Wesley Publishing Company, 1969.

Stiegler, Bernard. *Technics and Time, 2: Disorientation*. Stanford, CA: Stanford University Press, 2008.

Still, William. "Abolitionist in the Underground." In *Slave Narratives of the Underground*, edited by Christine Rusdisel and Bob Blaisdell, 21–38. Mineola, NY: Dover Publications, 2014.

Stockman, Farah. "'We're Self-Interested': The Growing Identity Debate in Black America." *New York Times*, November 8, 2019. www.nytimes.com/2019/11/08/us/slavery-black-immigrants-ados.html.

Strate, Lance. "The Medium and McLuhan's Message." *Razon Y Palabra*, 2012. Accessed October 2, 2020. www.razonypalabra.org.mx/N/N80/V80/00A_St rate_V80.pdf.

Subramaniam, Banu. *Ghost Stories for Darwin: The Science of Variation and the Politics of Diversity*. Champaign: University of Illinois Press, 2014.

Swaine, Jon, and Oliver Laughland. "Darren Wilson Will Not Face Federal Charges in Michael Brown Shooting." *The Guardian*, March 4, 2015. www.theguardian.com/us-news/2015/mar/04/darren-wilson-federal-criminal-ch arges-michael-brown-shooting.

Taylor, Keeanga-Yamahtta. *From #BlackLivesMatter to Black Liberation*. Chicago: Haymarket Books, 2016.

Taylor, Keeanga-Yamahtta, and Adolph Reed. "The Reparations Debate." *Dissent Magazine*, June 24, 2019. www.dissentmagazine.org/online_articles/the -reparations-debate.

Terry, Jermont. "City of Evanston to Use Cannabis Revenue for Reparations Fund for African-American Residents." CBS Chicago, November 27, 2019. https://chicago.cbslocal.com/2019/11/27/evanston-recreational-cannabis-re parations-african-american-residents/.

Towns, Armond. "The (Black) Elephant in the Room: McLuhan and the Racial." *Canadian Journal of Communication* 44, no. 4 (2019): 545–554.

———. "Black 'Matter' Lives." *Women's Studies in Communication* 41, no. 4 (2018): 349–358.

———. "Rebels of the Underground: Media, Orality, and the Routes of Black Emancipation." *Communication and Critical/Cultural Studies* 13, no. 2 (2016): 184–197.

———. "Toward a Black Media Philosophy." *Cultural Studies* 43, no. 6 (2020): 851–873.

Ture, Kwame, and Charles Hamilton, *Black Power: The Politics of Liberation*. New York: Vintage Books, 1992.

Tyler Bonner, John, and Robert May. Introduction to *The Descent of Man, and Selection in Relation to Sex*, edited by John Tyler Bonner and Robert May, vii–xli. Princeton, NJ: Princeton University Press, 1981.

"Voices Remembering Slavery: Freed People Tell Their Stories." Library of Congress. Accessed April 4, 2020. www.loc.gov/collections/voices-remembering -slavery/about-this-collection/.

Wark, McKenzie. *Capital Is Dead: Is This Something Worse?* Brooklyn, NY: Verso Books, 2019.

Watts, Eric. "Border Patrolling and 'Passing' in Eminem's *8 Mile*." *Critical Studies in Media Communication* 22, no. 3 (2005): 187–206.

———. "Postracial Fantasies, Blackness, and Zombies." *Communication and Critical/Cultural Studies* 14, no. 4 (2017): 317–333.

Weheliye, Alexander. *Phonographies: Grooves in Sonic Afro-Modernity*. Durham, NC: Duke University Press, 2005.

White, Derrick. *The Challenge of Blackness: The Institute of the Black World and Political Activism in the 1970s*. Gainesville: University Press of Florida, 2012.

Williams, Raymond. "The Analysis of Culture." In *Cultural Theory and Popular Culture*, edited by John Storey, 48–56. Athens: University of Georgia Press, 1998.

———. *Culture and Materialism*. New York: Verso, 2005.

———. *Television: Technology and Cultural Form*. New York: Routledge, 2003.

Woods, Clyde. "'Sittin' on Top of the World': The Challenges of Blues and Hip Hop Geography." In *Black Geographies and the Politics of Place*, edited by Katherine McKittrick and Clyde Woods, 46–81. Toronto, ON: Between the Lines Press, 2007.

Wootson Jr., Cleve. "A Black Yale Student Fell Asleep in Her Dorm's Common Room. A White Student Called the Police." *Washington Post*, May 11, 2018. www.washingtonpost.com/news/grade-point/wp/2018/05/10/a-black-yale-student-fell-asleep-in-her-dorms-common-room-a-white-student-called-police/?utm_term=.d91d97c17c90.

Wynter, Sylvia. "The Ceremony Found: Towards the Autopoetic Turn/Overturn, Its Autonomy of Human Agency and Extraterritoriality of (Self-)Cognition." In *Black Knowledges/Black Struggles*, edited by Jason Ambroise and Sabine Broeck, 184–252. Liverpool, UK: Liverpool University Press, 2015.

———. *"Do Not Call Us Negros": How "Multicultural" Textbooks Perpetuate Racism*. San Francisco: Aspire Books and Magazines, 1992.

———. "1492: A New World View." In *Race, Discourse, and the Origin of the Americas: A New World View*, edited by Vera Lawrence Hyatt and Rex Nettleford, 5–57. Washington, DC: Smithsonian Institution Press, 1995.

———. "On How We Mistook the Map for the Territory, and Re-imprisoned Ourselves in Our Unbearable Wrongness of Being, of Désêrtre: Black Studies toward the Human Project." In *Not Only the Master's Tools: African-American Studies in Theory and Practice*, edited by Lewis Gordan and Jane Gordan, 107–169. Boulder, CO: Paradigm Publishers, 2006.

———. "Unsettling the Coloniality of Being/Power/Truth/Freedom: Towards the Human, after Man, Its Overrepresentation—An Argument." *The New Centennial Review* 3, no. 3 (2003): 257–337.

Vaidhyanathan, Siva. *Antisocial Media: How Facebook Disconnects Us and Undermines Democracy*. New York: New York University Press, 2018.

Yuen, Nancy Wang. "Playing 'Ghetto': Black Actors, Stereotypes, and Authenticity." In *Black Los Angeles: American Dreams and Racial Realities*, edited by Darnell Hunt and Ana-Christina Ramon, 232–242. New York: New York University Press, 2010.

Yusoff, Kathryn. *A Billion Black Anthropocenes or None*. Minneapolis: University of Minnesota Press, 2018.

Zoubir, Yahia. "The United States, the Soviet Union and Decolonization of the Maghreb, 1945–1962." *Middle Eastern Studies* 31, no. 1 (1995): 58–84.

# Index

Founded in 1893,
UNIVERSITY OF CALIFORNIA PRESS
publishes bold, progressive books and journals
on topics in the arts, humanities, social sciences,
and natural sciences—with a focus on social
justice issues—that inspire thought and action
among readers worldwide.

The UC PRESS FOUNDATION
raises funds to uphold the press's vital role
as an independent, nonprofit publisher, and
receives philanthropic support from a wide
range of individuals and institutions—and from
committed readers like you. To learn more, visit
ucpress.edu/supportus.

Printed in the USA
CPSIA information can be obtained
at www.ICGtesting.com
LVHW090351151123
763992LV00004B/444

9 780520 355804